INTERNAL ALCHEMY

The Natural Way to Immortality

INTERNAL ALCHEMY

The Natural Way to Immortality

By Hua-Ching Ni
Teacher of Natural Spiritual Truth

The Shrine of the Eternal Breath of Tao
College of Tao & Traditional Chinese Healing
SANTA MONICA

*Acknowledgement: Thanks and appreciation to
Suta Cahill and Janet DeCourtney for typing,
proofreading, editing and typesetting this book*

The Shrine of the Eternal Breath of Tao,
Malibu, California 90265

College of Tao and Traditional Chinese Healing,
1314 Second Street #208
Santa Monica, California 90401

Library of Congress Cataloging-in-Publication Data

Hua Ching, Ni
    Internal alchemy : the natural way to immortality / by Ni,
Hua-Ching.
        p. cm.
    ISBN 0-937064-51-3 : $15.95
    1. Spiritual Life. 2. Alchemy--Religious aspects. I. Title.
    BL624.H83   1992   91-50618
299'.51444--dc20   CIP

This book is dedicated to all people who are interested in learning the depth of their lives through practicing internal alchemy. I also wish to express my appreciation to the first group of students and friends who gave great support to my work and teaching upon my arrival in the United States.

To female readers,

According to natural spiritual teaching, male and female are equally important in the natural sphere. This is seen in the diagram of T'ai Chi. Thus, discrimination is not practiced in our tradition. All my work is dedicated to both genders of human people.

Wherever possible, constructions using masculine pronouns to represent both sexes are avoided; where they occur, we ask your tolerance and spiritual understanding. We hope that you will take the essence of my teaching and overlook the superficiality of language. Gender discrimination is inherent in English; ancient Chinese pronouns do not have differences of gender. I wish that all of you achieve above the level of language or gender.

Thank you, H. C. Ni

Warning - Disclaimer

This book presents information and techniques that have been in use throughout the orient for many years. These practices utilize a natural system within the body; however, there are no claims for effectiveness. The information offered is to the author's best knowledge and experience and is to be used by the reader(s) at their own discretion.

Because of the sophisticated nature of the information contained within this book, it is recommended that the reader also study the author's other books for further understanding of a healthy lifestyle and energy-conducting exercises.

Because people's lives have different conditions and different stages of growth, no rigid or strict practice can be applied universally. Thus, it must be through the discernment of the reader that the practices are selected. The adoption and application of the material offered in this book is your own responsibility.

The author and publisher of this book are not responsible in any manner for any injury that may occur through following the instructions in this book.

Contents

Prelude

The Subtle Essence conveyed by the teaching of the Integral Way is the deep truth of all religions, yet it leaves all religions behind to be the clothing of different seasons or worn in different places. The teaching of the Subtle Essence includes all things of religious importance, yet it is not on the same level as religion. It serves people's lives directly as all religions wish to do, but it surpasses the boundary of all religions and extracts the essence of all religions.

The Subtle Essence as conveyed by the teaching of the Integral Way is also the goal of all serious science, but it leaves all sciences behind as partial and temporal descriptions of this Integral Truth. Unlike any of the partial sciences, it goes beyond the level of any single scientific search.

The Subtle Essence is the master teaching. However, it does not rely on any authority. It is like a master key which can unlock all doors leading to the inner room of the ultimate truth directly. It is not frozen at the emotional surface of life and does not remain locked at the level of thought or belief with the struggling which extends to skepticism and endless searching.

The teaching of the Subtle Essence presents the core of the Integral Truth and helps you reach it yourself.

Preface

The contributions of ancient achieved ones to the spiritual development of humanity are deeply related to universal and individual spiritual reality. The term "internal alchemy" is actually derived from external alchemy. Both types of alchemy originated in China with the "Scholars of Formulas" who used certain methods or "formulas" to try to achieve immortality. During the time of Spring and Autumn (722-403 B.C.), the Warring time (403-248 B. C.), the Chin Dynasty (248-207 B.C.), the Han Dynasty (206 B.C.-219 A.D.), and the Jing Dynasty (265-419 A.D.), the Scholars of Formulas were especially active. Master Kou Hong recorded their activities in the book called *Pau Po Tzu*, and references to them appeared in many other important spiritual books, too.

In one book of Kou Hong's collection, there is a description of vermin and bacteria that the people of his day frequently experienced on their bodies. Some remedy was needed to destroy such objects. This was one motivation for the development of chemical substances produced by external alchemy. Natural minerals had been used for medicinal purposes for a long time. Cinnabar, for instance, was commonly used in small doses combined with an herb tea to help the stability of the mind.

During the Han Dynasty, the Scholars of Formulas concluded that the physical body needed specific amounts of certain minerals to support health and longevity. This was another reason why external alchemy was pursued. Young babies, for example, are easily startled by a loud noise or other type of disturbance that might cause them to cry all night, so there was a formula which contained gold combined with herbs in order to calm children down. (Babies cry for different reasons such as hunger, overfeeding, coldness or heat, etc. If a baby is crying from a scare or fright, or if you yourself have one, you might repeat some of the invocations from *The Workbook for Spiritual Development for All People* as a kind of first aid; this might stop the symptoms. It is merely a suggestion.)

In ancient times, certain formulas using metals and herbs were applied for many special medical situations. This all furthered the development of external alchemy.

External alchemy is different from internal alchemy. This class will follow a totally different direction from that of external alchemy. People have tried to use external alchemy to achieve physical immortality, but failure is common. The truth of internal alchemy can be proven, however, with deep awareness. One can experience personal body spirits and then develop sensitivity to the spirits of the mental and spiritual levels. There are truthful practices that can reveal such things to someone of sound mind and objective attitudes. These practices can also bring good health and long life. I feel responsible for not allowing this knowledge and discovery to be lost when it could be taught to people who would like to open a new frontier which ordinary scientists shy away from.

This kind of teaching can be an especially helpful supplement to and shed new light on the shortcomings or insufficiency of modern medicine. Realizers of spiritual truth know life more deeply than general medical doctors, because life is more than just physical. Although physicians established physical knowledge of the body and physical treatment for the body, their achievement and understanding is incomplete. For this reason, I offer my knowledge in this area. I would like to go forward step by step, first to help the understanding of people with open minds and broad attitudes. Then, possibly the high secrets can be passed on.

It is a simple truth that once people become ideological, then it is difficult for them to open up to new facts or points of view. I choose to do this task for the benefit of all human life. I will slowly give away the secrets I experienced, experimented with, and learned. For me to teach these high practices is not a matter of how much people pay me, but of whether it is right for me to teach everyone. Because there is a spiritual responsibility involved, this information is not public nor given to all people. I will try a new way and new attitudes in my teaching. It will take a while before this becomes common knowledge to all people of future generations.

Some people will take a detour before they are ready for this knowledge. Yet the work must be started. This was my motivation, and so I started by giving these classes so that people would understand the reality of spiritual achievement.

The Scholars of Formulas enthusiastically pursued immortal life. They understood that on the physical level of life, precious metals could exist for centuries without decay. This guided them toward the refining of precious metals for immortality through alchemy. Gold was the metal that lasted the longest, so they tried to refine gold to make a substance which they called Golden Immortal Medicine. This substance was supposed to be ingested to bring about physical immortality, but it failed. They made attempts to refine other precious metals to be Immortal Medicine, and they also tried to refine base metals to be precious metals, which met with the same result: failure.

Through experimentation, they discovered that when some minerals were combined during refining, a highly poisonous substance was produced which could be used as an external medicine to cure certain diseases. They also discovered that when gold and other minerals were cooked in a concoction of herbal tea, the resulting beverage had the property of calming upset children. Thus, there was some benefit to the efforts of alchemy, but it did not bring about the immortality which was sought.

Basically, the results of external alchemy were false gold and new chemicals which could only be used for medicinal purposes. This partial success caused some people to move away from external alchemy altogether. As far as I know, nobody has directly swallowed gold and silver for the purpose of pursuing immortality, but some people have swallowed gold to commit suicide.

The results of the refineries were hidden secrets; the true masters always kept them secret from people who were not directly involved. The true masters did not tell people that the gold produced was not real gold. However, the language of external alchemy was employed to describe the operations of internal alchemy, which is the transforming of lower energy into higher energy.

Thus, metaphorically, writers or teachers used the terminology of precious metals or minerals to explain human energy transformation. For example, mercury stood for spiritual or yang energy, and lead for sexual or yin energy. People who succeeded in practicing internal alchemy discovered that integrating the two energies could produce a certain light or ray during spiritual cultivation. Thus, the processes of external alchemy are a proper description for internal alchemy, but in my view, the language is still too indirect and causes confusion.

During the Han and Jing Dynasties, many people who did not receive the secret teaching died from ingesting mineral formulas in a misguided attempt to achieve physical immortality. Especially during the Tang Dynasty, the emperors did not know that the instructions for immortality were written metaphorically, so they were all fanatic about using external immortal medicine to support their sexual capability. The external medicine may have lead them to experience more sexual pleasure, but all of them suffered an early death. They believed that they achieved immortality because they immediately experienced the restoration of sexual strength, but other observers had reservations about that type of achievement.

Actually, the practice of internal alchemy existed long before external alchemy, but a different secret code was used to describe it. Of course, the process is the same no matter what terms are used. After the development of external alchemy, its terminology was used as a metaphoric description of the internal human process of personal energy transformation.

Ingesting external substances is not absolutely helpful in the attainment of either spiritual achievement or immortality. Only the original internal alchemy is helpful for possible spiritual achievement.

Alchemy, as a subject of knowledge, started in China. Arab traders who came to China brought this knowledge and its practices, as well as other important ancient inventions, back to their homelands, and from there the knowledge of alchemy spread to the West. The achievements of modern civilization have been made from the contributions of all peoples in one way or another.

Unfortunately, as the knowledge of alchemy traveled from place to place, it did not always remain intact. Many incompletions and misunderstandings occurred. For example, although immortality is related to sexual energy, this does not mean that the way to reach immortality is through excessive sexual practice.

Besides internal alchemy, two other traces of the search for immortality have been found, one in Egypt and the other in China. In Egypt, the ancients used mummification and built pyramids. In China, mummification was done by using spices and dehydration to preserve the body. Many statues in Chinese Buddhist temples and in Taoist folk temples were made by this process. The statues were people's actual physical bodies. The Chinese did not use pyramids, but they developed the knowledge of geomancy, which can determine whether the energy characteristics of a location are suitable for a grave or tomb. However, the true development of immortality of the Integral Way, which has not yet been totally disclosed to modern scholars, is spiritual immortality, not physical immortality. Spiritual immortality is built, nevertheless, on the knowledge and skill of how to live a long and healthy life.

As a student and a teacher of this ancient tradition, I obtained my training and confidence through actual spiritual development, not through religious beliefs. People of profundity know that the religious way only touches the surface of spirituality; it cannot reach objective achievement. For the purpose of avoiding confusion, I therefore differentiate the religious approach from real spiritual development.

I hope that through my books and other work I am able to help the spiritual development of each individual and the entire society by gradually disclosing the ancient secrets of life and the skills and practices developed by the Scholars of Formulas. This is a big task. Its purpose is to teach the high truth of the subtle sphere of life rather than establish faith in external things.

Introduction

I arrived in the United States on November 4, 1976. During the first years, I began my teaching activity alongside my busy Chinese medical practice. I continued my practice of Traditional Chinese Medicine until five years ago, when I started a full schedule of travel and retreat for the purpose of writing. The class I gave in 1977 and 1978 on internal alchemy was important, and is the material on which this book is based.

The class on internal alchemy made an impact on all the students who attended it. Most of them were greatly benefitted by the intensified revelations of deep mental and physical levels. Because this type of internal work can bring old difficulties to the surface, people must take it a little easy during this process of self-release. Spiritual achievement is closely related to personal life attitudes, and I hope that all of my teaching material can respond to the spiritual challenge of modern times.

Some people imagine spiritual life to be free of all worldly responsibility and obligations. Ordinary religions have long developed such imaginary goals which cannot be reached in any time, modern or ancient. A true spiritual life is built on a foundation of spiritual health; one must have the strength to be able to deal correctly with all types of responsibility, obligation and pressure.

In modern times, there is not much opportunity in most people's lives to evade responsibility, obligation and pressure. Although a few people have such exceptional lives, anyone who tries to escape responsibility or work and calls this "spiritual" lives a life of self-deception. There are some people who try to push responsibility for their own lives onto other people. This is a new political and social trend.

Worldly renunciation can be a philosophy, but spiritual dignity can only be found when people support their own lives through their own strength or labor and give help to others with their own hard earned crop or harvest.

Giving up the troublesome world and its pressures cannot prove more spiritually truthful or meaningful than finding one's own true sacredness or holy being in secular life. When one finds holiness in the ordinariness of life, when good and important disciplines are applied to oneself, spiritual value is also found and spiritual mellowness is reached.

A carefree life of no worldly obligation is supported by some religious teachings in places such as Thailand and its neighboring countries. However, that type of lifestyle is only a way to escape personal trouble or responsibility, it is not spiritual development. It is questionable whether the practice of merely being a "lotus eater" brings true spiritual fruit. Unfortunately, the ideology of Buddha is used as negative support for this type of lifestyle. Typically, to live in the world and experience contention, struggle or evil competition is considered unspiritual. It is unfortunate that the ideology of God is made to support worldly contention and wars. Yet, cooperation, mutual help or giving help to others are considered moral strengths. These moral strengths are all demonstrated through working and living in the world, not by staying in a secluded forest or monastery.

Giving help to others, cooperating and being of mutual assistance is the typical message of the ancient spiritual teaching. Unfortunately, it is neglected and twisted to support both people who escape from the world and those who wage war upon others.

The difference between true spiritual practice and psychological practice is the difference between growing through realistic living in the world while giving help and living in seclusion and offering imaginary help to the world in order to save one's own dignity. If you accomplish a task and give help, and you withdraw from the group or mass when your work is done and the help has been given, this is the ancient and highest morality.

Trying to avoid life comes from one's emotional attitudes. Renouncing life is not the result of a clear understanding of life. All people have cycles. During a low cycle, people do not like to be active or face the financial responsibility of life, etc., but would rather withdraw. This is human nature; nothing is too amiss with that. A student of spiritual truth knows when he or she is in a good cycle relative to life energy and applies the good cycle in a positive direction. In a low cycle, the student of spiritual truth remains calm and peaceful to modify the possibility of external pressure or disturbance.

Although a spiritual teacher has the role and responsibility of helping other people in their spiritual development, he or she must first be a virtuous person. As a spiritual teacher, I may be tricked by people, but I cannot trick others. There must be no unrighteous practice in my life, so that I will not feel ashamed to serve the public. However, not all teachers are suitable to teach certain types of students. Students have different needs, and not all of them can be met by one teacher.

People and environments are all subject to change. We could not expect it to be otherwise. People may receive new stimulation and change their attitude for better or for worse. A spiritual expression says that the "first heart" is valuable. It does not matter what change happens later, the first heart should always be appreciated. If I could respond to the demands of all people, I think I would be happy all the time, but I still have not achieved that capability.

It is not the heart which creates trouble. It is the thought, and the behavior that supports the thought, which is the source of harm to other people and to oneself too. All spiritual students and teachers would benefit from taking heed of the way they set up their mind and realize its goals. I have strong feelings about people who say that their spiritual goal is to renounce worldly life. When I was ten years old, I experienced the strong attraction of religions such as Buddhism, folk Taoism and Christianity, but not the small occult groups. My parents did not agree with my direct involvement with religions when I was a teenager, because I was still very young, although they supported my spiritual learning with an open attitude. They were open to the discussion or experience of all types of religions as spiritual education.

Because my parents had a deep spiritual understanding, they could use the terminology of any religion to discuss or explain any type of worldly experience, including frustrating ones. They often gave spiritual instruction to patients with different spiritual backgrounds using the religious language most easily understood so that the patients could derive maximum spiritual support from their own religion. My father and mother never used the words of Tao or used spiritual teachings to deny any religion. They understood that spiritual truth is in everything, including every religion which is useful and unbiased.

My father and mother were spiritually developed people. My family had friends in different temples, mountain retreats and nunneries. My father's College of Tao had many kinds of students. I was the classmate of several Buddhist nuns and was quietly impressed by their purity and their interest in renouncing the world. My family also frequently visited Buddhist or Taoist temples in the high mountains or in open fields next to lakes. I was born and grew up next to a network of canals. The canals were main waterways which could be used to travel anywhere. This wide variety of religious and spiritual experience, and using the canals near my house, shaped my personality as one who does not hold oneself in one spot or closed up in one house. In other words, I accept the same truth through different languages. Words are only different ways of expressing the same deep truth.

When I was 15 years old, I lived in a spiritual retreat called The Company of the Clouds which was in South Mountain by the Lake of Kindness. It was a place I frequently visited during my youth. My experience of living in a rural place and learning from different teachers made me understand that renouncing the world was not what I wished to do. The care-free life I admire is a spiritual achievement rather than the reality of life. A person may go to a temple to renounce the world only to find that there are just as many problems in a temple as there are outside the temple. The key to resolving one's problem is working on improving oneself.

Thus, a spiritual life is not determined by where you live, but by how open your mind is to transcending your current situation and setting up the correct self-discipline. Some people do not have the desire to go to places like Hollywood or Las Vegas, but few people can avoid some unnecessary glamour. It is not a matter of denouncing or renouncing the world of glamour or it denouncing or renouncing them. Some people just choose a more natural lifestyle without going to extremes to avoid some less essential worldly involvement. All cities have some glamour; some of it is unavoidable.

Is a religious person who renounces the world saved from worldly responsibility? My own experience is that being religious is just a different lifestyle; the responsibility of life cannot be avoided. In other words, if you do not take responsibility for your own life, you need someone to take care of your life for you. In the end, you put energy into making somebody interested in supporting you through donations or help, etc. That is one way of fulfilling the responsibility of life; it still takes energy, but is just a different way to go about it. I do not think that a person living in a temple is more respectable than someone who works in their own field, sweating and toiling most of the time. I have more respect for the average working person than for those who try to renounce the world.

I do have sympathy for people whose destiny, fortune and interest are different from my own and thus choose to renounce the world. Not everyone is well suited to living and working in the business world. Fortunately, there are other choices for them.

For my students and friends who wish to avoid the conflict between worldly life and spiritual life, I would like to offer some advice: be selective. Select the things you do, and accept only the things which cause no conflict with your spiritual study. Try to avoid those things which would cause the downfall of your spiritual attainment. I salute those who live in the world and earn their daily bread with their own hard work and at the same time are spiritual. They never lose their own spiritual cultivation and self-discipline. I also respect those who have already solved the problem of how to make a living and have some free time to offer themselves to help the growth of the younger generation.

My conclusion is that it is correct to live in the world and to be selective spiritually and maintain your purpose of living a complete, healthy spiritual life.

The idea of renouncing the world comes from people who are psychologically worn out by their life experience. They become more attracted to the spiritual path of renunciation rather than the living of a balanced life. In some ways, this is the conflict between my teaching and other teachings. I teach that responsible life is spiritual life, and irresponsible life is unspiritual life. I do not mind that other spiritual teachers do not agree with me.

There are two types of spiritual teacher. One type of teacher announces that money is evil, but that the students should give money to the teacher. The other type of teacher respects one's hard-earned money as the support of one's own spiritual cultivation.

A balanced way of life is the reality of spiritual growth. This is what I teach. I exercise no dominance over anyone, close students or readers of my books. My hope is only that people have true experience of spiritual learning and attain a certain growth so that they can use the same subtle frequency of visual power to see the spiritual truth.

My experience and spiritual attainment still reveal to me that renouncing the world is self-deception. Perhaps it is helpful for a short time in one's learning, but no one can really renounce life. I advise my friends to live differently from the worldly pattern, to be selective and wise. A person can still be active in the world during the daytime or business hours, and renounce the world during your quiet time or meditation at home. Any person who wishes can thus alternate between a worldly and a spiritual life each day without moving or retreating.

Life is precious; we need to be spiritually developed by living a truthful and earnest life. No one could give up this life expecting to live a better life somewhere else at some other time in some other condition.

Deceptive spiritual learning has attracted many people who did not receive any spiritual fruit from their practice and died as fools. The spiritual flower or spiritual fruit is to maintain your soul or spirit intact and safe while living in a world filled with poison and harm. You do not renounce your responsibility to improve yourself and the world. Improvement is the correct direction for all those whose mind and intelligence have reached the understanding to move away from making trouble, causing harm or brewing poison due to their own thoughts, which are incompatible with the world in which they live.

My teaching is to support people in working in the world and living a normal, healthy life. All spiritual people have different degrees of escaping the world. Most people would like to live a carefree life, but I do not consider it dignified or a high spiritual achievement to become a burden to the rest of the world by living upon other people's charity.

All the help of all my students is appreciated, whether they learned well or not. On this occasion, allow me to dedicate this book to the spiritual merit of all my students.

October 28, 1977

I

We are all born into life with different personal energy formations of body, mind and spirit. Everyone knows that physical life does not last forever. The mind is even more unstable than the physical body. We have a thought or idea one minute, and the next minute it is completely gone, yet this intangible aspect of our lives is always stirring us up and causing trouble of one kind or another. Only the spiritual part of life, the soul of your conscious center, remains unchanging and everlasting, but it should not be taken for granted. The opportunity of human birth is precious. Unless you take advantage of it, you could be reborn into a lower form of life. You might wonder how to take correct advantage of your life to avoid that misfortune. It is not difficult to improve yourself and move to a higher reality of life. I will continue to address this task throughout the course of this and all my other classes.

God or spirit is the process of universal life, the subtle law of universal life. Each individual life is a small process that mirrors the process of universal life. When one's own life process matches the subtle spiritual reality, everything is okay. When your process of living goes against the subtle energy reality, consciously or unconsciously, you have trouble right away or you sow the seeds for later trouble.

How or what is spiritual reality, and what is the subtle law? I will answer you as a teacher of the universal subtle law. However, whatever I tell you is not enough. The best knowledge that you will obtain about your spiritual nature and the truth of spiritual reality is not what somebody else tells you. The best knowledge is a product of quiet observation and understanding of your own life. The best knowledge comes through your own experience. Through studying yourself, you attain the most truthful knowledge of life.

The ancient sage Lao Tzu said, "Do not overdo anything because of the demand of the mind's desire." I modified his saying, but basically, what Lao Tzu means is that one needs to be natural in order to harmonize or follow the subtle spiritual law. Good fortune or misfortune is defined by the mind, but fortune is still not nature. What is considered fortune is external physical reality, not spiritual reality, which in truth is more important. Generally, people are concerned about their fortune and thus they compare themselves to others. We spend too much time judging our lives and so little time living our lives. I am talking about this very moment! Many of you are thinking this moment instead of living and experiencing this moment. How foolish we are when we move our thoughts away from the reality of our bodies and our lives! Can we live our lives fully in this moment, and in all moments, rather than just thinking about our lives? Let us all keep learning and experimenting in our lives, in society and in the world of all times.

How does one break through the limitations of physical existence and mental obstructions to connect with the spiritual part of life? To begin with, we must increase our consciousness. Consciousness is the ability to be aware of more subtle levels of life. We increase our consciousness by removing the obstacles to consciousness, which are energy blocks within the mind and body. This is different from just working with the mental and emotional levels. There are a lot of spiritual paths and religions on the market today which offer different mental and emotional toys and tools. They have many followers, but they are more concerned with social education and control than with actual spiritual development. They do not tend to increase one's consciousness. In ancient times, people's minds were not highly developed and something was needed to pacify people in order to maintain social order, thus religions were formed to teach behavior modification. Today it is not enough to just be good boys and girls in a religious model of a correct life; we must continue to develop ourselves. Once we deal effectively with the physical and mental aspects of life, it is time to move forward in the direction of spiritual maturity.

Here are some questions to help you understand yourself. Are you self-responsible yet, or are you still looking for a personal savior? What is a spiritual life? Do you pay attention to your immortal self, or are you only concerned with your body and your mind? Do you concern yourself with the meaning and purpose of life and death, or are you too busy to think about such things?

If you have concerned yourself with these and other questions, it has probably been through reading and thinking about them, which can stimulate a person's search but does not ultimately bring one in touch with the immortal self. This class will not spend a lot of time in sitting around discussing the great issues of life. This will be a class of doing the practice. This will be a class of real service for your real self.

No one in the world can escape difficulties. Everyone who was ever born has had problems in life. Birth is trauma. Getting along with your family and society is often hard. Adolescence is painful. Working is difficult. What methods can be used to heal yourself of these past and present problems? Do you think I will use herbs to try to help you? Wine or drugs? Do you think I will try psychology and have you scream and shout your problems out? I am not going to use any of these methods, because you can play those games and still hold on to your ego. The method I am going to teach you was developed over 10,000 years ago. What method is it? It is called energy manifestation.

It was through subtle energy response that pre-historic people were first able to communicate with each other. Language is a relative late-comer in human development, yet how dependent we have become on it! People are proud of their Ph.D.'s and so forth, but what good does a degree do a person who is on his death bed? Can language or a degree save your soul? Can language add one more second to your life? It cannot. For this reason, we will not be doing any talking or reading in the main section of the class. The communication can be done at the end of each class.

How did enlightened people impart their wisdom and other experiences to students before language developed? It was done by subtle energy transference. That is the method we will use here also. Energy transference is done to help another person attain a state of balance or equilibrium. As a trained master, I can see by your movements whether your energy is balanced or not. Balanced energy does not ultimately come from mental improvement.

Thus, we will not be developing your minds here; they are already developed too much and have become overly restless. Mental development has nothing to do with life and death on the level of spirit. You can remain totally insensitive to many levels of existence no matter how many books you read, hymns you sing or rituals you perform. Many Christians, for instance, talk about knowing God's will, but most of them are not even aware of the lower levels of the psychic realms, much less the divine realms within their own subtle beings. How can someone hope to become immortal without even being able to see the immortal realm? Proving the existence of such things will give a person true self-confidence for spiritual development. A person who believes in something without actual experience has a kind of faith or belief, not knowledge. Faith or belief is where most people start in spiritual learning, but I do not recommend that you stay on that level without making progress. Thus, if you say you believe in the immortal realm without actually experiencing it, you are just being foolish. I recommend that you develop yourself to find out more about it. How do you do this? The first step is to work on your energy composition. It is the raw material you will work with to later form your spiritual fetus.

The second stage of spiritual unfoldment is to develop your sensitivity to subtle energy. A person who is sensitive is able to sense when I am near him even if he cannot see or hear me - even if I am 30 yards away. You can also develop a sense of the future in the same way, through energy sensitivity. In ancient times, people did not have telephones to announce to a friend that they were coming for a visit, yet the friend would start preparing the feast several days in advance. How did they know their friends were coming? They knew by intuition. You can develop the same sense as they did. When you do so, when I tell you that the shiens have come to visit us, you can see them also. You must learn to raise your vibrational level so your energy can respond to them, or else you will be unable to see them. After you learn this, then we will go onto the third stage.

The third stage is to become a shien or a spiritually achieved being yourself. Only after you have a good foundation of energy control can you hope to achieve this. If you have no self control, you can achieve nothing. If you truly gain control over your body, mind and spirit, then it is possible to control your destiny, including your life and death. You will know the future and everything else, but right now, there is much work to be done.

What is a shien and how do they differ from ordinary people? Shiens are pure spirit. Spiritual shiens do not have bodies. Earthly shiens have bodies but have transcended them. The most important thing is that shiens find happiness in spirit itself. They are not much interested in social benefits or artificial pleasures. Their interest and amusement is in the simple, natural things of life. They still retain a sense of awe and majesty in everything they do, no matter how simple or ordinary it is. We will not discuss the shiens any more now, we must focus on the first stage, which is self-release.

Self-release is the first step of self-discovery and it is done by uncovering your energy composition, which is affected by your psychological condition. The purpose of self-discovery is not to find out whether a demon or an angel is inside of you, because there are no demons or angels. It is to find out the patterns of your thinking that need to be improved and to discover and release any negative energies inside your body which might direct you to be *like* a demon or an angel. The purpose of self-release is self-purification. Then you put yourself back together in one piece.

For true and total integration of spirit to take place, you do not live your life for your parents, your boy or girl friend, or your society. Neither do you live a selfish life. You live a life of naturalness and completeness with all three spheres of body, mind and soul. Your internal composition and external life will function correctly. Thus, you will live a life for all people, including yourself.

During the course of this class, you are welcome to bring your questions. Since true teachers of natural spiritual truth are not spiritual dealers, I am not going to push anything on you, but I respond to your level of growth.

I am not here to tell you only what you want to hear; I am here to help you become shiens if that is your interest. As long as we do have language, we might as well take advantage of it and make use of it in a helpful way.

II
Commentary

When you begin to practice internal alchemy, your first discovery will be the latent life energy in the body. Quite often, people experience their eye muscles twitching or their limbs shaking. Modern people call such involuntary movements reflexes of the nervous system. They ignore them rather than study them. Even modern scientists do not talk about the latent physical or semi-physical energy which everybody has within their bodies. In this class, the first step is to discover this latent energy.

We are going to do a practice called self-release to expose the internal energy so you can experience, regulate, harmonize, refine and develop it. After you do that, you can begin the practice called Internal Alchemy. Thus, the first part of my teaching has the purpose of discussing the basics of your life energy in ways that are different from what you already know.

This class will continue for around four months to enable you to sufficiently experience your own latent energy.

The self-release of latent energy can be done in all kinds of positions; sitting, lying, walking and standing. Because our space is limited in this class, we will do it in a standing position, about an arm's length away from each other.

Let me now tell you what to do. It is simple: you just stand there. However, you must remember one important principle in your standing. Do not use your mind. Do not tell your body what to do. In general, we use our minds to command our bodies. When you are practicing self-release, allow the body to be natural in its behavior; this is the ancient instruction. Do not use your mind to form spiritual reality, do not use any artificial approach to interfere with nature. You only stand there and allow your body to make all kinds of adjustments to itself, by itself, just as it needs.

I call this self-release because you do not know the existence of your latent energy which is one important partner of your life. While this energy is exhibiting itself within your body, you find out what is inside of you. However, absolutely do not use your mind to conduct or guide what you feel, the sounds or movements you make, or try to connect the energy released with any past emotional experiences you have had. If you try to do that, some subnormal phenomenon might occur.

When all of you do the self-release, close your eyes so you will not see what any of the other people are doing. In that way, you are not affected by what you see, nor will you start to imitate what other people do. Thus, your movement will be natural and it will be your own. Also, I will play some gentle music which you are not familiar with that will not cause any stimulation to your mind. It will keep your ear or consciousness from searching for any sound which would give you any hint or suggestion that might form your reaction in any way other than totally natural.

In other words, when this energy is released, do not allow your mind to command it, or your emotion to help it; then you will fully experience your latent life force.

It is suitable to do this type of practice for three months or so, up to one year. Then you can go to a higher step to recognize the higher energy. You might wonder if you can move directly to a higher step of learning. I say you can, but spiritual energy is subtle and you might miss it if you are not paying attention. It has five levels, each level more subtle than the other. The highest subtlety is almost like nothing. That is what I call the subtle origin.

The energies that you are releasing in this class are on the first of the five levels. The first three levels of energy have certain forms. To describe it more correctly, I would say that the latent energy is not really a form, because it is deeper than form. It is what supports the form of life.

All of you are modern scholars or intellectuals. You may not believe in latent energy at this time, so this practice will have great value as a process of self-discovery at a level of energy which is new to you. Hopefully it will be strong or forcible enough so that your mind can experience and recognize it as the basic foundation of your life.

If you feel that you have not fully released all the latent or stored energy that is in your body during the course of this class, then you can continue to do this practice at home in the mornings. When you do it in the morning, the purpose is just to let your body absorb the morning energy. That will be new energy plus old energy. If the energy releases itself through some kind of emotional expression, it is not suitable to link up the release with past or present emotions, external stimulation or trouble; that will be of no benefit and will only delay your achievement.

For many people, releasing internally stored energy will cause a temporary new excitement. You take responsibility when doing the self-release not to associate it with your mind, I take responsibility for the method I teach. When you feel that it is unsafe or you are overdoing it or become unable to control it, just open your eyes and stop the direction you are moving in or totally stop the practice and do something else for a while. Then do it later when you feel okay about it. I have asked all of you to sign individual statements which extend this type of understanding.

Definitely, self-release is a class of discovering your own life energy. I am a spiritual teacher, not a psychologist or therapist. Although all life is related to all spheres, the main purpose of this class is not psychological or emotional. Some amount of release, if it does not verge on breakdown, is okay; I will not stop you. If you have deep-rooted psychological or emotional difficulties, you might prefer to consult experts in those fields. That is your responsibility. The statement that you signed is mainly to help you avoid coming to any quick conclusion or becoming judgmental about your new experience. Once people understand this practice, they participate in it fully and reap its benefits. Many people have expressed tremendous gratitude that they went through the release and transformed their lives so that they would continue further study to reach the truth of life. No textbook in any school can teach this.

Your personal energy belongs to you alone. Usually, people are guided by parents, society, school, culture and friends to do certain things rather than guiding themselves in proper behavior. Whether it is someone outside or yourself, either way, you are being guided by the mind. We experience enough of that. Now, in this class, it is time for you to put that aside totally and experience something different. Now you need to experience the body's nature. Then you will find out that you have the possibility to achieve yourself as God through your self-cultivation. You can do this if you are not dependent upon any church to act as an agent between you and God.

With this understanding, if you do not misconduct yourselves, this will be a great class and a great experience with high enjoyment. It is not some kind of toil or labor. It is simple. You just do nothing with your mind in the class. I ask you to do nothing about your partner the mind. I ask you to listen to nobody but your body. During this practice, you think of nobody and nothing but your own body. By standing still, you allow the body's nature to behave naturally by itself. Then the latent energy shall find its release.

During this class, I will only speak when I give a comment at the end of each class. This will help your mind attain correct spiritual knowledge, which is not the teaching of the church, nor is it meant to conduct you. It is the spiritual education from a broad background, the natural spiritual truth.

During this first class, I have seen that all of you were on the right track in self-releasing your energy. The energy was generating in different patterns.

Although energy transformation and formation is accomplished in many ways, to sum it all up, it is *your* energy. You are safe with your energy as long as you do not conduct it to a different direction of life. Different directions can be harmful if they turn out to be emotional sensitivity, excessive anger, sadness or sensuality. Everything is natural; if we do not get carried away by the mind and overdo anything, and allow nature to take its course, the experience of this class will be peaceful, harmonious and enjoyable. May the divine energy of Heaven be with all of you.

November 13, 1977

I would like to briefly touch on the importance of generating and refining energy. Everyone knows the principles of cooking - even if they are a lousy cook! You need fire - or in today's world, a stove - a pot, and some food to put in the pot. Then, you can boil, fry, steam or stew the food. The important thing is to use the right amount of heat. If the fire is too hot, the food burns; if there is not enough heat, the food remains uncooked.

When you practice internal alchemy, also called spiritual cultivation, you work with the same principles as cooking. "Cooking" in spiritual cultivation refers to increasing and refining one's energy. Many religions destroy you with too much heat, too much emotionalism. Some religions do not generate enough heat, and the food stays raw. The trick is to refine your energy at just the right temperature.

It is impossible for anyone to achieve themselves if their energy has not been refined. Without working to refine one's energy, a typical person stays on the worldly level and cannot achieve higher spiritually. Those who are open minded and listen to new ideas from an experienced cook can learn to refine energy and achieve themselves. Some of you will have to go through our internal alchemy class a second and third time because your cooking skills are still so basic. Some of you have not even started cooking yet.

I would like to pause for a moment to tell you a little bit about my teaching. I teach the subtle methods of refinement because that is what I have learned. I will direct you in one particular method - that of the Integral Way of natural spiritual truth - in order to keep you from scattering your minds by trying too many different methods from too many places. However, the divine energy is universal, and there are many ways to reach it. This is one I know to be true, which originates in China.

Our tradition started in pre-historic times. The reason we know this is because the earliest writings in Chinese show that people already had knowledge of divination.

Divination is not refinement, but it indicates an awareness of the influence of energy. Some religions say that humans are inferior to God, but the achieved ones of spiritual energy think people can control divine energy. Achieved ones of my tradition believe that all people were born with a divine nature, just like the Gods.

The earliest people were always trying to understand and conduct the subtle energy. The big events in their lives were all preceded by ceremony and divination because they understood that divination can reveal energy and that ceremony can affect energy, and thus one can change or control destiny. This is true to a certain extent.

Today most modern Chinese, and modern people in general, are skeptical or just do not believe in those things any more. They use their inductive and deductive reasoning and they deny the existence of spirit and the usefulness of divination and ceremony. Most modern Chinese do not understand that prehistoric people did not have any sophisticated intellectual development to confuse them. Their minds were not spoiled yet, and so they were not separated from life itself. They were still natural and used their intuition to discern things.

Now, in modern times, we have the written word. We have books written by achieved ones such as Lao Tzu, Chuang Tzu and Lieh Tzu, etc. Only part of the original spirit of universal subtlety has been told in those books. Finally, civilization became so corrupt that all the Chinese sages and achieved ones went to the high mountains to live and stopped writing completely. Sometimes they would come down to help humanity, but mostly they stayed away.

You must understand that the mountains I refer to are not like the mountains in America where there are a lot of ordinary people running around. You cannot even go into certain mountains in China unless you have some spiritual power. For one thing, the monkeys would stone you if you tried. You must negotiate with the head of their families before they even let you enter.

Anyway, about that time in history, during the Han Dynasty (206 B.C.-219 A.D.), Taoism was the established religion of people who still lived in cities. What they called

Taoism was different from the older and more natural tradition. The new Taoist leaders just performed rather superficial ceremonies so they could earn a living. They did not have the depth of the achieved ones of the pre-historic original spiritual culture.

My tradition mostly concerns itself with cultivating the pure spirit. That is our main purpose. Sometimes we work to help the world, but it is with the same purpose, because the world is a big life that is yours also.

During the Tang Dynasty, Chinese people were heavily influenced by Buddhism. Before Buddhism arrived, farmers were only interested in being good farmers to support their own lives, and scholars were only interested in getting prestigious positions in the government, etc. When Buddhism arrived, the Buddhists told them that being self-sufficient was not enough - they needed to be a Buddha too. No one was content to just be a good farmer or an achieved scholar anymore; they all wanted to become Buddhas.

A little later, some highly evolved people came down out of the mountains and learned the ways of the Buddhists. These interactions gave birth to Zahn (Zen) Buddhism. That influence is why Zahn (Zen) puts more emphasis on knowing your own true nature than on knowing the details of Buddha's life. The essence of Zahn is one's self-nature rather than the external trappings of Buddhism. However, today Zen is still attached to the shell of religion. It is not like the teaching I do, which is to adopt no single religion in order to present the plain truth.

Zahn (Zen) seems to have become the new Buddhism as religion and lost its originality. They sit too much. It is unnatural and is bad for energy circulation, thus they are unable to directly reach the truth of enlightenment.

Who today knows anything about energy circulation? Who knows what day is a good day for making money? Who knows what is a good day for having sex or training a horse? Because the energy is always changing, we must change our activities to harmonize with it, so that everything will go smoothly. If we do not attune ourselves to the energy, then there will surely be trouble. Most people do not realize this, but if you have sex at a bad time, you may get V.D. or something. Even worse, you may conceive a child and give birth to a criminal or some other kind of inferior being. You see, a child that results from a bad exchange of energy between a man and a woman will have bad energy.

Also, by not following the energy cycles, you may invest your money at the wrong time and lose it all. Money, you see, is only a form of energy. If it is manipulated on a "broken day," it will be taken away. A broken day is a day whose energy causes you to lose, or gain at first, then lose. With regard to investments, of course, there are many cycles to take into consideration besides your personal cycle. Market cycles are also important. This is just an example.

The concept of the "broken day" came from the calendars that were made by the Scholars of Formulas during the Han Dynasty. The "broken day" was considered to be one day of the twelve-day cycle. Unfortunately, the Scholars tended to apply their knowledge and invention of the twelve-day cycle somewhat rigidly instead of actually flowing with the energy of the day. The term "broken day" is not related to the term "broken line" which describes yin energy. In general, it means a day on which you lose energy. For example, if you initiate a business liaison on such a day, sometimes you gain at the beginning, but eventually you lose again. As I view the twelve-day cycle, it is too external.

Because a person's activities tend to follow one's internal energy cycles, when you do things on low energy days, you will tend to lose energy in all of its forms, such as money, property, etc. Thus, investments are not affected only by external cycles of the market, they are also affected by internal cycles of one's own energy. I am using the general trade market as an example, but this can be applied to many situations in life. All these kinds of things can happen if you are ignorant of subtle energy. This is why I say that Zahn Buddhism is limited to the mind. It does not cover all aspects of life.

In addition to the knowledge of subtle energy, you must also develop control over yourself in order to eventually be able to generate and refine your own energy. Many people know when they are going against the energy flow, but because they are so desirous and weak, they cannot stop doing so and they end up hurting themselves. Sometimes living in a spiritual community where everyone tries to live a natural life can help that situation, but typically it is something that a person has to learn by oneself.

We do not ask you to be a Buddha, or wait to go to Heaven after you die, or anything like that - just enjoy your own good nature. By enjoying your good nature, I do not mean enjoy yourself by indulging in pleasures. I mean enjoy your calm and peaceful internal energy. Do you know that your own energy is as complete as the energy of the universe? You are a complete little universe yourself. Not only that, the three levels of your energy can connect with the three energy levels of the entire universe. You have Heavenly energy, earthly energy and human energy. Unfortunately, most people do not know anything about their Heavenly energy, which is the level of refined energy. This is why it is necessary for people to cultivate themselves in order to understand more deeply.

There are many ways to cultivate oneself. Helping others can be part of your cultivation, but it is not meant that you go around and look for people to help. Many well-intentioned people waste all their good energy on people who are not really interested in improving themselves.

People of spiritual achievement usually try to help others in subtle, formless ways. We are not interested in becoming popular or starting any kind of social movement.

People come to me wishing to learn the subtle truth. I am in the role of helper, but basically one helps oneself rather than just follows me. The learning of the spiritual nature of the universe is something that you must accomplish by yourself. All spiritual service is given to help you find the spiritual reality by yourself. You are the purpose of the spiritual service. You are here to restore your true nature. Once that is accomplished, then you may help the world in turn, but remember that the world is different today than it was in the old days. You cannot hope to suddenly return today's world to its natural state. If you try, you will only exhaust yourself. Your time would be better spent in making a living for yourself in order to support your cultivation. Once you are self-sufficient, you can work gently and subtly on the world for however long it takes without hurting yourself.

Anyway, back to the Tang Dynasty and what I was wishing to tell you about the spiritually achieved ones. As I mentioned, many poor people were seduced into learning Buddhism at that time. It is interesting that on the general level of religion at that time, if you had no money, you studied Buddhism to save your soul, and if you were rich, you studied Taoism to try to live forever! Even though mostly rich people studied Taoism, there were many restrictions placed upon them so that only the most sincere students with deep spiritual roots were ever allowed to learn the more profound secrets.

Also, I mentioned how rigid Buddhism was before the naturally achieved ones influenced it. They sat too much and ate only vegetables and told people not to have sex, etc. The achieved ones came out of the mountains and said, "It's holy to do sex!" You might find it interesting that with the proper knowledge or training, sex can be part of your cultivation. You know, if everyone had become a Buddhist monk or nun, none of us would ever have been born. The truly achieved masters actually taught people how to have sex as a part of cultivation, but that is not all that cultivation is about. Do you know how much that information would cost you today at our inflated prices? At least $100,000 American dollars.

Anyway, when Master Lu, Tung Ping, a well-known highly achieved master, came down from the mountains, he watched the Buddhists meditating every day and saw that they were getting more and more sallow looking. This is why he instructed them in how to generate their own energy. Without any energy generation, meditation is like water boiling in an open pan; the water soon boils away and the pan will burn. Perhaps that is not the best description, but we might say that many meditations and cultivations stagnate your energy and leave you cold and dry, but a rapidly boiling pan leaves you hot and dry. Therefore, it is important to learn the correct meditation and energy generation. Adjustment in one's cultivation and meditation is important, just like tuning a musical instrument.

Otherwise, your mastery can be damaged. Good meditation makes you warm and moist. Dead things are cold and dry, but living things are warm and moist.

This important and necessary method of energy generation we call the "fiery dragon" method. It is the good result of internal energy generation. The fire is your own energy, and with this method it is even possible to restore withered organs and tissues.

Old men tend to become impotent. Once this energy is restored, they can be like the fiery dragon again. They become rejuvenated. Many older people were helped by this method of energy generation. If your energy is already good, meaning if you are not sick or weak, the fiery dragon method can help you refine and balance it. I wanted to discuss this method with you today so you could see how valuable and important it is as a foundation for further spiritual growth.

Master Lu showed us this method. That statue over there is him. It shows him traveling, which is something he enjoyed very much. He went all over China teaching and helping people in subtle ways. He was also a poet and enjoyed life greatly. Who says a divine being cannot enjoy life? I will tell you more about his life some other time.

Now I would like to read you a poem written by Master Kou Hsiao-Hsieng who was active around 160-300 A.D. He was known as the Immortal Kou to most Chinese people until the last generation, but not by name. He was the grand-uncle of Master Kou Hong.

The rolling pearl of my ambitious mind commanded my life.
It made me run everywhere
        and search in many hard-to-obtain books.
Although I tried hard,
        I still did not find the truth of immortality.
I was only thinking about my own stupidity
        by trying all kinds of metals
        and testing all the precious minerals
        hoping to discover ancient sacred spiritual alchemy.
Even when I was sixty years old,
        I was still wandering in search of truth.

I spent my entire fortune looking for it.
Finally, sighing, I sat and held my knees.
Then, I finally found my teacher
*   and he kindly revealed the truth for me.*

Subtle vitality is not found in substantial materials.
It is found in the evasive and illusive interplay
*   of yin and yang within oneself,*
*   by which it produces chi and sen.*
Nurture the subtlety of evasiveness
*   and illusiveness of mind,*
*   flow with the interplay of yin and yang*
*   expressed through deep, gentle and relaxed*
*   inhalation and exhalation*
*   to allow the two forces to help*
*   brew and renew vitality.*

In order to refine the Immortal Medicine,
*   first set up the Inner Golden Cauldron.*
Then, allow the stove beneath it to be fueled
*   by the five energies.*
As a rule, the fire of Li should descend under the ocean,
*   your lower tan tien.*
The water of K'un should rise to the sky
*   of your upper tan tien*
*   to refine the body fluid.*
Then newly produced and harvested jade fluid
*   moistens the pure land of your life.*
The rain of fragrant balm also reaches everywhere.
Then the actualization of immortality is near.

No other way can bring true success.
The truth helps only the person
*   of deep spiritual awareness.*
Realize that it is not the physical universe
*   which is everlasting*
*   but the truth of immortal being*
*   which is truly everlasting.*
Immortality can be achieved with true sincerity.
The words I give need to be studied carefully.

November 20, 1977

Master Ni: Today, let's take some time to answer your questions.

Q: After the last class, you took us outside and showed us the Big Dipper and the North Star. You mentioned finding "your" star. I'd like to know more about that. Does each person have only one star?

Master Ni: In general, so-called fortune is external. When you were born, there were many stars and planets in the sky, and together they composed or structured a kind of picture that describes your life. The stars are posed in the sky according to the time, and they express a specific type of energy. Some stars and planets have a strong influence and others have a weak influence, but the whole view of a person's star chart gives clues about a person's life, not just one specific individual energy. The whole energy formation is what is important, because that is what affects one's personal disposition and tendencies. Yet, real characteristics and one's personal virtue are not decided by external destiny alone. Your destiny depends upon what and how you conceive yourself spiritually.

Q: Is there any special thing that we should do on our own birthday every year?

Master Ni: Ordinarily, spiritually achieved people do not emphasize birthdays because they remind us of our mortality and physical limitations. Your birthday is the birth of your physical life, not of the true you, which experiences all processes of life. It is the everlasting you which participates in the evolution of your self and the world. The real birthday is the time when one achieves a breakthrough in finding or establishing the meaning of life, especially spiritually. Then you are born spiritually.

The physical body influences your life and mostly gives you a lot of inconvenience. You are not free anymore when you have a body. If you travel, you must get a visa for it and you must also buy it a ticket. You must pay for its food and clothes too, so having a physical body is a great limitation, except for further spiritual development. The main reason you take all the trouble to have a body and experience that kind of life is for your spiritual fortification.

To answer the question, birthdays do mean something. They mean external fortune or destiny. As I mentioned, the position of the stars at the time of your physical birth affects your external life. After you become a serious student of spiritual reality, you might like to try to reform your fortune, to change it so you do not need to follow your physical destiny. If you want to follow your limited physical destiny, then you can study another kind of philosophy or belief other than the Integral Way, which goes deeply to the root. If you follow your external destiny, you limit yourself to being a certain kind of person.

In your current lifetime, you have the possibility for change and improvement. However, if you accept your birthday, you also accept your destiny. Nothing can be done; you will surely have trouble. I do not accept my birthday. Do you? If you are tied down by your birthday, it means that certain events are predetermined, such as whether you will marry or not, how many children you will have, how much money you will make, etc. If you have birth, then you have death. There must be an end to your life if there was a beginning.

To a student of the Integral Spiritual Way, life is a beginningless and endless journey. One day you just find yourself here. You pick up the customs and the clothes and the language, etc., and one day you will go away. Perhaps you will pay another visit, perhaps not. Maybe you will visit many times because you love Earth very much. Who knows?

Q: When I suppress sex I end up thinking about it more.

Master Ni: Sex is a kind of physical release. Sometimes you are tense and you cannot deal with your mind and desires. Thus, when you have sex, you can release the tension and relax. It is a kind of self-adjustment.

In learning spiritual reality, we use sex in two ways: as a cultivation or as a self-attunement. Sexual attunement is only for physical purposes, but it can also be applied to someone who has an overactive mind. Under careful instruction, sex can be used as a cultivation and can even help your body, but this is not the vulgar or ordinary way of sex.

Ordinary sex is a physical relief, but at the same time, it is a self-chaining. By self-chaining I mean your habitual reliance on it will chain you. Now that you have begun this class and are interested in increasing your self-awareness and are cultivating subtle energy, try to stop having sex altogether for a while, if you can - or just do it less. For the time being, my suggestion is to decrease it. If you do it too much, you will hurt your energy. If you have too much sex, you will have no fire in your body, so how can you connect with the Divine Energy? You will be like a candle without the wick; you cannot make any light.

I would like to tell you the truth. The correct way of having sex as a spiritual cultivation is deep, profound knowledge. If you know how to do it correctly, it is good medicine and can help your life. If you do not, it is a poison, but I think you all still enjoy your poison!

This internal alchemy class deals mostly with your gross and rough energy. It will take a number of years to refine it because you still live in a society which continually feeds you bad energy. Even if you refine yourself now, later, in a day or a month or a year, or every sixty days, you will need to release the contamination you have picked up from the world.

Each time you do self-release, your energy changes. Ordinarily, your mind is quite active, but now you have a new energy in your body because you have done the self-release. The energies that compose you are attracted from the different energies in your environment, such as the energy from people, from stars, natural forces from every dimension and every direction. All of these energies cause you a lot of automatic and responsive movement, as you have experienced in the class. Each individual experiences self-release differently; there is no unified way to describe what each of you experience, because the experience is not controlled by your mind. Your mind must relax its control during self-release. Some of you can do this better than others. It is okay to think, but your energy will not pay attention to what you think.

For many years your vitality, your vital power, has been controlled and suffocated by your mind. Now it is time to relax that control and let your energy express itself by natural automatic response and self-adjustment. I might describe the activity of self-release that I taught people, but it is not suitable or needed for everyone in the world.

Normally, what people call a good mind is a highly intellectual mind, which is also called a brilliant mind. I have made some observations about that. People who are considered intellectually brilliant usually have a larger brain cavity and are physically weaker than ordinary people. They often have physical problems such as stomach trouble, liver trouble or ulcers, etc., and tend to be emotionally unbalanced. This is because they are controlled too much by the negative, untamed mind. They always see the world as their enemy. This person's approach at all times is to label and describe everything. They overuse the mind, and the result is not positive. Even if he or she does well in life, this person cannot enjoy it. They usually live a shorter life and have more suffering.

However, wisdom, or having a truly good mind in the spiritual sense, is different. Wise people keep their original sincerity, earnestness and simplicity. Nobody can take their enjoyment away from them. If a person always worries that someone will take his enjoyment away, then he will always be afraid. Fear itself causes trouble and is an indication of the loss of wisdom of the spirit.

Many people try to cheat themselves and say that they are happy. This is not true achievement; it is ignorance and is pathetic. They are not really happy, because they are following their mind and not the wisdom of their spirit. So you see, the best way to live is with the spirit and not with the happiness and fears of the mind.

Some churches teach you to say every day, "Oh God, you give us all protection. You give us what we need." This practice eventually makes your mind and nerves numb to reality. It is not the thorough way of spiritual self-responsibility. When you become spiritually self-responsible, you accept the truth of life which contains both good fortune and misfortune. From misfortune you learn to be prudent. There is a wise saying, "From what is needed, you learn to create." In English you might say, "Necessity is the mother of invention," but the thought is that difficulties bring about growth, creativity and strength. Do not be afraid of knowing the truth and following the truth of spirit. Pain or no pain, happy or not, it is not necessary to create a mental wall to keep pleasure in and unpleasantness out. Walls do not work; nobody can build a wall strong enough to keep unpleasantness out, because whatever is out there is also within you. In reality, there are no walls.

If you are healthy and if you are strong enough to deal with things, everything can be pleasant. I hope that your next question is: "How can I become healthier and stronger?" My answer is, both come from your cultivation.

Your cultivation can begin with self-release. At the first stage of your self-release, perhaps you will laugh or cry. Even if you cry, it is not true sorrow; it is just some bad energy coming out.

Also, as an important part of one's cultivation, you need to get up early in the morning, because it is the morning's energy you need for health, anti-aging and to live a happy and long life. Some of you stay up late at night because you are city people. You do not know that the energies of the late hours are poisonous. The more you partake of them, the more you are weakened spiritually. If you cultivate the energy of the early mornings, you will have good energy, and you will have an enjoyable life at all times. Are there any more questions?

Q: Should we meditate in the evening?

Master Ni: It is okay, but you see, quiet sitting is only one aspect of natural spiritual cultivation.

The natural spiritual way of cultivation is a whole series of training. The Chinese normally call it "Tao Kung." Tao means Tao, Kung means techniques or methods. The purpose of the many methods is to encourage your mind and body to have intercourse. This means to keep your body and mind joined at all times and not let your thoughts wander away from what your body is doing.

I mentioned before that if your mind is not developed and you lack spiritual ability, then you cannot prove the many levels of spiritual realms. The training of this class is to begin your cultivation so you can develop your high sensitivity to penetrate the deep realm of spirit.

In natural spiritual cultivation, we concentrate on one thing: the energy. Energy has many different manifestations, but most manifestations cannot last long. Only the Divine Energy is everlasting. It is the most powerful force in the universe. This is why the Divine Energy is the center of our cultivation and the center of all truly spiritual ceremonies. If you are achieved in Divine Energy, you will be a shien in your next life, a whole person, or a Buddha, if you prefer that title.

Now let's focus on the importance of the body. With your body, you can verify the existence of the subtle spiritual reality. With your body, you continue the evolution of humankind. Do you believe that this planet and the human race is in its final stage of evolution? Surely not. Do you think that if people are successful in destroying all life through nuclear force, that man would re-appear on earth? Spiritual people think so, because they believe that with the same environment and the same atmosphere, the same living beings will reappear.

I would like to give an illustration of this. In China, there was a place where a forest burned to ashes. For a thousand miles, no living beings existed because of this big fire. Even ten feet down into the earth was ashes, and in this area there were no birds or anything moving. According to Western scientific biological knowledge, life would re-appear by the wind bringing new seeds, but spiritually developed ones say that a place will grow a certain kind of tree because the energy arrangement was a certain way. Anyway, ten years after the fire, the same trees were growing there beautifully; not just a few, but thick groves. Nature grew them spontaneously.

Thus, according to spiritual nature, we are the products of our environment and we are here to fulfill one great purpose: to use your body as a laboratory to do the work of self-refinement, which is also called internal alchemy. In other words, you refine yourself to produce a new spiritual self, a new spiritual life, because the human species is short-lived and bound to the physical world. The new spiritual species is free and everlasting.

There are two methods to accomplish internal alchemy: one is to cultivate individually and the other is dual cultivation. If you are young and your energy is strong enough, then you can do it alone. If you come to middle age and you are not too strong and need something to balance yourself, then one can do dual cultivation between man and woman. If you are old and your energy is gone and you need a renaissance of body, mind and spirit, then we teach you dual cultivation to help you.

Vulgar sex is a kind of self robbery, because your essence (the energy and the spirit) is the most important thing in your body. Your sexual energy is the material or base of your cultivation. It is the capital you can use to start an enterprise. Sex is attractive; even if you are a sage, it is hard to control yourself and keep yourself from losing your energy.

Some of you are younger, so this is an appropriate time to lay down a strong foundation for high spiritual development. When you have a good foundation, even if you become old, the enjoyment of youthfulness will be boundless. You can avoid physical illness and also lengthen your years and especially develop your sensitivity. You can also communicate with all different levels of beings; thus, your life will not be limited to what you can perceive with your eyes, ears and nose.

Have you heard the story of the three blind men who were having an argument about what an elephant was like?

One blind man felt the side of the elephant and said, "An elephant is just like a wall." The second blind man felt the leg of the elephant and said, "An elephant is just like a tree trunk." The third blind man felt the elephant's trunk and said, "An elephant is just like a snake." Each one was so insistent upon his knowledge of the elephant, that they almost came to blows. Well, all people who have not achieved themselves spiritually are just like the three blind men - none of them have a complete idea of what the spiritual realm is like. It is a partial understanding.

Now I am asking you if you are ready to give up your blindness. After your development of spiritual powers, you can connect and communicate with all realms of beings. Your view of life will change. You will not live the way you do now. Surely, you are still what you are, if you choose to stay that way, but you will not live merely to make more money or become famous. Those superficial things will not be as important in your life anymore. If you know that people can survive after death, if you know that there are other worlds and if you know that even in your lifetime you can connect with those other worlds, then your view of life will change drastically.

One thing I must state so that you do not become confused: when I say that you will not live to make more money or become famous, I do not mean that you will quit your job and stop talking to people. I mean that you will quit seeking excessive wealth or excessive fame. I mean that wealth or fame is no longer the main goal of your life. It does not mean that you do not earn your way or that you disregard others. A true student of spiritual nature always works for one's own living and is kind to others, but is not excessive in either of those regards.

When I was young, I lived in a small town. I visited metropolitan Shanghai, which had millions of people, and was considered a big city. In my town, anyone who had friends or relatives who lived in Shanghai and corresponded with them felt superior to everyone else in town. However, when you connect with all the different levels of beings, you do not feel a need to be more important than your neighbor, because that kind of thing is too petty to care about any more.

This is the start of your cultivation. You are starting by learning and by releasing negative energy to make room for positive energy. If you continue your cultivation and eventually become successful at taking it to a certain level, the opportunities for spiritual development are boundless. The more you cultivate, the more you discover about yourself and the universe. The more you cultivate, the more your energy is refined. At least, you become subtle and spiritual.

In the past, some masters actually flew away physically in broad daylight; we have historical records of that. They enjoyed a new kind of beingness, and so can you. In the ancient teaching of natural spiritual truth, our main work is to refine our energy.

We are pursuing the nurturing or development of our subtle energy. Energy has at least three levels: physical, mental and spiritual. There are many different ways to train your energy. One way you have seen a lot is through the expression of Kung Fu. The word "Kung" means method and the word "Fu" means the accumulation of time and practice. After successful Kung Fu training, a finger can penetrate a wall or your hand can break anything. Some martial art masters who achieve the subtle levels of Kung Fu training can damage an opponent's energy without even touching him. A higher form of physical energy transmission is called "Hit the wild oxen on the other side of the tall mountain." It uses the energy to attract water from inside a deep well. At first nothing will happen, but eventually you will get a response from the surface of the water. After some years, when you draw back your hand, some of the water will come out. I was not highly interested in these methods; at the time of Pau Po Tzu, over a thousand special skills were developed, but they are not the pursuit of a student of natural spiritual truth. They are not the value of life. They are limited practices. Even the best Kung Fu practitioner knows only how to kill. Those practices do not give life, so we cannot consider this as the learning of high spiritual truth.

Ancient China was different from today's China, or the China of thirty or fifty years ago. Our land was our fathers' gift to us. Since most people had enough to eat, they tried to achieve themselves spiritually. Some people liked to practice Kung Fu, some were good at poetry, some achieved other special skills. Only the ones who achieved themselves in the high subtle truth had nothing to show because they do not look for special learning or for something that they could have to show off.

After you work to support yourself, that is not all you can do because you still have energy to achieve yourself spiritually. Today's society has the tendency to require everyone to be the same, which sometimes causes people to feel that their lives lose all individual meaning. However, although we face social trouble, we are also individual beings. We can achieve ourselves and not necessarily live life in a uniform manner.

Some of you may think that the powers a person can develop from practicing Kung Fu are imaginary, but in China people question them because they would like to do them too. If you were to take time to practice it, you would be able to do many unusual things also. Some people can jump from the ground up to the rooftop of a house. Please bring a star down for me!

Many Kung Fu practitioners, after achieving the ability to do something with their powers, discovered that they were not using their energy or power in a positive way, so they decided to change their purpose and become spiritual. Spiritual people do not use energy to hurt or kill people. Instead, they use their energy to help people and achieve themselves spiritually.

The energy that is generated in Kung Fu practice and in spiritual cultivation is the same energy. The difference between them is the instructions that are given and the direction in which the energy is applied. In learning the Integral Way, your energy achievement is on a much higher level. It is the same energy, but it is the direction you take it that determines the function.

II

Q: I have studied Buddhist yoga and am interested in the kundalini energy. How does this relate to the philosophy of natural spiritual truth?

Master Ni: We have some experts and teachers of that subject in our class. I only know that all people have Divine Energy, only their attitudes and philosophy of life are different. For example, Buddhism looks away from life. It does not love life or the world. However, a spiritually achieved one, at age 80, still thinks, "I have not been born yet; I am still in the universal womb." That kind of statement indicates that life causes neither bitterness nor happiness. Once a person conceptualizes what life should be like, the person is self-troubled.

Everybody has kundalini energy. The natural spiritual teaching calls it by a different name, and the way of handling it or nurturing it is different too. We call it tsing (jing) or sexual energy. You can experience it in this class or in the T'ai Chi classes.

I once received a book on the subject of kundalini energy by a writer named Gopikrishna. He was a devoted Indian practitioner of kundalini who had profound experiences. I spent almost a whole summer afternoon reading his book.

Kundalini energy is interesting to beginners in spiritual practice. They are attracted to experiencing a kind of phenomenon that cannot be experienced through the ears, eyes, touch, etc. Practically, in the deep meditation of internal alchemy (spiritual cultivation), those experiences are considered phenomena or happenings which occur in the beginning stages. Manipulating the kundalini energy in a manner of children playing with a kaleidoscope is not the purpose of spiritual cultivation. It is neither the goal nor the achievement, it is only one possible experience. The exhibition of kundalini energy is similar to seeing the scenery of the countryside as you travel in a car, boat or train; the scenery is not your destination; the fact that you are going somewhere is more important. Similarly, the kundalini is only a passing show. The Indian spiritual tradition usually stays at the stage of experience such as seeing visions, transforming head energy into the blossoming of lotus flowers, or seeing lots of different lights in your head. All of these experiences or sensations are the result of tantric practices that hold sexual energy so that it is not absorbed or digested and then evenly distributed to support all the organs. When that unrefined energy is transported to the head, the person only experiences exciting phenomenon. Drug users have similar experiences.

Q: Does this stage of seeing visions include seeing spirits, shiens or immortals? Are they only visions?

Master Ni: Not completely. A certain development is necessary before the mind can discern what is merely a vision and what is a real subtle fact.

The basic principle from the valuable, ageless Integral Way, whether you are single and celibate or do dual cultivation, is to control the semen (sexual energy) to return to your body as Immortal Medicine to feed yourself. This necessarily needs all kind of conduction, such as physical conduction, spiritual conduction, all of which is called Dao-In. All those practices refine the medicine you receive from that stimulation or from natural cyclic production. Without the refinement process, merely keeping the energy inside is only half the knowledge, and this incomplete practice will give you more trouble than benefit.

Gopikrishna wrote only about his personal experiences, but he was a respectful author, because he earnestly described his personal difficulties. He was searching and going to many Hindu saints expecting to receive help or some kind of useful instruction from them, but there was none. If someone did an objective, comparative study of Hinduism and the subtle, natural practice of the Integral Way, you might appreciate and use it to develop yourself further.

Reading his book about kundalini energy enabled me to appreciate the ageless experience of the ancient achieved ones. You can find all kinds of suitable instruction in their writings or direct teachings. The stage of energy training called kundalini by that author can also be found in the knowledge provided by the spiritually developed ancestors.

There are two mistakes which are made by most beginners and which were made by Gopikrishna in his spiritual pursuit. The first is to stay with the experience of seeing different scenes when one spiritually enters the depth of nature. In the terminology of the Integral Way, you project your soul outside your head; when you do that, you are not living with your body. This does not happen to general souls. It happens only to people who have already gathered spiritual energy through natural processes. Projecting the soul outside of the head is like prematurely giving birth to a child; the soul or child will be weak and have trouble and misfortune. The mother, or body, experiences a great energy depletion and becomes extremely weak. There is no chance of any medical cure because the cause is not physical; the problem is that the mind has been allowed to release the gathered essence due to incomplete knowledge and lack of control.

Ancient guidance teaches us that in the last stage of immortal cultivation, after the gradual cultivation of the immortal foetus, when your new spirit is out of the body, you see light like a blossoming flower. You need to allow the flower to experience the natural stages of growth: budding and slowly opening should last for at least three months to one year. Once you have a certain experience with opening the flower and seeing the light, you need to allow around three years for the flower to become strong. In ancient terms, this was called "Be a mother who breast feeds the baby for three years." The ancient masters also instructed that the first time the spiritual baby is allowed to leave the mothers' body it should only be allowed to go one step. The next time, it can go three steps; the next time, a little farther; the next time, one mile; then several miles. All this time, it stays connected with the mother. In the *Tao Teh Ching*, this hidden instruction is in chapter 52:

> When you know the son,
>   you know the mother.
> The son should keep to the mother.

Then the spirit will help the life. The mother will continually provide nutrition or a worldly residence or villa for the spiritual baby until both grow to maturity. When the mother's body can no longer be used, then the spirit of the mind and the spirit of the body join the spiritual baby to establish a new life outside the old body. Then the possibility of immortality is achieved.

Here I provide two important sketches of immortal cultivation.

Table A: Essential Guidelines for Immortal Cultivation

1) Refine energy in forms such as food intake and body energy to become Tsing, reproductive energy.

2) Refine Tsing (reproductive energy or sexual essence) to become chi. (Here chi means the physical spirits.)

3) Refine the physical spirits to become shen, pure spiritual energy.

4) Form spiritual energy to become the subtle life.

5) Reunite the subtle life with the physical life to fulfill the reality of God and man/woman in one.

Table B: The Steps of Spiritual Sublimation

1) 100 days to build the foundation.

2) 1 year to receive the mystical conception.

3) The holy fetus gives signs of the holy pregnancy.

4) The birth of the holy baby.

5) Three years bosom nursing the holy baby.

6) Nine years of maintaining the oneness of the baby and the mother.

7) Decide whether to forsake the old body like a suit of clothes or pair of shoes or to continue worldly service in a "non-showing off way" with the life of God and man/woman in one.

From this, we can see that the writing about kundalini energy is just a description of an early stage of spiritual development. People enjoy playing with discoveries about the subtle sphere because it makes them marvel that they have come in contact with it; but this does not bring about any real spiritual achievement. I talk openly about this knowledge but it may be risky to give such knowledge a little too early or a little too fast. I suggest that you take what I say here for your future reference in case you have a chance to make progress and come to a similar stage.

Spiritual development does not focus only on the wonders of experience in a different sphere or only on the practical development of life. I am concerned that you have a balanced life that is developed physically, spiritually and mentally.

In order to achieve this, you must stay alert. Do not go in one direction too fast before doing something for the physical world, which needs the correlation of a sound mind and a sound spirit. By this I mean, do not fly away to the spiritual realms before accomplishing your virtuous fulfillment on earth.

Many students believe that the spiritual baby must be in the shape of a human baby. That is a great mistake. Many people cannot achieve themselves because they do not make this conceptual breakthrough. The spiritual baby is an energy baby. Your sexual energy can be transformed into particles which, after convergence, become the spiritual baby. Those crystal particles are invisible, but you definitely can feel some of the transformed energy like a piece of silk or thread. Thus, the first step to immortality is to produce the crystal particles with threads which begin the formation of the spiritual energy baby.

The second step is to transform those particle-like energies into light. This will be more secure and give better control than proceeding directly into light. When you see the light, you could imagine moonlight going through a small window or skylight into a house, but it is not moonlight, it is the sign of the conception of the spiritual baby. At this stage, it is not suitable to think about the baby going out traveling; that is appropriate only when the holy baby becomes a strong gold color, stronger than you have ever experienced, like exposing yourself at noontime in the desert sunshine.   Before that happens, there is a sign.   You suddenly see snow, but it is not real snow. It is a sign that occurs one or two days before the strong gold light happens. When that happens, guide the spiritual baby back to your body, and train it step by step as I described.

When the spiritual baby stays with the person, the person will become wiser. Wisdom is different than intelligence.   Intelligence is probably what you are born with, although it can continually be improved.   A wise person does not necessarily make a show of it. Lao Tzu said:

You know what is bright,
     but you would rather keep to the dark
     as though you knew nothing.

This means that your wisdom is not for sale or exchange unless you fulfill your spiritual mission and do what is necessary to fulfill your virtuous attainment in life. Lao Tzu hid important immortal practice behind his lines and words.

The process of sexual energy control is the same for both men and women.   It is a process of conducting the energy, step by step, to become an asset for your spiritual achievement.

In religious art, the best portrayal of the spiritual baby is pictured in the Western tradition as cherubs, baby angels who fly on wings. Although it is a metaphoric representation, it will become the truthful fruit of your spiritual cultivation if you succeed.   Although in the Western religious traditions there is no practice similar to internal alchemy which is objective and scientific enough to reach this reality, any creation of human culture can be used for positive and truthful purposes.

The Western tradition portrays the spiritual baby in terms of Jesus' teaching that only childlike people ascend easily to Heaven. This was the inspiration of the artists who produced these great images.

People of intelligence apply their mental capability to their lives in order to do better in all aspects, but high intelligence does not necessarily mean a happy life, nor does it mean the ability to attain any spiritual reward. Only people who are kind, wise and virtuous earn a spiritual reward. However, when you practice kindness, you must have the foreknowledge to know that your kindness can cause you trouble. You will be exposed to contact with people and the world and will have some negative experiences in your external affairs. This is to be expected. Whatever happens, the most important thing to remember is: never become spiritually damaged through any temptation regarding your spiritual virtue. That is your insurance for the possibility of attaining immortality.

In life's circumstances, when people know you are kind, they will exploit your kindness to get something. When they try to do that, you must become like a simpleton so that people will not be able to abuse or misuse you. Therefore, there is another guidance called being natural. Being natural means that in a life situation when it is correct to respond, you should respond. Being natural and responding correctly is similar to not allowing poison oak to grow in the flower bed of your front yard; it is being aware of danger when you are traveling in a world of people who are not totally developed.

Lao Tzu teaches that there are three virtues that must come together. The first is kindness, the second is effectiveness, and the third is moderation. If you are missing any one of them, you do not have complete virtue.

Before the time of the Three Kingdoms (220-264 A.D.), the usurper Tsao Tsao (155-219 A.D.) succeeded in obtaining the throne, from which he could manipulate the whole known world at that time. His ambition, like that of all powerful, determined leaders, was physical immortality. He therefore ordered all achieved teachers, masters and individuals to gather at his palace. The invitation made to each of them said it was to show respect for their achievement, but Tsao Tsao was looking for the formulas for longevity and spiritual powers. Some gave the foundation, some gave false formulas, some played with him. Tsao Tsao's real plan was to kill them. Some masters were totally aware of Tsao Tsao's intention before coming to the palace. Master Tsu Yuan Fung, whose popular name was Tsu Tzu, exhibited his powers to Tsao Tsao. (Since the names Tsao Tsao and Tzu Tzu sound almost exactly alike to westerners, I will use his scholastic name.) That made Tsao Tsao afraid of him and the dictator ordered that Tzu Yuan Fung be arrested and executed. Tzu Yuan Fung was standing among a group of people, and suddenly, every person there looked exactly like Tzu Yuan Fung! The soldiers could not decide which one was the real Tzu Yuan Fung. Tsao Tsao was not easily discouraged, and the search for Tzu Yuan Fung continued. One time, a soldier discovered Tzu Yuan Fung in the countryside where there also happened to be a flock of sheep. The soldier wanted to capture Tzu Yuan Fung, but suddenly Tzu Yuan Fung could not be seen; there were only sheep! One sheep started to speak and told the solider, "I am Tzu Yuan Fung." Again the soldier tried to arrest the sheep but then all the sheep began to say, "I am Tzu Yuan Fung."

Tsao Tsao developed an intense pain in his brain, and his doctor Master Hua Tu, an acupuncturist who was over 110, suggested that the head be cut open and cleaned so that the pain could be cured. Tsao Tsao dared not entrust himself to this procedure so Hua Tu went back to his home town. Tsao Tsao ordered Hua Tu arrested and killed. After that, the surgical aspect of Taoist or natural medicine was discouraged. However, natural medicine such as acupuncture and herbs always played an important role among powerful people like Tsao Tsao and other dictators, who were jealous of those who became immortal but were still dependent on the traditional practitioners to help them with their health. This was how natural medicine stayed alive and continued to be respected by general society. The art of immortality has always been a hidden teaching given only to qualified, virtuous students.

Spiritual freedom is invaluable for each individual because it is the opportunity for spiritual development. For example, a unified and peaceful China is necessary, but become an open and free society. When communism became the only regime in China after 1949, its enemy was the freedom of the people. All people and all things were put under a clumsy control that killed the organic function of a natural society. They used their ideology to control people, having learned from some socially dominating religions that ideology is an effective tool to control people who are not yet developed intellectually or spiritually.

China has deep roots from its ancient society. Many spiritual traditions have survived in China because China was a natural society. It remained natural up to the time the communist party took over in 1949. One old monk in Shanghai told about an event that happened during the so-called cultural revolution. Mao Tse Tung invited all the spiritual leaders such as the abbots of Buddhist and Taoist temples, religious community leaders, etc., to come together to discuss traditional matters. Thousands of the most influential spiritual leaders of the country came together, honored by individual invitations. Once they had gathered in a rural place, the communists put them in concentration camps and killed most of them. Only a few escaped.

I hope this helps you understand that spiritual freedom is not a gift. In a backward society with narrow-minded leadership, spiritual freedom does not exist, and you must remain under cover or in hiding. Spiritual freedom is so important. The darkness of religious intolerance in history and the darkness of communist rule in China are both matters of spiritual undevelopment. In places and times when spiritual development abounded, people have a much better life. Spiritual development is not a lofty or selfish pursuit of dubious value; it is a practical aspect of life which affects all people's lives. Everyone needs spiritual development, especially people who have the personality and capability for leadership.

The world is looking for a solution to its problems, but the most fundamentally used solution - military means - is not a good choice. The alternative to military action, political activity, is better, but not ideal. Religion has been used in the past and is employed in the present to solve the world's problems, but religions tend to bring further confusion and lead people to hold onto their prejudices. As I see it, the only true hope for the problems of the world is the spiritual development of all people. This is the direction in which I devote myself and I also recommend it to you, because it is everybody's business to have a better world. A healthy world depends upon the health of its individuals. A healthy individual depends upon spiritual development. Your individual spiritual immortality will become your reward for having helped the spiritual development of all people. This is what I call virtuous fulfillment.

November 24, 1977

I

Good evening, everybody. Today, I had an unusual vision or illusion. At noon I felt a spiritual call from a remote place to give a treatment to a 27-year old woman who was in critical condition. I could not get away at the time because I had a lot of patients here to take care of, but the request kept coming, and I became restless and ill-tempered. It was not until late in the day that I was able to hurry to my room and go into a deep, meditative rest. When I returned to my body, it was already 5 minutes past 7, and that is why I was late tonight.

This kind of spiritual phenomenon, visions, dreams and illusions are popular spiritual experiences. They helped develop religious and spiritual practices, but most of these experiences cannot be verified in terms of everyday life. It is not easy to decide whether such an experience is true or just a psychological expression which is conditioned by things in the surroundings which function as non-verbal suggestions to the mind.

As a professional healer and spiritual teacher, I have seen that some patients, when troubled, pray for my help. My living soul responds to such spiritual messages for help. This is my experience. Some time later, a real letter comes from those patients to express their gratitude.

Q: Master Ni, how do you treat someone in that way? Do you perform "spiritual acupuncture" on somebody who is unaware or just give healing energy to help someone else who is performing the treatment?

Master Ni: The spiritual sincerity of an individual can cause a response from nature which is consistent with physical shape and spiritual energy. Natural spiritual response has no mind. For example, your internal response to a person, which is an energy event, will be sensed by the other person, who will respond in kind, although in our daily activity only an oral or written response counts. You might not accept this as a fact, yet it is true: your sincere prayer can also cause your own spirits to respond.

If a person has physical trouble, rather than using his or her own mind and spiritual energy to try to treat the problem, it is usually better to seek outside help such as acupuncture or herbal medicine. In this way, the healer's energy also assists the patient. Healing power or the resilience of life does not rely on spiritual intention alone, it needs cooperation and response from the complete foundation of all one's life energies.

You asked whether I do a type of spiritual acupuncture when I work on the spiritual planes. Not exactly. My spiritual energy is healing energy. My energy alone heals people, because all people are made of energy.

Although some people have frequent experiences of leaving their bodies to do things in the spiritual realms, it is not safe or healthy. I remember one time when I was seven when my mother was planning to take me to a celebration at a temple. Thousands of people were going to be there for the activities and it was going to be a joyous occasion. Because the temple was over 10 miles away, she arranged for a boat to take me and my brother and sisters there. My hometown is similar to the Italian city of Venice, with lots of canals, so we went everywhere by boat. I was excited about going but suddenly, one night before the event, I became restless and irritable. I think the stimulation of going to such a big event caused some kind of over-stimulation to my young, sensitive mind. My mother became immediately alert; she preferred that I stay peaceful rather than experience a spiritual illusion. Finally, I fell into a deep sleep and held my own spirit within. My mother still took me to the celebration and carried me around for several hours until I woke up. The most subtle things can be fulfilled in sleep; you might find evidence of this afterwards, but it might encourage you to become illusive. Practicing illusion was not the spiritual education I received and is not what I teach.

Unfortunately, the celebration had just ended when I awoke, so I missed the whole colorful ceremonial activity.

However, the subtle level of my mind was still able to experience it. To my spiritually developed mother, spiritual peace and oneness of spirit, mind and body was more important than any exciting spiritual experience. Not following this principle would have caused my spiritual cultivation to be without benefit.

I remember another, similar occasion that happened once when I was in Shanghai. I was a big fan of Chinese opera then and a friend invited me to see an outstanding performance. The leading role was played by a male actor made up to look like a woman, a character called Mei Lan Fan. It was not considered strange in those days for a male performer to dress like a woman to play a female role. For the most part, women were not allowed to act, so men typically played women's roles. Because he was so famous, those tickets cost a lot; only rich people could afford it.

No sooner did I arrive at the performance than I felt drowsy and fell asleep. Again, I missed most of it, only this time I wasted my friend's money! On the subtle level, I had missed nothing, although I think that I fell asleep because of the noise.

Actually, it is necessary for all of us to cultivate ourselves. A spiritual person is not a special person; we all need discipline. I cannot be sure how you will receive these stories. Most of you are fairly well balanced and can use this information to further your understanding of life, but others may desire illusory power and try to imitate it, which could cause trouble. I am telling you these stories so that if this sort of thing ever happens to you, you will understand it for what it is: a reaction to too much stimulation.

Spiritual learning has many aspects; there are some things you must be careful about or avoid. Just recently one of my students tried to develop psychic power prematurely and hurt his energy. These things must develop slowly and naturally; they cannot be forced. Some of you who have this tendency to rush things must be careful.

Tonight, I have a more important message for you. I want to share with you the way I discipline my mind. Once you hear this you will know that I could never be involved with unreal fantasies or illusive thinking. I first received this kind of mental training when I was little. I was born into a family with spiritual training. All their spiritual experiences served as examples for me and greatly impressed me. I wrote down one of my spiritual guides for you to use in ordering your own minds. This is one of the treasures I learned as a boy; I hope it will be of great use to you also.

This work is titled: "Instruction from a Great Master to the Students of Deep Truth."

Do not be troubled by your dreams.
Do not be fascinated with your visions.
Do not be carried away by your illusions.
Even in real life, do not allow the mind to fool you;
　　if you do, you will overreact to situations
　　with emotion.

When you look at things and lives
　　and see that they have form,
　　you take the forms for solid objects,
　　but they are not.
You also think the good or bad treatment
　　you receive from the world is real.
It is not.
It is only circumstance.
Nothing can be held onto as being good or bad.
You also think the thoughts in your mind
　　are real.
You behave according to them.
You live according to them.
You use them with partiality or prejudice.
You are stubborn in holding onto them.
But they are not real either;
　　they are phantoms formed
　　from fragmentary elements.

Water flows in rivers;
　　above there is wind,
　　below is the shape of the riverbed.
What part of thought is real?

What part of thought can be defined?
Thought is formed by internal and external pressures
    and stimulation.
How can you call it real, my beloved friends?

You think that the behavior
    and actions of life are real, too.
It is necessary to do them,
    and yet they are not necessary.
They cannot be taken as absolute,
    one way or another.
There is no need to bring about conflict
    or confrontation in one's behavior.
Just do what you must do that is right,
    and then let it go.

Then, finally, you are attached to your knowledge.
You have attained it through years of collecting.
You are so widely knowledgeable.
Is all this knowledge really helpful?
Is it the final or ultimate truth?
The truth itself is continually forming and reforming.
No one can afford to be a foolish dictator
    and try to stop people from learning and discovering.
The life of the entire universe
    keeps revealing itself to our minds.
At what point of knowledge can you decide you have the
  final truth?

How can you recognize the truth?
Do you depend upon your eyes, nostrils,
    tongue, ears and skin?
Is that information trustworthy?
For example, how do your eyes see?
Your eyes are dependant upon the light.
When the light changes,
    the information your eyes gathers is different.

What the ear hears is also not reliable.
The ear cannot even hear all sounds;

the highest pitch is too high to hear,
and the lowest pitch is too low to hear.
Things that are too far away cannot be heard.
Things that are too close cause distortion of sound.
How can you say that what you hear and see is accurate?
Temporal truth is subject to condition and circumstance.
In all, how do you decide what is the real truth,
    the truth one can insist upon?

A truth can be presented relatively,
    but not absolutely.
Since things are not absolute,
    how can people be so definite?

A person of deep observation has a truth.
It is that the formed world
    is equal to the unformed.
The experience we gather is equal
    to having no experience at all.
The thoughts we hold are useless,
    or are equal to nothing.
Our actions are equal to non-doing.
The knowledge we have collected equals ignorance.
This is the reality which is much deeper
    than what is observed on the surface.

This new understanding can help you with your troubles.
However, I am not telling you this
    to help you escape your obligations.
The deep world is just as it is,
    according to its energy.
The deep world does not increase or decrease.
It is not a dirty world,
    nor is it a pure world.
It is just like this.
There is no vista that the eyes can see.
There are no concepts that can be considered real.
The feelings of soft or hard, warm or cold
    and the sensations of color, sound, smell and taste
    are not real in the deep world, either.

The perceptions of eyes, ears, nostrils,
 tongue and skin, and the mind's intent,
 cannot be held as real or as absolutely correct.
Nothing can be called absolutely dark or bright.
There is no need to remove darkness.
There is no reality to aging or death.
Real things can be illusion.
Illusion can be real.

There is no such thing
 as birth, old age, sickness and death.
There is no such thing as the bitterness of life,
 the collection of life experience,
 the extinction of life,
 or reaching eternity.
By learning this,
 and thus reaching the deep understanding,
 no more dreams or illusions can trouble you.
You do not need to be searching for dreams.
The integral truth and integral mind can be attained
 by following the most sacred, powerful teachings,
 which helped many lives to achieve
 the Ultimate Spiritual Truth.
It is the most truthful spiritual message
 and can remove the troubles from your mind.

There is a river called the River of Troubled Water.
People on both sides of the river
 always think the other shore is better
 than the one on which they live.
People on both shores wish to cross the troubled water
 to get over to the other shore.
While trying to cross to the other shore,
 many people are swallowed by the vicious waves
 of the troubled water.
Nobody has ever really reached the other shore.
The only ones who have reached the other shore
 are those who do not accept
 the River of Troubled Water
 and do not accept that there are two shores.

Here, in this moment, right now,
you can reach safety.
This teaching needs to be confirmed.
Thus I repeat to you the following.

Your own true wisdom is what carries you
across troubled waters to the safe shore.
If a person has unobstructed perception,
he can see that the accumulated data
from the five sense organs are empty bubbles.
When one sees through the solid shadows
of sensory creations,
one can overcome all troubles.
To people of absolute spirit,
things with form are no different
from that which appears to be emptiness.
Emptiness cannot really be distinguished
from that which appears to have form.
That which has form is in fact emptiness.
Emptiness, at the same time, is that which has form.
Your suffering, thinking, doing and knowledge
are all of the same quality.
All things and beings form themselves with what is empty.
In reality, you have nothing to bring about
and also nothing to take away.
There is nothing that may be thought of as clean,
and nothing that may be thought of as unclean.
There is nothing to which something can be added
and nothing from which something can be taken away.
In the eternal emptiness,
there are no things which can be called form,
thinking, doing or knowledge.
There is nothing to be seen, heard, smelled, tasted,
felt or thought about.
There is nothing to approach
and nothing to move away from.
There is nothing for you to set your eyes upon
and nothing to which you can
apply your consciousness.

There is no darkness or anything that can be called
the elimination of darkness.
Furthermore, there is no old age or death.
Therefore, there is nothing that can be called salvation
from old age and death.
There is no such thing as having a troubled mind
or calming down.
There is no such thing as thoroughly eliminating problems
or finding the perfect pathway.
There is no such thing as wisdom,
and nothing to be obtained.
When a person connects with high wisdom
by following his true wisdom,
there is no longer any obstacle in his mind.
Because there is no obstacle in his mind,
there is nothing to be afraid of.
Then one can leave all troubles and nightmares far behind
and reach for the final completeness of one's being.
High beings of the past, present and future
all follow their own true wisdom
to gain the highest awareness and
achieve the greatest clarity.
Hence, you may know that your true wisdom
is the spiritual key to self-liberation.

More of these valuable instructions can be found in Lao
Tzu's *Tao Teh Ching*.

The following is the most enlightening incantation that
exists. These magical words have an all encompassing
mystical power. They can take away all your spiritual
troubles and are very true. Now I will tell you the secret
incantation; remember it well and practice it often.

BEI AN, BEI AN
DAO BEI AN
WU BEI AN
TZU RAN DAO BEI AN

To save your minds from wandering, the meaning in English
is:

There is another shore.
You are expecting the other shore
     to be much better than this one.
Reaching another shore,
     there is no other shore.
In this way you have reached the other shore!

(Everyone practices the incantation many times.)

II

I just got a new shipment of herbs today and I happened to notice the picture of the famous Lu Shan mountain on the container. Lu means villa and Shan means mountain. It is a beautiful mountain. Lu Shan is in Jan She province. Many spiritual practitioners went there to cultivate themselves, and some attained high achievement. There is a particular spot on that mountain where immortals gather; you can see them on certain nights in a valley where only special people can go. You can see there are many lights. They come in many sizes and colors. Some are like lanterns, while others are as big and bright as the sun or the moon. Ordinary people cannot see them, but I think some of you might be able to see them clearly. They look like huge phosphorescent balls floating above the ground. Another place they gather is a mountain called O Mei Shan in Sze Chuan province.

People cultivated themselves at Lu Shan and it was there they saw Master Lu. The great immortals do not need our recognition but sometimes they appear to truly sincere people who have cultivated themselves well.

When I was young, I wondered whether the immortals were real or not. I wanted most of all to see them, but my energy was not yet converged. Only after years of cultivation can a person become subtle enough to meet them. However, the purpose of self-cultivation is not to satisfy one's curiosity; it is for self-development. It is possible to prove the existence of the subtle reality by your achievement; then you do not need to bother searching elsewhere.

When I speak about Lao Tzu and other immortals and their teachings, I am referring to subtle beings and principles. When I refer to things like "Wu Wei" and "the form of emptiness," these are at a more profound level. The other day, someone told me she had been practicing Wu Wei, or "non-doing" as you would interpret it in English, and she felt guilty about how dirty her house was getting from not cleaning it any more. This reflects lack of understanding; Wu Wei does NOT mean doing nothing. It means not being entrapped by whatever you do. I practice Wu Wei everyday and although I am busy, I do not feel that I am busy at all. Do you understand now? To practice Wu Wei your mind must not cling to any particular thing. If you form your mind in any way or attach it to anything, you have not reached Wu Wei.

On one hand, there is spiritual emptiness and on the other hand, there are worldly desires. Most people ignore their spiritual emptiness and only pay attention to their desires. Vulgar people go from desire to desire and never realize the power and effectiveness of spiritual emptiness. In their endless pursuit of desires, they go from one extreme to another and never realize that the middle way is the only way to rise above their troubles. Some people think they are practicing Wu Wei, but the truth is they are still attached to their personal preferences. Thus, what they call non-attachment is really not non-attachment, and it is a poison. Wu Wei can be a vehicle to carry you away from all worldly troubles, but most people do not understand it, so they are just fooling themselves.

You all have more or less the same intelligence, but your abilities to understand the deep truths of life are different. Even if I pass a certain truth to you simply and directly, some students still cannot grasp it. They will misunderstand what I say because their minds are clouded. Even the ones who think they understand usually do not get it. Maybe after several years, some of you might begin to grasp part of it at a deeper level. When I was only nine years old, I already knew all these things, but it was many years before I truly became a real being.

Some of you are more advanced and do understand these truths immediately. In spiritual learning, it does not matter whether you are advanced or a beginner. You must start where you are. If you think you are more advanced than you truly are, you cannot make any real progress. You must start from where you really are - not from where you think you are.

November 25, 1977

Truthfully, there is no higher enjoyment in life than the movement of one's own subtle energy. Subtle energy is your birthright but you have ignored it for many years because you have been ignorant of it; you put your mind above your real life. Society has also helped you to create an unnatural lifestyle. All of this is why you lost your naturalness. Today, you have come here to purify yourself and wash away all unnatural influences.

The best cultivation is when there is not too much mental control. Some of you have too much control; you still follow your brain instead of your whole being. By this I mean that your entire body and the space around you are communicating to you all the time but most of you listen only to the singularly narrow voice of your repetitive thought patterns. For most people, cutting off all other communication is a form of self-defense or self-protection from the difficulties of life, but this kind of protection, when continued over time, becomes a kind of self-suffocation. Those of you who are here now have realized this on some level, thus you have come to a place where you can begin to relax and open yourselves up. When you stand in this shrine, your whole being can be present, not just part of yourselves.

If your whole being is not present in a situation, then your movement will reflect it. It can be observed.

In this society, when you eat, you also watch TV. When you are on the toilet, you read. When you sleep, you leave the radio on, etc. When you do this, you do not have your being in one piece. In other words, your being is always divided and you are never concentrated. These unnatural habits must be corrected. In this class, try to make your whole being totally present.

Tonight is a special night. It is the 15th day of the 10th moon according to the Chinese calendar, which is special because it is the first mid-month of Winter, and it is also a full moon. How much do you really know about the moon? Let us compare the Western and Eastern approaches to it.

Westerners know the distance, speed and size of the moon, and send men up to dig a lot of holes in it. It seems to me that this is not much different from an ant sent to research a person's body. He would report back to the other ants that it is not a good place to be. It smells bad and is covered with a lot of hair. Could the visiting explorer ant be aware of your soul? Certainly not. Well, Western science is like that. Scientists can travel and explore, but even with scientific methods they can never know your spirit. Sure, they can find out some small data about the aura or human energy fields and so forth, but using machines and instruments gives only limited or partial information, not the complete truth.

All Western scientists believed, and rightly so, that Einstein had a good head on him, so after his death they cut it up to see how big his brain was. Did they find that his brain was different from other peoples' brains? No, they did not. This kind of investigation is a waste of time. You can never touch the real being or real energy with a scalpel.

Western knowledge has some truth to it, but it is partial rather than whole. How big the moon is and how far away it is does not tell you about the real moon and its energy. We owe a lot to the moon, because without it we would not have any mental evolution. We get our intelligence from the moon. If you cultivate for three years at midnight under the full moon, with the right ceremony, you can become a wise person. However, if the ceremony is not right, you become a lunatic, because the energy is so strong.

In China, we say that if you want to see a woman's real beauty, look at her under the full moon. The moon's yin energy enhances her beauty. If you want to enjoy the handsomeness of a man, you must also look at him in the moonlight, because the yin energy pulls out his yang energy. If you know how to use the energy of the moon, it can be a big part of your cultivation for immortality. If you do not know how to use it, it can cause a lot of trouble between a man and a woman or just cause sexual desire.

It is important to know how to control your energy correctly. When it is blocked and cannot get through certain parts of the body, like some joints and organs, it will result in death or sickness, so you must be careful. Use energy to help energy; do not always rely on the mind. The mind itself is a kind of energy, but the mind can also rob your energy. I will tell you how: All day long you use your mind and emotions. These all steal your energy. With every flash of energy, your energy dies partially. It is not actually that it dies, but it moves away from you. Thus, if you keep up a busy, hectic life, you will send away your energy until all of it is gone and your soul becomes black.

The most important thing in life is energy itself. In the teaching of the Integral Way, the soul means your subtle or divine energy. Certain ceremonies can help you connect with your own soul, because certain words and movements have the same frequency as divine energy. We use these ceremonies as a discipline to develop one's sensitivity. Divine energy exists not only in your soul, it also exists abundantly in the universe. After you develop your sensitivity, then you can prove to yourself that divine energy and divine beings exist everywhere.

Do you truly know that there is divine energy? You can always tell when there is bad energy around because something does not feel right, but why can you not tell when there is divine energy around? It is because today's people only look downward, not upward. I would like you to share in the good energy. After you learn sufficiently about the high energy, you can become a higher level being. It is a true enjoyment and reward to become a higher level being.

Spiritual energy is natural but it is not a religion. That is why we respect the moon, sun and stars, etc. Why do we respect natural things? Because they have a message for us and also give us energy.

Some of you are more intelligent than others. Some have more energy. Do you think it all comes from the food you eat? Scientists count the calories you eat, but calories are nonsense when it comes to talking about how much and what kind of energy a person has. Each person consists of many different kinds of energy.

Each person lives in a total environment which consists of various kinds of energy necessary for human life. If we left it for one minute, we would die. If you went to a place where there is no atmosphere or sun, it would be hell. If you were completely cut off from nature, you would end up in a shadow world or "underworld."

It is not the goal of this tradition to help you go to the shadow world; the goal of this tradition is to help you improve your energy so that you can become a shien and return to the subtle origin. How can you become a shien? A shien has the kind of energy that connects with natural energy. Even without being in a physical body, a shien still has the energy source of the sky and nature to sustain its existence. If you learn the method of sublimation and become divine energy, you can still connect with the natural energy without having to reincarnate and go through the process of passing through the birth canal of a new mother to endure a lot of painful and pleasant experiences here on earth again.

The teaching of spiritual energy appreciates nature differently than science, but that is no reason to discount the value of this learning. Do not laugh at what you do not yet understand. Scientists worship machines, bacteria and fossils. They can create small things, but can they create the moon and sun?

The kind of "nature worship" practiced by the Integral Way is not really nature worship at all; it is the study of the source of all life. We value natural energy, especially the energy of the North Star, the Big Dipper, the sun and moon, etc. Tonight there is a beautiful moon. Let us respect or pay homage to the moon, not just think about it in a scientific way. I will tell you what to do in just a minute.

Man has been the dominating force on the worldly stage for only a few tens of thousands of years. Before man, there were only plants and animals. Plants and animals also found the secret to gathering good energy. They even learned how to transform themselves into higher living beings or the subtle life at will. As a Chinese folk story tells, a fox or a fox spirit can become a beautiful woman. Some foxes even live to be old by gathering energy for a long time. Every night they dig up a girl's skull and then worship the moon. When enough energy is gathered, a fox can transform into a beautiful woman right before your eyes and become so beautiful you will want to marry her. There is tremendous spiritual value in a fox having such high spiritual ambition.

It is interesting to know that both in English and Chinese the word "fox" can describe a beautiful woman. In Chinese, it can be either a male or female that bewitches the opposite sex to become the victim. Since their tails cannot change, when you are with a beautiful woman for the first time, you must reach behind her and check to see if she has a tail or not! Having a tail means she or he might try to damage you or harm you at the end and proves that this was not true love from a developed being. It is the undeveloped beast nature that starts to become active and make trouble, and brings about an unhappy ending. The spiritual value of the story in this chapter is the teaching that the harmful intention can only be shown in the end. This is to warn you not to enter into a bad relationship or keep bad friends. The most useful spiritual value to us, man or woman, is to avoid bad relationships or a marriage that pulls you down spiritually.

I know this sounds like something from a fairy tale, but please understand that this kind of story has spiritual meaning. It did not originate with me or with China. All ancient natural cultures knew about this type of thing, and similar stories are told on all the continents.

Q: Where does the fox get the skull?

Master Ni: It digs up graves. It is believed that for an animal to take human energy is the first step toward achieving itself spiritually. It means that it is worthy of respect to have a human form of life, but people do not respect their own form; they act like beasts sometimes.

You know, even trees and stones can gather energy and become active. You may say, "Nonsense!" but it is true. You accept that trees can fall down onto the ground and become gasoline and diamonds, so why can you not accept this?

Once a person told me that his family liked to hunt with old flintlock rifles. One day they saw a white shadow go by and followed it, thinking it was a rabbit or some other animal. When they came to a hole under a tree, they felt strange, as if they were controlled by some energy. Then a whole group of white foxes came out of the hole one by one. They all showed their disdain for the offenders by pointing at the men with their front claws as they stood on their rear feet. The family tried to shoot the foxes but their guns would not work. The person who told me that story later thought: if foxes have this kind of power, surely people can have even stronger power if they know to cultivate themselves. The true spiritual value of this story is seen in the last sentence.

Tonight I have used some folk stories to illustrate an important teaching. I would like to emphasize some useful knowledge that I hope you can adopt into your everyday lives. You know, people enjoy good relationships. We also like to be open and make many friends. Of course, anyone who enters into a relationship would like it to succeed, but things do not always turn out that way.

However, do not give up too quickly. All people who grow together experience difficulties, so do not be too hard on other people. You yourself are also in the process of growing; you may make mistakes and may offend people at times, but if you are always good-hearted and well-intentioned, you will be on the right track of life. Just work on learning how to keep your good heart and good intentions from causing you a lot of trouble! Sometimes you are tested by being good-hearted and become upset and do the extreme. Being good-hearted does not mean that you do not guard yourself from other people. If you do, you lose your balance.

It is not right to harm people with evil intentions. Some people are friendly and helpful at first when they come to you, then slowly they try to use you for their purpose and you suffer from their schemes. To have an evil intention is to try to get something for yourself in a situation and to not care about the other person's interest.

You know, on some bad occasions, you may meet or see people who are not people. They are beasts who put the skeleton of a human head covered by human clothes, but they have tails. That cannot be hidden in the end. It is not only that their beast nature is not improved, but also their evil intentions are deep within their conscious minds.

Human society everywhere needs spiritual education. For example, in China, all spiritual education, direct or metaphoric, was taken away, destroyed and forbidden by the communist regime. They trained the young generation to adopt a newer, more extreme ideology. Once people began to believe in the survival of the fittest, the law of the jungle became the only standard of their deep minds. Bestial habits were all restored.

What I teach is spiritual self-cultivation. Cultivation is the process of improving yourself and not allowing the beast nature to be the dominant factor of your life. We need to achieve ourselves above that. The human form evolved from animals, but it is necessary to attain spiritual growth to be truly successful over the animal nature.

It is a great opportunity for a spirit to be born into a human form. For all of us who are in a human form, it is important to know how to use this opportunity to work toward our own higher evolution. This is the purpose of this class. I am here to share this information and give the correct message to all of you.

Do not expect everyone around you to be angels, but you can cultivate yourself to become one. It is the most important thing you can do.

Since we are high-level beings, it is natural for us to gather energy for our intelligence and our immortality. Some people do not like the word "immortal," they prefer the word "divinity," but it does not matter what word you use; the reality is what is important. There is nothing divine or undivine in nature. There is nothing mortal or immortal in nature. That is to say, all things are both divine and undivine, and all things are both mortal and immortal. Some things are more subtle than others but all are divine and immortal. If we come to the correct understanding, then we can become divine and immortal, too.

Anyway, to enjoy the good energy of the moon, you must first quiet your mind. Calm yourself down and be open-minded or receptive. Choose a good place to go where you can see the moon well and bow to it. Then stand up straight, holding your hands around your tan tien, and see if I have been fooling you or not. If you feel nothing, you need to increase your awareness or sensitivity. I do not mean that you are supposed to feel something with your hands. I mean that you are going to feel something different inside of you; your energy condition will be different. You do not feel agitated, excited, emotional pushing or rushing. You should feel calm and clear, as bright as the moon. The moon has a gentle and lovely energy; see if you can open yourself up to receive some of it.

Q: Should we look at the moon?

Master Ni: That depends upon your own intention or inspiration. You must feel like you are with the moon or kind of like you have dissolved yourself into its light.

The day before the full moon is a good day to cultivate lunar energy because it is not full yet. Today the sky is somewhat cloudy; that causes the energy to be less strong. You will still feel gentle, but perhaps also a little stuffy.

Many years ago, when I was a young traveler, I visited some achieved people who gave off energy like the sun and moon. They radiated light. If you saw them, you would be overcome with awe and your nerves would become shaky and soft. They were not self-important, they just had good energy. With good energy, a person can do anything.

Those masters were men of divine energy. In my personal cultivation, most of my achievement or gain comes from the moonlight. One time, when I was cultivating in a garden in the late hours, a lot of divine beings came to visit the spot. For 30 miles all around, the wolves would not cry. Normally wolves always cry, but that place is where my masters cultivated themselves, so all the animals in that area had become domesticated.

It was a quiet, cold night. My impulsive energy had quieted down. Because my food was so clean and my speech and human contact was so pure, my energy was also clear. There were only good beings, and trees and caves on that mountain. You could say I was in Heaven, at least a kind of Heaven. I finally went into a deep meditation. Three beings riding on energy descended to where I was sitting on a stone. I was under the trees and near a stream. The three beings took me away.

First the moon was as big as a silver coin and then the closer I got, the bigger it got. Suddenly there was no moon, only light. I was invited to a party. Many male and female shiens were there. They were all achieved humans, so they showed gender differences, or perhaps it was just my vision that saw them that way because of the stage of my mind's development. Whenever they moved, it was graceful. I was invited to sit at a table that was green like jade. Everything appeared to me to be lucid and clear, but again, perhaps that was just the way I saw things because of the stage of my mind. I wondered why everyone moved so naturally and did not move like me. My movement seemed to be tense. It was because their energy was different. I saw true colorful energy. True color is energy, it is nourishment. It is edible and you take it in not by mouth but by absorption.

If you love knowledge, than every inch of space and every second of time is knowledge. If you love beauty, then everything you see is beauty. In this realm, a person could experience anything that he or she desired. This experience was so beautiful and lucid. Everything that I held by the mind felt so soft and flexible, just like something that had been soaked in water. The only thing that was not soft was the tension I felt from my own muscles. Things were so sublime because everything was so gentle.

After that party, the three divine beings took me back and then they disappeared. I had been gone from my body for hours, but my legs were not even sore from having sat for so long. This story falls in the category of spiritual illusion, like the summons to heal someone or the soul having left the head, which is the separation of body, mind and spirit. That is not correct practice. It can only be viewed as a spiritual experience or phenomenon. The highest spiritual practice is still to remain in one piece. I only tell you these stories to illustrate my main teaching of spiritual oneness.

Do you think this is fiction? In spirit, if you think of a stone, a stone comes. If you think of food, then food comes.

If you think of light, light comes; death, then death comes. Every word or thought you choose has a result. It is true. On the earth plane, our minds are spoiled and we cannot manifest things quickly. For the most part, things you need for your current stage of growth will still come to you, but in the human commercial and social world, most things are hoaxes. I tell you, in spirit, there is no truth because there is no hoax. A hoax can only happen when a person has desires. If you have no desires, you cannot be cheated.

If you accept this as fiction, then you can relax and say it is just entertainment. If I tell you it is the truth, you will have difficulty because it is beyond your experience.

You know, everybody must leave their bodies someday, and when you do, you will become the energy you gathered from this world. Do you want to become the ghost of money, hate, jealousy, vanity, good cars, alcohol, drugs, television or junk food? You will become exactly what you gather. Do you think I can tell all of you apart by your faces? No, the difference I see between you is in your energy arrangement. Everyone has an invisible form, but to me it is visible. The students who live in this house sometimes have a bad time because I do not let them continue to solidify bad energy as their true being. Thus, their true beings also have an image, but it is not of bad quality.

Tonight I talked quite frankly, perhaps a bit too much. My spiritual friends will laugh at me and ask, "Why do you talk about the snow to summer cicadas? Summer cicadas have no understanding of winter snow because they have not lived long enough." I tell you, there is winter snow; there is a spiritual reality. It is not that you have not lived long enough to know the spiritual reality, you have not developed a deep enough interest yet. You are not summer cicadas, you are my precious students and disciples. You are all honest and sincere in your cultivation. You know true from false because of your spiritual development. I hope that someday you can also embody the truth.

You know, if two people check out the temperature of the water in the same swimming pool, one will say the water is cool and the other will say it is warm. With spiritual matters, it is the same: each person must experience it by oneself. Who can say who is correct? Do not merely listen to what other people tell you. The things you hear, the books you read, are only information obtained by your senses. Your senses can cheat you, so do not depend upon them for everything, especially spiritual learning, because it does not rely on the senses at all. Listen to what people tell you, read the books, do whatever you think is helpful until you get tired of it; then work on the real achievement, put yourselves together and make a whole being. Now, your life is fragmented - it is in pieces.

Q: How long should we sit under the moon?

Master Ni: As long as you wish. Sitting or standing are both good. Choose a good place so you will not disturb others or be disturbed by them.

Tonight I have told you some stories which might have caused a disturbing response if I had told them in some village of Sangtong or Hunan province where people strongly believe the fox spirits should not be offended. However, I will give you a better story from the Tang Dynasty as compensation to the fox fairies.

Wei Yin, ninth son of the daughter of the prince of Shinan, was a somewhat wild young lord and a heavy drinker. His cousin's husband, Zheng, whose first name is not known but who was the sixth child of his family, had studied military arts and was also fond of drinking and women. Since he was poor and had no home of his own, he lived with his wife's family. Zheng and Wei became friends and were inseparable. In the sixth month of the ninth year of the Tian Bao period (750 A.D.), they were walking together through the capital on their way to a drinking party in the Shinchiang quarter, when Zheng went to take care of some private business and left Wei at the crossroads saying he would join him later at the feast. Then Wei headed east on his white horse, while Zheng rode south on his donkey.

On the road Zheng came upon three girls, one of whom, dressed in a white gown, was exceedingly lovely. Pleasantly surprised, he whipped up his donkey to circle round them, but lacked the courage to approach them. Since the girl in white kept glancing at him in what seemed an encouraging way, he asked jokingly:

"Why should such beautiful girls as you travel on foot?"

The girl in white countered with a smile: "If men with mounts aren't polite enough to offer us a lift, what else can we do?"

"My poor donkey is not good enough for such lovely ladies as you," protested Zheng. "But it is at your disposal, and I shall be glad to follow you on foot."

He and the girl looked at each other and laughed, and with her two maids teasing them, they were soon on familiar terms. He went east with these young women to Leyuan Park, and dusk had fallen by the time they reached a magnificent mansion with massive walls and an imposing gate. The girl in white went in, calling back over her shoulder, "Wait a little!" One of her maids stayed at the gate and asked Zheng his name. Having told her, he inquired the name of the girl and learned that her last name was Ren and that she was the twentieth child in the family.

Presently Zheng was invited in. He had just tethered his donkey at the gate and placed his hat on the saddle, when the girl's sister - a woman of thirty or thereabouts - came out to greet him. Candles were set out, the table spread, and they had drunk several cups of wine when the girl, who had changed her dress, joined them. Then they drank a great deal and made merry, and late at night they went to bed together. Her coquetry and charm, the way she sang and laughed and moved were exquisite and something out of this world. Just before dawn, Ren said, "You had better go now. My brother is a member of the royal conservatory of music and serves in the royal guards. He'll be home at daybreak and he must not see you." Having arranged to come again, Zheng left.

When he reached the end of the street, the gate of that quarter was still bolted. But there was a foreign bread shop there where a light was burning and the stove had been lit. Sitting under the awning, waiting for the morning drum, Zheng began chatting with the shopkeeper. Pointing to where he had spent the night, he asked, "When you turn

east from here you come to a big gate.   Whose house is
that?"

"It's all in ruins," said the shopkeeper, "There's no
house left."

"But I was there," insisted Zheng.   "How can you say
there is no house?"

The shopkeeper understood in a flash what had happened.   "Ah, now I see!" he exclaimed.   "There's a fox fairy
there who often tempts men to spend the night with her.
She has been seen three times.   So you met her too, did
you?"

Ashamed to admit the truth, Zheng denied it.   When it
was light he looked at the place again, and found the walls
and the gate still there, but only wasteland and a deserted
garden behind.

After reaching home, Wei blamed him for not joining
him the previous day; but instead of telling the truth, Zheng
made up an excuse.   He was still bewitched by the fairy's
beauty and longed to see her again, unable to drive her
image from his heart.   Several weeks later, in a clothes shop
in the West Market, he once more came upon her accompa-
nied by her maids.   When he called out to her, she tried to
slip into the crowd to avoid him; but he called her name
repeatedly and pushed forward.   Then, with her back to him
and her fan behind her, she said: "You know who I am.
Why do you follow me?"

"What if I do?" asked Zheng.

"I feel ashamed to face you," she replied.

"I love you so much, how could you leave me?" he
protested.

"I don't want to leave you; I'm only afraid you must hate
me."

When Zheng swore that he still loved her and became
more insistent in his request, the girl turned round and let
fall the fan, appearing as dazzlingly beautiful as ever.

"There are many fox fairies about," she told the young
man.   "It's just that you do not know what we are.   Do not
think that we are so strange."

Zheng begged her to come back to him and she said,
"Fox fairies have a bad name because they often harm men;

but that is not my way. If I have not lost your favor, I would like to serve you all my life." Asked where they could live, she suggested, "East of here is a house with a big tree towering above its roof. It's in a quiet part of town - why not rent it? The other day when I first met you south of the Xuaping quarter, another gentleman rode off on a white horse toward the east. Wasn't he your brother-in-law? There's a lot of furniture in his house you can borrow."

It so happened that Wei's uncle, absent on official duty, had stored their furniture with him. Acting on Ren's advice, Zheng went to Wei and asked to borrow it. Asked the reason, he said, "I have just got a beautiful mistress and rented a house for her. I want to borrow the furniture for her use."

"A beauty indeed!" retorted Wei with a laugh. "Judging by your own looks, you must have found some monstrosity!"

Nonetheless, his friend lent him curtains, bed and bedding, dispatching an intelligent servant with him to move the furniture and to take a look at the girl. Presently the servant ran back, out of breath and sweating. "Well?" asked Wei, stepping forward, "Have you seen her? What's she like?"

"Marvelous! I have never seen anyone so lovely."

Wei, who had many relations and had seen many beauties in the course of his numerous adventures, asked whether Zheng's mistress was as beautiful as his own.

"No comparison!" exclaimed the servant. Wei mentioned four or five names of other beauties, but still received a negative reply. His sister-in-law, sixth daughter of the Prince of Wu, was a peerless beauty, as lovely as a fairy. "How does she compare with the sixth daughter of the Prince of Wu?" he asked.

Again his man declared that there was no comparison.

"Is that possible?" Wei exclaimed, clasping his hands in amazement. Then he hastily asked for water to wash his neck, put on a new cap, and went to call on Zheng.

It happened that Zheng was out and Wei, entering, found a young servant sweeping and a maid at the door, but no one else. He questioned the boy, who told him with a laugh that there was no one at home. Making a search of the rooms, Wei saw a red skirt behind a door and going closer discovered Ren hiding there. Dragged out from the dark corner, she was even more beautiful than he had been told. Mad with passion, he took her in his arms to assault her, only to meet with resistance. He pressed her hard, until she said, "You shall have your way, but first let me recover my breath." However, when Wei came on again she resisted as before. This happened three or four times. Finally Wei held her down with all his strength and the girl, exhausted and drenched with perspiration, knew she could hardly escape. Limp and inert, she gave him a heart-rending look.

"Why are you so sad?" he asked.

With a long sigh, she answered, "I pity Zheng with all my heart."

"What do you mean?" he demanded.

"He's over six feet tall but has failed to protect a woman - how can he call himself a man? You are young and rich, and have many beautiful mistresses. You have seen many like me. But Zheng is a poor man, and I am the only woman he loves. How can you rob him of his only love while you have so many? Because he is poor, he has to be dependent on others. He wears your clothes, eats your food and so he is in your power. If he could support himself, we shouldn't have come to this."

At this, Wei, a gallant man with a sense of justice, desisted, composed himself and apologized. Then Zheng came back and they exchanged cordial greetings. And thence forward Wei looked after all their needs.

Ren often met Wei and went out with him on foot or by carriage. He spent almost every day with her until they became the best of friends, taking great delight in each other's company. And because she was everything to him except his mistress, he loved and respected her and grudged her nothing. Even eating and drinking he could not forget her. Knowing Wei's love for her, Ren said to him one day, "I'm ashamed to accept such favors from you. I don't deserve such kindness. And I can't betray Zheng to do as you desire. I was born in Shangshi and brought up in the capital. My family are theater people, and since all the women in it are the mistresses and concubines of rich men, they know every single courtesan in the capital. If you see some beautiful girl and cannot have her, I would like to get her for you to repay your kindness." Wei did not accept her offer, saying, "I have corrected my sexual attitudes toward women. You are the true teacher of my life. I have stopped the endless pursuit of sexual pleasure; people should work on their spiritual development."

Sixth Class

December 4, 1977

Master Ni: Are there any questions about your cultivation from last week? Did any of you have unusual experiences that you think relate to this class?

A student talks about a dream he had in which he had a nocturnal emission and asked how they can be avoided.

Master Ni: The problem of nocturnal emission is an energy disturbance which relates to the question of sex. In order not to have a nocturnal emission (or in the case of women, nighttime or early morning orgasms) from practicing celibacy, there are a few things you can do.

Typically, when someone begins to cultivate for spiritual immortality, what they want to know is this: "Is it all right to have sex or not?" Most of you know that the first principle of the teaching of the Integral Way is to refine your physical essence to be mental essence. Worldly people lose their physical essence through sex; they do it to have children or just for fun. Whether for children or for fun, sex can cause many problems and is actually never completely satisfying. Now, do not get the idea that I am saying that strict asceticism is part of the Integral Way. Most of the monks in the monasteries who have abstained from sex often have a lot of wet dreams because they are violating their nature.

I will tell you one interesting thing about that. For you men, if you ever notice a bad mood coming over you for no reason at all, it often means that you will have a wet dream that night. For the women, it can mean that you are about to start your period. Try to observe that connection.

Anyhow, I hear that many of you try to deal with this problem by taking cold showers or by masturbation. These are not healthy methods either. Normally, a healthy male cannot keep his essence over six months. Achieved ones have a secret method to deal with this problem. A clue to the method can be found in the Chinese classic called

"Monkey." I do not know if that section of the book has been translated into English or not. It is the part where it talks about a treasure the monkey has called the "Golden Hook." It is a point on the body where, if you focus your energy there, it acts like a net and holds in the essence.

I must tell you this: if you are sufficiently advanced on the spiritual path and you lose your essence through improper sex with a woman of bad energy, you will lose everything else too. If you are a rich business man, you will lose all your money. If you are a famous politician, you will lose your fame, etc. This happens because your success was based on your energy level, and if you lose your good physical essence, you will lose everything else that was based upon it. By this, I am only referring to improper sex or masturbation. Normal sex or a wet dream is not that serious. We Chinese call a wet dream "losing your chicken," because having a wet dream means you must replenish the amount of energy a good chicken dinner can provide.

Another thing I want you to know about is the connection between the wind and your discipline. The wind is the disciplinarian of a practitioner of the Integral Way. If you lose too much essence, the wind will come and warn you. It will get windy outside as one energy response. I am not referring to ordinary people. They lose their essence every day and the wind does not warn them. However, for a person of cultivation who has some sensitivity to the divine beings, the wind becomes an early warning system. If you are achieved enough, this is a valuable thing to know.

For women, the way to avoid trouble while you sleep is to always sleep on your side, never on your back, and always keep your legs together. If you lay around thinking of sex, you will invite negative energy to you. You can also lose energy if you are not careful. Images you project while you are awake can unconsciously become active while you are asleep. It could be a physical reason or a possible external intrusion. If this is the case, then the image or the thought you emit while you are awake becomes the invitation for the outside response which then invades your mental control.

Ordinary people can have sex regularly and it will not hurt them, but to a person who has been cultivating and refining their energy, it can be damaging. The laws are different because the energy composition of the two types of people is different. Having sex and producing babies is the only way ordinary people have to continue their lives after they are gone. Achieved ones in the Integral Way transform lower energy to be high energy; the result is the conception of a spiritual baby, born to be a god.

According to the developed ones, the world already has too many people in it and too many people make the quality of life go down. Man's reproductive energy is too active nowadays. The larger the population, the more complex life becomes and the more complex it becomes, the sicker people get. Just look at all the big cities in the world and how degrading life has become. When people think that their lives have no more meaning or purpose than that of ants, it is reflected in their lives. They work hard all day and come home tired and frustrated. When they have sex with an improper attitude, they need not wonder why their children are born deformed or are disturbed in some way. We have a huge population of low quality people nowadays and they have spoiled the world. This is so sad.

First of all, try to keep your essence. If you cannot and you want children, then make sure you have good ones. A person's inclinations are formed at the moment of conception, so be sure you have sex only under the best conditions. Many people have sex when it is not appropriate. If it is stormy out, or if it is a new moon, or if either partner is physically or mentally disturbed, do not have sex. If you are both drunk, you may attract a bad person to be born to you. If your children are bad, then your family will be troubled. If the family is troubled, society will be troubled. So, the health of the whole planet comes down to how a man and woman perform sex! Most people do not realize how important this is.

Now, I will go into the practical matter of how to decrease your sexual desire. American society is no help in this matter. Everywhere you turn, you are seduced and stimulated by sex. Advertisements, magazines, movies, TV, etc., all keep you artificially stimulated. Sex is not bad, it can actually be beneficial when done correctly, but the way it is encouraged in this country can only be harmful. So be careful about how you nourish your minds. Some of you think you are not affected by all that stuff, but you are. All that social pollution has a cumulative effect on you. The first way to decrease sexual desire is by giving up stimulating or unhealthy books, magazines, movies and television, and using spiritual or healthy books or television, etc.

Another thing you must be careful about is your diet. Most people do not realize how much diet stimulates them sexually. Many people are rich and can afford all kinds of foods, but in discipline and understanding, they are poor. For example, many Americans eat rare steaks; don't you think all that beef affects their disposition? If I ate like most Americans do, after three weeks I would become a master of sex. Not only does that kind of food make you desirous, it also leaves a lot of toxins in your body. Please be careful about what you put in your bodies. You must also watch how much you eat. Just eat enough to stay alive, why do you need more? It is a superstition that you must eat three meals a day, unless of course, you are doing a lot of heavy physical work and you really need it. If you are an office worker and you eat like a physical worker, that just makes you an eating machine. Most of you would be better off if you ate only half of what you eat now. Most of it is junk anyway. Coffee, spicy food, greasy food, shellfish, raw meat, cheese, etc., are not good.

Those are two ways to slow down your sexual desire.

Now the only thing left for you to learn are the sexual techniques, but first you must understand some of the basic principles involved in sublimation. Right after midnight is the time that males produce their essence. If you are not overworked, your body uses that time to produce sperm. This is why achieved ones sit up from midnight to around 2 or 3 o'clock to do our cultivation; we refine that essence to become chi. The very act of sitting up causes the energy to rise and move away from the sexual organs.

In one of the classes, I talked about the necessity of keeping the "mouth of the dragon dry" (the end of the penis).

This means not to ejaculate. This week you must learn how to kill the "White Tiger" and the "Red Dragon." The White Tiger is sperm and the Red Dragon is menstruation. Men use up a lot of energy just to produce sperm. If you do not intend to have children, then why waste all that energy? Likewise, women go to a lot of inconvenience just to produce and get rid of an egg. You all are just sperm and egg producing machines.

Q: Are you saying that through our cultivation we can control our menstruation?

Master Ni: Yes, but it does not happen spontaneously. You must know the correct technique. Today, though, I only want to give you the basic principles involved. I realize that modern scientific people think this is impossible, but it is not. What you must learn to do is to turn your sperm and egg producing machines into machines of divinity.

I am willing to teach you these techniques if I see you are really willing to control yourself instead of just talking about it. In this country, there are a lot of institutionalized people with mental problems, all caused because they did not learn to control their sexual energy. If you are willing to make a total commitment to your cultivation and new way of life, then I will consider teaching you.

Remember the two things I told you earlier this evening that will help you to control your essence and refine it to become higher level energy. First, avoid cultural pollution. Second, watch your diet. Then we will talk about techniques such as "Cut the White Tiger and Red Dragon." Some of you men imagine yourselves having sex with every woman you see on the street. This is because your White Tiger is too uncontrolled. That kind of energy also disturbs your mind. You wonder why you cannot meditate better than you do. It is because your sexual energy is so strong. If you can successfully do those two things, you will be benefitted. This beginning process in self-cultivation is important.

I am not so sure you are so willing to control yourselves. It takes a lot of time and energy to do it. Are you willing to invest it? Are you sure? Some of you are already wondering if you can ever have any fun any more. We realizers of the Integral Way have a lot of fun, but it is fun of a high level of energy. Fun is not limited to your sexual organs. I tell you, every part of your body can be a sexual organ when your energy is high. Every cell in your body is capable of sex. Your energy can connect with someone ten miles away when you are achieved. When I was young and had good energy, just making eye contact with a girl at a distance could send a shock through my whole body. Nowadays, your energy is so bad that you go around hugging each other all the time and you feel nothing! This is a pity.

Sex between ordinary people is done at a level of energy that is so insensitive. They cling desperately to each other in the night and call that fun and excitement! I tell you, much greater excitement awaits you if you learn to refine your energy. The secret to better sex is to have higher energy.

December 9, 1977

I

You all know that in the Bible it says God created man. In Genesis, it said that because man was lonely, God took one of his ribs and made woman. This book of Genesis has had a lot of influence in the Western world, but in China, we do not think that man and woman were creations of a God who is like a person in the sky. We think man is the combined creation of the sun, moon, stars, earth and other energies. Spiritually achieved ones conceptually divide all energies into categories of yin and yang; when these interact, a new species may appear. Also, identical environments will produce the same types of living beings because all beings are images of their environment.

The distances from the earth to the sun, moon, planets and stars, etc., has been about the same for millions of years, so their influence has been around for a long time. Why, all of a sudden, did the strange creatures called humans appear? Without a new energy coming here, it would have been impossible for man to have appeared upon the earth. Where did this new energy come from? The human species is definitely a mutation, so where did it come from? Humans came from the stars.

We know how the sun gives life to all things, including human beings. Without the sun, nothing is possible. Everyone accepts this, but many still do not accept the notion that the moon also has a great influence on us. It is now generally accepted that the moon influences the tides, people's emotions, how crops grow, women's menstruation, etc., so it is important. However, modern scientists still do not know how the moon affects people's intelligence, their brains and all their thinking. The moon has a definite effect upon people.

The extent to which people know the influence of the energies of the sun and moon is still shallow. With the sun and moon we have life, but it is a general kind of life. If the only influence that was available on earth was that of the sun and moon, there would only be plants and simple animals. The power that produces humans and makes one person different from another is the stars.

Some people have special powers and special areas of development. Even in the same family, the talents and inclinations of its members are different. These differences come from the subtle influence of the stars. The sun's energy is certainly not subtle. The moon is more so, but the planets and the stars near the path of the sun are the most subtle of all.

In the Integral Way, we call the annual path of the sun in the sky, the ecliptic, the Yellow Road. The equator or celestial equator is called the Red Road. Because the earth moves around the sun in a yearly cycle, there are seasons. This is also the reason that the apparent position of stars in the sky is constantly changing.

The stars near the Yellow Road are influential in a person's birth and destiny. They are the constellations of the zodiac and they account for all differences between people. Tonight we will talk about the energy of the stars.

Each of the four major directions has seven constellations connected with it, making twenty-eight constellations in all. The differences in the energy formation of these powerful constellations and their locations at different times accounts even for the drastic changes that occur within societies and also subtly affects individuals and leaders. Among all stars, the North Star is king. We say all stars bow to the North Star because they all appear to revolve around it in the sky. Without this order and stability in the sky's energy environment, it would be impossible for human life to have developed. The North Star is the head of the astral order in this particular system.

Even the North Star gives up its position as leader. In about twelve thousand years, the star Vega will be the pole star for three thousand years. Then the pole will slowly recede from Vega, and in another twelve thousand years Polaris will again become the pole star.

As the head of our star family, the North Star is the emperor with all the other stars surrounding it like ministers and people. In spiritual practice, it is correct to embrace our spiritual center which is symbolized by all the stars embracing the North Star. In society, the North Star heading the sky system expresses the order in human society, but it is a great mistake for ambitious leaders to become attached to their power and want it to last for all time, when even the pole star changes.

As you know, the Integral Way is concerned only with energy. Although we sometimes talk about gods, deities and sages, etc., they are only different transformations of energy. Some energy is strong, some is wise, some is graceful, etc., but it all comes from the stars, so we must learn to connect our energy with the energy of the stars, especially the North Star.

A photographer took a time-lapse picture of the North Star that showed all the other stars as streaks of light circling it. That picture clearly shows how the North Star is the leader of the other stars. It is beautiful.

Most of you are probably able to recognize the Big and Little Dippers. The last star on the handle of the Little Dipper is the North Star. The last two stars on the ladle of the Big Dipper point to the North Star. If the Little Dipper could fall down, it would land in the ladle of the Big Dipper. Do not ever point at the stars, because it is against their energy.

(Master Ni then took the class outdoors to show them the sky with its starry energy system.)

I hope you use more of your time in deep meditation to find the source of your energy and life. By standing safely with closed eyes, you can feel where and in what direction the pull comes to you and makes you turn yourself to it. If your life existed before you were formed, where did you exist? Do you think that some of your mother's blood and your father's essence formed you? A certain kind of energy is what made you what you are. I would like all of you to tell me about your energy connection to the twenty-eight constellations.

In the East, the seven constellations are in the shape of a dragon and are thus called the Green Dragon. These constellations are the Horn, the Neck, the Bottom, the Room, the Heart, the Tail and the Basket. In Western astronomy, these seven constellations correspond approximately with the area of the constellation Scorpio.

In the South, the seven constellations are in the shape of a bird and are called the Red Bird or Phoenix. These constellations are: The Well, the Ghost, the Weeping Willow, the Star, the Drawn Bow, the Wing, and the Carriage.

In the West is the White Tiger. These seven are called: The Champion, the Hump, the Stomach, the Rooster's Crown, the Fork, the Beak, and the Interwoven.

In the North is the Black Turtle, or Warrior, and the names of its seven constellations are: The Pipe, the Ox, the Damsel's Room, the Void, Danger, the House, and the Wall.

In the East, where the sun rises, is the Sun Gate. When you go to Heaven, you must pass through the Southern Heavenly Gate. The "Heavenly Gate" is also within oneself, it means the head, or something that comes into creation within oneself rather than externally.

(Now Master Ni passes out the sheet with the sources of the Heavenly rays and reads the following incantation).

With the sun I wash my body.
With the moon I refine my form.
With the divine immortals I am supported.
With the eternal beings I perpetuate my eternal life.
I unite myself with the enduring energy of the
*   twenty-eight constellations.*
Within and without, all impurities are cleansed
*   with divine water.*
Most respected Heavenly treasure of divinity,
*   console my body.*
Saturate my souls and energy with the light
*   of all stars in the enormous "bushel" of space.*
The Eastern stars of the "Green Dragon"
*   lead me forward.*
The Western stars of the "White Tiger"
*   protect me from behind.*
The Southern stars of the "Red Bird"
*   guard me from above.*

The Northern stars of the "Black Turtle"
*   guard me from below.*
So it is commanded and confirmed.

When our human ancestors' spirits came from the North Star or Big Dipper to this new home, the Earth, the first thing they did was to locate where they were in relation to the influence of the five directions, the relationship with the stars and the constellations. The sun and moon and the Earth itself are not easily located except by time change and the different positions shifting to create the change of day, month and year. This is old knowledge or methodology. Because human spirits came from the stars and migrated here, they first had to decide from what direction the different influences were coming in order to use them properly. Those first people who came here had the same ambition to control the universal energy, which they expressed through incantations. We are not sure how successful they were. I hope you use this for your cultivation in order to connect your energy with positive energy in the five directions and as you try to develop yourselves spiritually.

Every direction has two kinds of energy: positive and negative. We only connect ourselves with the positive. Positive means life, negative means death. You must understand that whatever kind of energy you connect with, you become. As the saying goes, "Birds of a feather flock together;" the energy that is around you reflects what you are. Our saying in Chinese is "The same breath blends together, the same voices harmonize." I am sure you all want to connect with divine energy and not with demons, correct? Because your thoughts are a subtle vibration of your energy, incantations can be recited orally to connect with and gather higher levels of energy. If you can accept that, then try it. It can influence your whole life.

Whatever you think about and hope for, the reality of the natural world will give to you. If you can learn to control the eternal force, it can even give you eternal life. The eternal force will not respond to emotional demands, but only to the calmness of mental vibration. Thus, if you can keep a calm mind, you will be sure to succeed and find happiness in your life. How best to do it? Avoid emotions.

Our shrine is the center of subtle energy here, so if you ask for anything in deep meditation here, there will be a response. If you ask for rain, it will come, so will money, friends, anything. However, you need to avoid vulgar desires because a strong desire will block the energy. The harder you try to hold anything, the more it will elude you. You must empty yourself first so there is a space in which things can be held. The *Tao Teh Ching* says: become void, become hollow. Never be too full. You cannot obtain anything new that way. Just sit quietly and let the impure energy go down and the pure energy reach to the Heavenly axis. That is the point I used, in the middle of your eyebrows, to pass the divine energy through. That point can respond to the North Star, which is the center of universal energy. I hope you use that point or physical location and build up your energy bridge to the universe.

Tonight there was good communication between us.

II
The Story of the Jade Mortar and Pestle

This story, a metaphor for internal alchemy, was written during the Tang Dynasty when spiritual achievement was at its peak in Chinese society. I am going to tell you the story but allow you to come to your own understanding about how it applies to your cultivation.

Over a three-year period (821-824 A. D.) in the Tang Dynasty, a scholar named Pei Hung, who had failed the governmental examinations, travelled around the country until he came to Erchow where he visited his old friend, Minister Quei. His friend the minister took pity on his plight and gave him several hundred silver coins, and Pei Hung determined to go back to the capital to study further and retake the exam. Thus, he boarded a large ship which was sailing up the River Hyan. As he sat in his chair, he saw another passenger, Madame Fan, who was a most beautiful lady. They exchanged remarks through a curtain, chatting

quite freely. Although he was so close, Pei Hung was unable
to see her face to face, so he bribed her maid, Misty Wreath,
to deliver this poem to her:

> *Were we as far apart as North and South,*
> *I would still long to meet you;*
> *All that separates me from you, goddess,*
> *is a silk screen.*
> *If you are bound for the Jade City*
> *of the Immortals,*
> *Let me follow your phoenix train*
> *up to the azure sky!*

For a long time, he received no answer to his poem. He
asked Misty Wreath about it several times, until finally she
said: "What can I do if my lady chooses to ignore it?"

Not knowing what else to do, Pei purchased some good
wine and select fruit the next time the ship docked and
presented them as a gift to Madame Fan, who then told
Misty Wreath to let him visit. When the curtain was raised,
he saw a woman whose beauty was as cool and bright as
jade, as lovely as a flower, with hair like clouds and eyebrows like the crescent moon. Madame Fan's poise and
demeanor were like that of a being from Heaven who had
condescended to visit a mere mortal. Pei Hung bowed and
became lost in wonder at her beauty.

The lady said, "My husband lives south of the River
Hyan. He wishes to resign from office to live as a hermit in
the hills to practice his self-cultivation. I am on my way to
see him to say goodbye. I am grieving and anxious that I
may not reach him in time. Thus, how could I be thinking
of another? I have enjoyed your company on the boat, but
I am in no mood for trifling."

"I would not dream of such a thing!" replied Pei.

After drinking the wine he had bought and chatting
with him for a short time, she withdrew. She was as cold as
ice, with a forbidding exterior. Later, she sent Misty Wreath
to him with this poem:

> *Drinking your wine I was deeply moved;*

Once the elixir is well ground,
  you shall see Yung-ying;
Lanqiao is the abode of immortals,
You need not climb to the Jade City in Heaven.

Pei Hung, reading this, admired her talent in writing verses but did not understand the meaning. During the rest of the journey, he was not allowed any further visits and could only send greetings through Misty Wreath. When the boat reached Shiangyang, Madame Fan and her maid took their suitcases and left without even saying goodbye, and Pei did not know in what direction she had gone. Although he searched everywhere for her, she had vanished utterly, leaving no trace of the direction in which she had gone. Then he gathered his belongings and continued his journey, which was now on horseback. At the Blue Bridge posting station, which is a town with a compound for traveling government officials to stay, Pei Hung, parched with thirst, dismounted to ask for a drink. He found a low, thatched-roof cottage of three or four rooms, in which an old woman was spinning hempen thread. Greeting her politely, he asked her for a drink of water.

"Yung-ying!" called the old crone, "Bring a bowl! There's a gentleman here wanting a drink."

Pei Hung was astounded as he remembered that the name Yung-ying was in Madame Fan's poem. While he was trying to collect his thoughts, from behind a reed screen appeared two slender white hands holding a porcelain bowl filled with lucid water. Pei Hung took it and drank thirstily. To his dry lips, the beverage was like a true essence of jade, and as he drank, a wonderful fragrance came to him through the door. When he returned the bowl, he lifted up the door curtain and discovered a girl who was lovely as a flower glistening in the morning dew or melting spring snow in the golden sunlight. Her face was smooth as jade but softer, and her hair was as graceful as thick clouds. She turned away shyly, hiding her face. Not even a vermilion orchid from deep in the valley could match her exquisite beauty. Pei Hung stood rooted to the ground, enchanted by her beauty. He could not tear himself away.

He told the old woman: "My servant and my horse are tired and hungry. May we stay with you and partake of your hospitality? If you grant me this request, I shall compensate you fully."

The old woman replied, "As you wish."

After the refreshing meal, Pei said to the old woman, "The young woman who assists you is a lady of astounding loveliness. To me, she is a peerless beauty. That is why I hesitated to leave. May I offer generous gifts and marry her?"

The old woman said, "Truthfully, she has already been promised to a different suitor, but no marriage date has been set yet. I am an old and ailing woman. Several days ago, an immortal gave me an elixir, but I cannot eat it until it has been pounded for a hundred days in a jade mortar with a jade pestle. Then I can live as long as Heaven. However, I do not have a jade mortar and pestle. You shall marry the girl if you can get me one. I have no use for gold or silk or the like."

Pei Hung bowed in thanks, saying: "It will take me one hundred days to fulfill your request. Please protect her until I return."

The old woman agreed to this and Pei left.

When he reached the capital, he ignored his customary business and went to all the public markets, small curio shops and jade carvers searching for the jade mortar and pestle. Yet there was no sign of such an item. He saw many of his friends, but ignored them, causing them to think he was out of his mind. After several months had passed, he met an old jade peddlar who told him, "Not long ago I had a letter from Old Ben who runs a medicine shop in Kuachou. He mentioned that he has a jade pestle and mortar for sale. Since you are so eager to find one, I can write you a letter of introduction so you can go to meet him."

Pei Hung thanked him heartily, for at last he would succeed in getting what he needed. The price, however, was several hundred pieces of silver, and to meet this sum Pei not only gave him all the cash he had, but also had to dismiss his servant and sell his horse. Then, taking his purchase, he returned on foot to Lanqiao.

When he arrived, the old woman was pleased and said, "I see you are a man of your word. I cannot keep the girl and not reward you for your services."

The girl said with a smile, "However, he must pound the elixir for a hundred days before we can talk of marriage."

The old woman took the elixir from her pocket, and Pei Hung started pounding it, working all day and resting at night, during which time the old woman took the mortar to the inner room. Every night in the dark, the sound of pounding went on. When Pei peeped in, he saw a jade hare manipulating the pestle, while a light white as snow lit up the whole room so that every little thing in it was clearly visible. This further strengthened his determination.

After the hundred days had passed, the old woman took the elixir and swallowed it. Then she said, "I am going to a cave in the mountain to tell my relatives to prepare the bridal chamber for you." She took the girl with her, requesting that Pei wait until he was sent for.

Shortly afterwards, a retinue of attendants and carriages came to fetch him. They escorted him to a great mansion which reached the clouds that had pearl-studded gates which flashed in the sunlight. Inside the mansion, there were curtains, screens, jewels and precious objects of every description, far surpassing what would be found inside the house of a noble. Pages and maids led him behind the curtain to proceed with the wedding ceremony. After the ceremony was over, he paid his respects to the old woman and expressed his regret that she was leaving them. The old woman said, "Since you are a descendant of the ancient immortal Pei, you will leave the world too. You need not regret this."

Then he was introduced to the guests, all of whom were immortals. One goddess, who wore her hair in a knot and whose gown was the color of the rainbow, was introduced as his wife's elder sister. When he greeted her respectfully, she asked:

"Don't you recognize me, Mr. Pei?"

He said, "We are not relatives, and I have no memory of having met you."

The lady asked, "Don't you remember that we traveled together in the same boat from Erchow to Shiangyang?"

Pei recognized her then and apologized cordially for not having remembered her immediately.

Later he heard from another guest, "Your wife's elder sister is Lady Yung-chiao, the wife of Lord Kahn, one of the well known immortals. She has already attained the rank of an angel and waits on the Jade Emperor in Heaven."

The old woman sent Pei and his wife to stay in Jade Peak Cave where he was given the elixir of Rosy Snow and Jasper Flowers which made him ethereal. His hair turned color, he could transform himself at will, and he became an immortal.

During the period 827-835 A.D., his friend Lu Hao met him west of Blue Bridge. Pei told Lu how he had attained immortality and gave him ten pounds of fine jade and a pill to help him achieve longevity. After conversing with him all day, he asked Lu to give his regards to his old friends.

Lu Hao bowed and said, "You have attained immortality. Can you give me some brief instructions?"

Pei said, "Lao Tzu taught us: 'Keep the mind empty and the belly full.' This is good instruction, but unfortunately, men of today keep their minds so full that they cannot attain immorality." When he saw that Lu was bewildered and confused by what he said, he added, "When the mind is full of vain desires, the belly cannot retain the vital spirit, that is what I mean. All men have enough power to attain immortality and keep the vital spirit; but it appears that the time has not yet come for you to learn this. I shall explain it to you some other day."

Lu Hao realized that Pei would not give him any further instruction. After a meal Pei Hung left, and that was the last time that he was ever seen.

December 30, 1977

(All the students first practiced their cultivation for around one hour, and then Master Ni gave his comments.)

Tonight was a good class. Most of you expressed yourselves well. The energy you have developed can be used to heal or to do whatever you want with it. It can even make you happy. But, to be happy or not happy is not the point. You could already be happy, so why aren't you? The reason you are not happy is because you are involved in too many outside things that depress and repress you. Your energy is under a lot of pressure, like a young tree under a pile of stones.

Our shrine and this class is here to provide you with the right environment in which to grow. I am glad to see all of you expressing your energy so well. Once you remove your repressive feelings, you will be free and will naturally feel happy, because there will be nothing covering you. You will be like the full moon with no clouds covering it. It is a beautiful thing to grow fully after removing the obstacles that used to crush you.

In the teaching of the Integral Way, there are two ways to develop or increase divine energy within you. One way is through gentle exercise such as T'ai Chi movement, Ba Gua, Eight Treasures, etc. The other way is to develop healing power by special spiritual learning, but you must know that healing is a little more difficult to learn than the movement systems. Once you learn the principles and become accustomed to the natural rhythms of the gentle exercises, the movements become easy to learn. Then you can teach it and help yourself and others to be healthy. It is also a good way to make a living, if you are the right kind of person to be a teacher.

The spiritually achieved ones also developed many systems of healing, such as herbs and acupuncture. Healing is all based upon intuitive power. When you are skilled at it, you can diagnose without even touching people.

By just looking at their energy arrangement, you will not only know the state of their health, but also how long they will live. You can also read their minds, because the mind is energy too. People's faces and speech, especially their eyes, tell their secrets. Emotional outbursts can also tell what is on their minds. Nothing can be hidden from the eyes of a developed person.

In addition to learning gentle physical movement, if you are interested, some of you can learn some spiritual healing to help yourself and your own children. You know, the spirit of a child is weak and can be easily influenced by bad energy. Normally, in traditional healing practice, we find out what the trouble is and then use the energy to quiet the child down. That can be learned, along with other things.

Some of you have been cultivating yourselves for some time now. You may have achieved the ability to untie all of your spiritual obstacles and physical problems. If so, then you will no longer be troubled by illnesses nor psychological problems. I know that some of you will be successful in doing this within one year. Others will take longer, but do not worry about how long it takes. One year or ten years does not make any difference. If you practice this method regularly, this attainment will come to you.

Right now, none of you have the ability to communicate with subtle beings, whether they are high level, normal, or from a lower level. Your level now is like that of a child who has entered a big book store. The spiritual side of life has many volumes, and it will take many years to learn them all. One day you learn or know this, the next year you know that. Spiritual learning is the same as learning anything. For most of you, it will take time. Even if you have a natural ability, you still need a good teacher to show you the right way to do things, or it could be dangerous.

Once your life has improved and you have become spiritually achieved, you will find that some of your interests in life are different. People who connect themselves directly with subtle beings usually make a profession of it, because they find it hard to do mental tasks after that. For example, when ordinary people have a relative or friend that dies, they cannot directly communicate with that person, so they often use the help of a medium. If you happen to be a medium who is engaged in spiritual cultivation, the ghosts come through you to talk to their loved ones and you use the money to keep your own cultivation going.

I would like to make a distinction here. Subtle beings (spirits) and ghosts are two different things. A profession using subtle beings (spirits) would typically be channeling, and a profession using ghosts would be mediumship. Do not confuse mediumship with channeling a subtle being (spirit), which is sometimes a form of healing. Other types of channeling are not real or helpful.

For a medium, sometimes there is the danger of a ghost coming again and again to bother you: "Oh, tell my daughter this or that, etc." Some mediums are genuine, but many are lazy or crooked and say all kinds of things, so I do not encourage you to go to people who say they are mediums. The only exception would be if your close friends really need help.

For instance, if a person has a strange disease for a long time and medicine cannot cure it, the illness may be caused by a demon or something. When you know that, and if you have been trained as an exorcist, you may try to make peace between the person and the ghost. This is more complicated and dangerous than healing work, but it too is a form of mediumship.

If you are a healer, and a lot of sick people come to you and your energy is not strong, then you can be badly influenced. In spiritual work, you sometimes use your whole body as a tool for healing. Because spirits cannot talk, they sometimes use your mouth and tongue, even at the same time you do. So you may say things like, "Hello, who or what are you?" If you are highly developed enough, you do not need to talk like this because you have enough sensitivity to know the situation to make things go smoothly. When their energy touches you, you immediately receive the communication. Sometimes wild spirits come, and especially if you do not know how to deal with that kind of energy, they will make your house their house. I am talking about your body.

However, all this is not the main purpose of self cultivation. Healing, channeling, mediumship, etc. are all superficial. These things can be done on a subtle level without needing a form. The main thing we do in self cultivation is develop our own spirit and help other people develop theirs, too. I hope that when you get a little power and ability, you will not think it is enough. You must continually cultivate yourself. If you do, you will open many new doors for yourself and allow the secrets of the universe to unfold to your growth.

Now we sit here next to all this vegetation. *(Master Ni points to the flower pots in the shrine.)* Just look at all those different expressions of energy! You all are just as different. Actually, you even hold more subtle and exquisite energy than they do. The only difference between humans and plants is different energy levels.

I would like to give you a suggestion that will help your cultivation greatly. Try not to have your mind fight itself anymore. By this I mean, keep your mind from having two different points of view about an issue and arguing with your own thoughts. It is far better for you to open up your mind and pay more attention to the truth: that all the phenomena of existence are just manifestations of energy. Whatever the energy goes through creates a different sound. Thus, each different channel of energy creates a different type of music. Make yourself a good energy channel and make a good melody. Is your personality a beautiful melody?

Another way to look at your life energy is to compare it with painting. Your life is just like a brush stroke on a beautiful painting. As you control the brush, you control the painting; likewise, when you control your emotions, you control your life. If you control your energy, you control your destiny. All the true or most important knowledge about life is concentrated on the energy level. Thus, how easy it is to learn about life! Everything is in the energy. All you have to do is learn about energy. If you read many books and if they are not directly about energy, perhaps they will lead you far away from the center of your mind.

Spiritual books can lead you back to the center of the existence of the universe. Unfortunately for some of you, your brain is already hard, and you are spoiled and ruined by modern education. It is truthful to say that mere intellectual education hardens people's physical brains. When this has happened, even if many truths come to you, your mental resistance prevents you from making good use of them. How can you make good use of them? First, give up all mental resistance. This means, consider as possible some of the unbelievable things you hear or read.

Do not think you are intelligent. There is really no such thing as intelligence, there is only energy differences between people. The energy difference between someone intelligent and someone who is not is subtle and slight. Intelligence that serves only yourself causes trouble anyway. True happiness is not built on intelligence. It is built on the sincerity of beingness, or your original energy arrangement.

All heroes and the heroic actions they perform are not necessarily constructive, nor do they contribute to the great harmony of the universe. You all have power, but you lose your power. How? By judging too fast; coming to conclusions too fast; eating too fast; making friends too fast, and tiring of them too fast. You keep something somewhere and when you forget where it is, then you try too hard to find it. In other words, you move too quickly and try too hard. I think if you slow down, you will find that it is easy to have power. Sometimes your mind is tense; this tension can also take away your power. Relaxation is important if you always wish to be with the power of life. There is no doubt that it is the tense boxer who always loses the fight.

Try, from this minute on, to come back to your own power. First find it and then do not let your mind trouble you with thoughts of, "Oh, Master Ni, I have no power!" If you think this, then you will truly not have any power. Even a small child can make trouble so large that sometimes many adults cannot fix it. If a small child has such power, so do you. It is easier to be destructive than constructive, but I recommend that you work toward the positive, constructive pole.

The idea that you do not have power is just a thought in your mind.   If you slow down the mind, then your spiritual power can become active.   If your mind is too active, you can suffocate your spiritual energy.

Who is your real enemy, and what is the worst obstacle to your spiritual achievement?   It is your own mind. Everyday you are too thoughtful - you try to express yourself through your mind all the time.   Some people are more developed and diplomatic than others, but being too diplomatic is close to hypocrisy.   If your mind is not developed enough, then it is too rigid and stubborn.   Those two extremes of a too developed mind or an undeveloped mind are not what we are aiming for in this class.   We are trying to discover and learn how to use our own spiritual energy in a constructive way.

The Chinese say: "The further you penetrate a bull's horn, the narrower it becomes."   Some people's minds are like that; they are too steep and sharp and narrow.   It would be helpful if they relaxed more and were more broad minded.   Their rigidity comes from being too tight and defensive.

There is nothing in our daily lives that needs protecting in a friendly environment, such as within a family or when you are together with your friends.   When you are too defensive, you make your personality too rigid, and your friends will lose interest and leave you.   If you are truly achieved, you have learned to untie all the tension, and can be relaxed and easy on any occasion.   This easiness is the foundation of your cultivation.

In our daily contact, we can talk to different people and find out who is narrow or broad, sweet or soft.   People's energy is kind of like honey.   Some people produce sweet honey in their lives and other people gather a type of sour or acid liquid.   The way your energy is depends upon what you feed yourself.   For example, if you read books with many poisonous viewpoints, your energy will be poisonous.

Why do you come to the shrine and attend classes? You come here for protection and to ease your tension. These are two of the most valuable things you learn here.

Spiritually achieved ones know that the natural spiritual energy is inherent within all of us. Originally we were all
equal because we all had spiritual energy. In the many
generations that followed the arrival of our ancient ancestors, we lost our true nature, original mind and positive
spirit. Now, through learning the teachings of this tradition,
we work on restoring our own position in the universe and
in the endlessness of time and space. We wish to restore
our right position of beingness. Our lives, destinies, self-
expressions, professions, etc. are all manifestations of our
individual energy, what we were born with and what we
have gathered.

As we begin to allow the process of restoration of our
original self, we must remember that at the same time that
we make a little effort, we must also let things happen
naturally. If you naturally become rich, then it is okay. If
you naturally become famous, it is also okay. However, it is
best not to force these things. They are not of great importance anyway. The point is to be relaxed about things. If,
for example, you do something and you are tense about it,
you will lose that which you wanted.

Tonight, a student gave me a good illustration of how
this subtle law behaves. She said, "Everyone's energy is
generating well, but mine is so poor." The reason that
happens to her is because she tries to control herself too
much. In other words, she is not relaxed and she is not
natural. That is causing her energy to be tight and rigid
instead of flowing. The more she uses her own mind, the
harder the shell of the brain becomes. This is true for
anybody. When you are natural, then the energy can
express itself. If you are rigid, you cannot express yourself
well because the energy gets suffocated.

Right now, many of you are almost as rigid as a board
in a coffin. When you are at home, when you are in this
class, you can relax and throw away your learned manners,
hostility and overcautiousness, and then you will not be so
rigid. Try to release your energy; it is your Heavenly music.
If you can learn to relax and release your energy, your
music might not be so beautiful at first. After you practice
relaxing for a while and learn to be more natural, eventually

it will improve and become lovely. I knew a young student who was learning to play an instrument. He started out with a old fiddle that had only two strings. At the beginning, his music sounded somewhat like a car whose brakes were badly in need of repair; terrible. He slowly improved his skill, then better music came which was more sophisticated and pleasing to the ear. It was not a miracle; it is the result of self-discipline and learning. Well, in a sense, it was a miracle, because not everybody does that. An earnest person and a fragrant personality come from a good deal of self discipline.

The income you earn from movement, music, healing work, work communicating with the subtle realms or exorcism, etc. can be used to keep your cultivation going. These are just some practical ways to keep your cultivation going. Those kinds of things are good for your cultivation because they help you maintain your sensitivity. This is, of course, not a complete list. I do not recommend that you do anything that would harm your virtuous character. The main thing is to cultivate yourself and achieve immortality.

Some people say, "I do not care if I die tomorrow. I do not care about immortality." Please understand that I am not talking about physical immortality. Surely, if you have an incurable disease, you do not want to live forever! You would rather die and come back with a clean body. By immortality, I mean your subtle body, which is immortal. Nobody can have physical immortality; even the older human shiens like my masters in China can only live a certain amount of time. According to the Chinese, the normal life span of a human individual is 120 years. Once a person dies, then he usually stays in the spirit world for 120 years before coming back again. According to the ancient ones of this tradition, this is the way the energy rotates on earth. Some come back, some go to higher places and others go to lower places. Some people have gathered a lot of material on the subject of reincarnation, but true spiritual teaching guides you to look forward by realistically improving yourself instead of looking back to complain about the past. We just pay attention to the true energy and to practical matters, not just theories.

In the cultivation of many of you, I think the attraction of Earth is not so strong now, but the attraction of Heaven is still far away. By this I mean, many of you are losing interest in worldly activities, but have not yet really begun to become interested in divine energy. Your head is not used to the Heavenly attraction. Sometimes this manifests as a kind of boredom, because you have outgrown the old but have not yet picked up the new.

At first, when you cultivate seriously, you might feel your head is heavy or have a slight headache, but after some time, the energy will circulate better. The center of life is in the upper part of the body, not the lower part.

I have written in the *Yellow Book*, (*Workbook for Spiritual Development of All People*) that there are some ways in which the body's poisons, whether emotional or physical, can be released and relieved. Some people give away bad physical energy such as toxins through diarrhea or vomiting. Some people give away bad emotional energy in unconscious ways, such as feeling heat in the throat, etc. There are a lot of different manifestations in the process of self-release or clearing oneself of negative or toxic energies. Illness is definitely one of them. If you wish to know whether your sickness is a release or not, just see how you feel when it is over. If you feel lighter and stronger than before, then it was a release. If you feel terrible after the sickness, like your energy has been hurt or you are weaker, it was not necessarily a cleansing.

Some of you mention that you lose your cultivation. You must work on it if you wish to be successful. If you wish to know the spiritual realms, your cultivation cannot just be something you do occasionally, it must be a daily habit like eating and breathing. If you backslide or forget, just get that positive effort going again the next time.

Q: How should we sleep?

Master Ni: Sleep is the most important time of the day for a person doing cultivation, because during the day, you must divide your time between external activities such as working, talking and meeting people, etc. Sleep is all your own time, so you must use it for energy accumulation or for spiritual activity. In the Integral Way we say: "Dreamless sleep is closest to the way where and when the mind ascends to a state of non-dualistic division."

If you eat too much during this festive season, that will also hurt your energy, so keep to the great principle of normalcy. Keeping things normal or balanced or constant is the first principle of a good spiritual life. If the sun did not come up one day, or if the Earth stopped rotating, there would be a great disaster. The reason we can trust this world is because of the normalcy and regularity of the Heavenly bodies.

Geng Shen day is a good day for purification. It occurs at the end of November. It is an a yang metal day, which means reformable metal. It is especially good time for people who cannot practice purification regularly. If you practice daily, then you do not need to choose that day in particular, but it is better not to have sex on that night. On Geng Shen morning, first wash yourself, then go to the West and blow air out of your mouth in seven "poofs" to cleanse your energy and refresh yourself. Western energy is cleansing energy. Then turn to the East to breathe in deeply as many times as you wish. Eastern energy is generating energy. Then go to the shrine and meditate. This is the best way to observe that day.

Some people also practice not sleeping during Geng Shen night. This practice is also considered a purification. However, if you sit up one night during Geng Shen and then for three days your energy is low, it will hurt you, so do not do it. It is far better to keep a regular schedule every day which includes time for purification, thus you can follow the greater principle of normalcy.

Too much rain or moisture outside is not helpful to someone cultivating. Too much thunder and lightning is also bad, so if it is stormy outside, do your practice inside. Full time cultivators always choose a place with good energy. Typically, this has not included being in general society for spiritual people in the past. Instead, they retreated to the mountains. Today, in the modern world, we must compromise.

Q: If we are in a room working or studying, what is a good direction to face? What about when we are meditating?

Master Ni: Indoor activity is much more complicated than being outside. The direction you face depends upon the layout of the house. Do not face the toilet or kitchen when meditating. Do not put your shrine on the bottom floor and have a lot of people walk or live over it.

No more questions? Then let us have quiet sitting.

January 6, 1978

We are sitting in our shrine, directly in front of the simple altar. A shrine is not just the building we are in; there are functional levels of a shrine like this. At the first level, it helps us to stabilize our minds so that our spiritual energy does not become scattered. Then there is a more important shrine; it exists within our bodies.

Thus, a shrine or altar does not only mean a location with a spiritual layout. That is external religion, it is not what you can carry with you all the time and everywhere. Physical buildings and altars are for beginners who do not yet know that the real shrine is inside themselves.

After discovering your own divine energy, you become a Divine Being. Everywhere you go, you are a Divine Being. Every movement you make, including speaking and think-ing, can cause a response from other subtle Divine Beings. For the student of spirituality, a shrine stabilizes one's Masterly Energy. For the experienced practitioner, the Masterly Energy lives in the shrine of one's body and life. This happens when a person cultivates and purifies himself for years by sanctifying and uniting himself with the Masterly Energy of the subtle realms. Wherever he goes and whatever he does, all the subtle beings live within and above his aura or energy body. The reason they take this position is that within and above one's aura, the divine energy exists and forms one's energy being. Images and pictures which represent this state of being have spiritual significance and spiritual truth, because these colorful energies connect with your deep spiritual energy, or Masterly Energy.

In learning spiritual truth, we do not depend upon images. When the primal energy of the universe manifests, then the myriad things come, and all beauties, wonders and miracles are her manifestations. In a broad sense, all things are transformations of the primal energy of universal nature. Thus, images are just transformations of that energy and are not the Divine Energy or the primal energy itself. The primal energy of the universe has been personified as the

Mysterious Mother of the universe. All things and all beings are manifestations of the Mysterious Mother. It is one energy. In this world, the reason why there are things and people that are good, bad, beautiful or ugly is because of self-distortion in adaptation to the influence of the external environment or one's internal environment. In depth, all things and all lives are one energy. This is how a student of the Integral Way perceives the world; it is different from how worldly people perceive the world. Most people perceive good, bad, beauty or ugliness through their own distorted perception.

Let us discuss this on a smaller scale. When you are young, you are innocent and do not know the difference between good and bad. If you do not have a strong external spiritual influence, then external worldly influences exert a bad effect on you and, after a while, you develop those tendencies.

In truth, the primal energy only gives birth to a life of wondrous beauties and miracles. This is especially true of human life which has attained spiritual consciousness. If a person yields to external influences, he changes and becomes a source of bad influence and bad energy to his fellows. Those who follow the teachings of the Integral Way do not look at that distorted side of life, they look only at the good side and work to develop it. As they do so, the other side naturally recovers its normalcy and health.

You are born into this world and then you come in contact with unfair and unrighteous treatment. You are educated with artificial concepts. All of these distort your true nature. To correct this, you must work on your understanding and your cultivation. I am here to help you. Because you are interested in restoring your true nature, you have come to this class. Those of you who are here are the most hopeful people, supported by the positive side of your own personality. This positive manifestation of being willing to explore the spirit is great.

You must understand that self-release will cause a lot of old stuff to come out. If these poisons are kept inside, then you will never have a chance to cleanse yourself. As long as negativity is not released from the body, your true self will continue to be contaminated.

Now you are on the road of continuing to evolve your life. In the process of self-cultivation, there will be many negative manifestations and a lot of obstacles. This is both natural and normal. Some of these things were accumulated during your childhood, some were accumulated during remote past lives. All of them need to be cleaned out, so do not feel strange. It is normal and regular. It happens to everyone who goes through this process, although it happens a little differently for each person.

In learning spiritual law, we learn to respect and value our internal spiritual reality. If you respect and value your internal reality, your internal spiritual energy has a strong manifestation, and you can make wherever you are a Heaven. If you do not have spiritual energy, then it is hard for you to say that there is any place called Heaven in the whole universe, because it has been destroyed by you yourself. It means your environment has created you. Your life can also create a Heaven for all people.

I am taking the level of Heaven down one step and relating it to everyday life so you can understand it better. Heaven can be considered a "good time," but not in the sense that most people think of it. Do not mistake a spiritual good time for a common "good time." A spiritual good time means everything is normal and peaceful. What most people think of as a good time is the cinema or a dancing party and so forth, but that only makes a person tired and exhausted. It upsets one's personal energy. A good time is a quiet, peaceful, sweet time with yourself, and having cordial, harmonious relationships with others like your roommate, housemate, relatives or fellow workers.

Some of you may get along well with others at times, but you cannot sustain supportive friendships over the long term. Do you know why this is? It is because you have not refined or worked through some parts of yourself.

The most wonderful thing in the universe is love. People give love to you and you give love to people. The love between a man and woman is especially beautiful. Unfortunately, what so often happens at the second sight or after living together for a while, one will become critical and say, "She's no good for me." The mind becomes proud and destroys all the beauty and wonderfulness of the relationship.

Heaven gave you beauty, wonders, and a miraculous life, but some of you destroy it all. Some of you have stable jobs and others do not, but jobs are external. You know, beauty and wonders are not necessarily external, they are internal. The reality is that if you cherish your work and love people, and if you are with people who love you, then your life can be a beautiful thing. Unfortunately, if you make trouble or are always critical, then you destroy the beauty and happiness.

Do you know what beauty and happiness really are? Beauty is not the physical appearance of your partner or the elegance of your house. Happiness is not having lots of presents at Christmas or a new car every year. Beauty and happiness are a feeling inside you that happens when you gently extend your loving energy toward other people, helping them, forgiving them or just being with them.

You must take responsibility for one small thing: your worldly life. Having a physical body is a nuisance to most spiritual people. However, we are already here on earth, and life on this planet is not easy. All of you are safe, with four limbs and five organs, so why are you sometimes unsatisfied? What would you like to be that is different from that? What do you hope to be? Your desire to be somebody in a high position destroys the enjoyment of life you could be experiencing right here and now. Your desire for greatness is unworthy and costs you dearly.

I would like to tell you a story about a boy I knew who was born to a rich man. He was a little foolish because he was young. His family always gave him nutritious food and provided him with good times. The family's friends who traveled abroad always brought back expensive toys for him from foreign lands, but the boy became tired of his good life. One day, he took his expensive toys and traded them all for some tasty, but unhealthy, food. He ate until he got a stomach ache.

Well, most of you do the same thing. You trade your assets in the form of your health, upright moral character, and pleasant personality for unworthy things. The most important thing is your good nature. If you are able to keep your good nature, you can then sustain yourself as Heaven, and every part of your life can be Heavenly. That's pretty abstract, but it is true: your calm, upright personality brings what you want in life. Unworthy things will not bring you what you truly desire. If you do not make yourself even-minded, your life will not improve. Also, if you do not make yourself even-minded, you will not reach the more subtle sphere of life and you will never know that there are spirit lives that dwell within you and work for you. Actually, your difficulty is not that you do not allow your spirits to help you; your difficulty is that you listen to your mind rather than your own internal knowledge.

To this, you might say, "You're wrong. I went to school to learn many different things that could help me make a living and make me superior to others." Or just, "I earned a degree from school." If this is what you think, I suggest that you open yourself up to the possibility that there is something more to life than what you know.   There is something more enriching, more rewarding than what you learned in school. Intellectual education helps a bit, but compared to spiritual learning, it is an external triviality. Do not trade your internal essence for any external triviality. I am not telling you not to learn intellectually; I am telling you not to think that intellectual learning is everything.

In learning about the spirit, we do not care if you are rich or not. What is more important than money is whether or not you have internal value. If you own a lot of property but you do not have any internal value, then you have no integrity.

What is internal value? Having internal value does not mean you are a knowledgeable person or that you have written a book. Internal value is what is within you. You might respond that your learning is within you, but I tell you that the intellectual level is not the same as the spiritual level. Intellectual learning comes from outside and becomes internalized. Spiritual reality is internal now, always has been internal and always will be internal. Do you see the difference?

Writing is sometimes intellectual and sometimes not. Being a writer does not guarantee anybody a good life with a healthy mind and healthy soul. It does not guarantee that a person has spiritual depth, either. Some famous writers exhaust their minds and kill themselves in the end because they cannot think of anything to write. Hemingway is one example, but there were many others.

On one level, you can understand that your internal worth is the energy within you. It is your source. After self-cleansing, you can connect with the source of positive energy within you and manifest your goodness in the world. The process is, first to restore or raise your internal spirit, and then to manifest yourself in the world. People who try to do this in the reverse order usually do not do well. For example, many people try to prove to the world that they are a "good person" before they have spent the necessary years training to become skilled at doing something. Thus, what they manifest is disordered or upset. People do not see them as helpful or good, they see them as unskilled or bad. When you see your creations, then you can know what kind of spirit you are manifesting.

In ancient China, the early achieved ones reconnected with their positive nature. What they did was make what people call "sacredness" a part of their daily lives, rather than just something they did on Sundays or when they had emotional trouble or when they were performing a ritual. One way to describe "sacredness" is to experience life as being full of wonders and miracles. Ordinary people like to see wonders and miracles but they never know that every minute of being alive is a wonder and a miracle. The simplest things are the most incredible and wondrous things. If you cannot see the wonder in your daily life, it could be that your eyes and ears and nose are not sensitive enough. It could also be that you are not looking at the right things; are you focusing on what is wrong with your life instead of what is right with your life?

The *Book of Chuang Tzu*[1] has a story in which one teacher tells another teacher not to discuss ice with summer cicadas, because cicadas, like people, do not understand what they have not experienced. In this class, many things I talk about are not completely described or developed, but I can give you a glimpse. This is why I am asking you to develop yourself wholly; then I can discuss more with you or you can know the rest by yourself. You shall embody yourself with all truth and all truth will become an expression of your life.

Another thing I would like to discuss with you is your spirit as the substance of your being. Each day you are alive, you have many experiences. These experiences will continue throughout all the days of your life, but the subtlety of your spirit will change. For example, the experience of being startled or excited is just a reaction to an experience. Experiences are not the essence or subtlety of your spirit. Gradually, all your experiences will not be just memories, but will also be subtle signs and images that internally tell you what will happen. Each event will tell the next step, because your life and spirit are a continuity. Typically, people live their lives on the level of emotional drama that is portrayed in soap operas. Obviously, no one can suddenly change that way of life to become highly achieved. However, you can eventually surpass the subtle range of experience and go deeper into the subtle essence that is the real substance of life. All kinds of things will still happen, but when you reach the subtle essence, you will have the even-mindedness to deal with them. When you are able to handle things better, you will not be disturbed by anything.

I would like to tell you again that to a student of the spiritual truth, every moment of every day is beautiful. If it is not beautiful, it is your responsibility to make it turn out to be beautiful. If something does not look beautiful to you,

---

[1]Master Ni's translation of this book is called *Attaining Unlimited Life.* - Editor

it is because you do not have a beautiful mind with which to enjoy it. You are troubled.

Something that happens in the process of cultivation is important; you can see light. This is important because it marks a certain stage or level of spiritual achievement. You can have dreams, some of which will make you happy. Both dreams and light are real and unreal at the same time. There is something behind all phenomena, which is the essence.

It is true that if you go through the process of spiritual cleansing your spirit will be able to connect with another kind of energy. You will experience that other energy if you persevere. It is so true and real; why deny it? Many people try to deny or belittle the importance of the subtle things without knowing that subtle things are stronger and more real than gross, material experience.

It is in daily life that your cultivation becomes complete. It can be practiced while you talk to others, walk, and in everything you do.

Do not be disturbed by the negativity in modern society. Let it go. Negativity will cause you conflict as you go through your day. If you experience it, just let it go. Most of you can arrange your lives or improve your personalities so that you will meet less external negativity.

One day a student drove me home after a T'ai Chi class. Some one drove poorly on the highway and made a bad turn. We almost ran into them, even though we were in the right and the other driver was at fault. Both cars stopped and the other driver got out and called my student a jerk. He thought that calling the other person a name was a way to tell others that he was right. If the student had insisted that he was right, there would have been an argument or a fight. I think if you are in the right, let them call you a jerk. So what?

It is relatively easy to drive your car well, but when you drive your mind, you do not always know what you are doing. If you call others names, it is because the world has conditioned you to think that the plaintiff is right or that having the first say means to win the argument. It is how you operate, and many of you have never learned how to control your mind to be able to do anything.

The teachings you learn from me have been tested over many generations and proven safe, like the natural herbs we use. They are the principles of harmony, simplicity and appropriateness. Try to use them in your lives; all can be useful. The teaching of the Integral Way is not just a matter of sitting still in meditation; the actualizing of spiritual truth in your daily lives is the most beautiful thing.

The one thing I cannot talk about is the reality of spirit. Any way of talking about it is only talking and not the real thing. You might start learning about the reality of spirit by learning about the things on the side that help take you there. The center of the teachings of this tradition is the unified spirit of the universe, and that is indescribable. It is a high achievement to extend our own spirit to connect with it. However, all the things I teach you are just so you can get to the point where you can try to develop your spirit. After you develop your spiritual being, you can unify yourself with the spirit of the universe.

When you come here, as in any Chinese household or shrine you take your shoes off. Thus, when you walk, you make no noise and the energy returns to your center. When you sit here I do not let you talk; this makes you quiet so the energy goes inward. When you are quiet and relaxed, it is easier for you to be aware of spiritual reality. The most powerful and most helpful thing in your life is your spiritual reality, which exists even as you sit here.

Before concluding this class, I have some verses I would like to share with you.

The primal energy of the universe
    is the Mysterious Mother of all.
She has never made herself seen.
She gives herself away
    by creating all things and all lives.
She cannot be pictured.
If she could be pictured by your mind,
    she would be what is beneath the center of the mind.
We call her the Universal Mystical Mother.

However, she would not consider herself as such.
The name we give her is not her own adopted name.
As the origin of Heaven, Earth, and all lives,
     she is shapeless.
As the Mother of the Universe,
     she is so named.

She envelops her wonders
     through the development of our eyes.
We can see the outer form of her offspring.
Through developing the ability to observe,
     we see the place where spirit and matter divide.
Both come from the same source,
     and each performs its own function.
The two opposites are really one.
The mystery is the gate
     through which oneness is reached.

When beauty is recognized as beauty,
     the mind gives birth to ugliness.
When goodness is perceived as being good,
     evil also comes forth.
Truly, the hidden and the manifest give birth
     to each other and nurture each other's nature.
Difficulty and easy complement each other.
Long and short depend on each other.
Voice and sound harmonize each other.
Back and front cover each other.

Therefore, the Mysterious Mother arranges the universe
     without adornment
     then imparts her teaching without words.
She disciplines without servitude,
     recognizing nothing particular but embracing all.
She nurses her offspring but lays no blame on them.
She accomplishes her task by just starting it.
She claims no credit for whatever has been
     accomplished by her,
     but it does not reduce her greatness.

By learning from her,
    the wise life absorbs her spirit in one's life.
Without exalting the talent but discouraging frivolity
    one attains contentment.
By not cultivating good,
    one deters coveting and stealing.
By not encouraging what is desirable,
    one strengthens one's heart to remain undisturbed.
Therefore, one governs everything through the heart
    by living in the body, weakening the ambition
    and strengthening the bones.

In this way, one learns from universal life
    without false knowledge and evil desires,
    and spares the knowing ones from any bother.
Practice non-concern and everything will be in order.

The Mysterious Mother is like an enormous valley,
    which is either empty or full.
Fathomless, she is the origin of all things.
Learning from her,
    the wise one restores spiritual flexibility.
The wise one also cannot be troubled.

She unravels all tangles,
    she harmonizes all aspects of life.
She denies the conflict of differences.
She is the subtle reality of the universe that is one whole.
Hiding in the deep core she seems to be
    the common ancestor of all existence
    even before Heaven and earth were born.
She has another name: Tao.

Now, take three quarters of an hour for meditation.

January 13, 1978

I

I can see your spiritual formation or exhibition of your spirit in your natural posture and movement, particularly your way of living and conducting yourself. The way that your divine body tends to display the internal spirit is like a composition of music. It was through the spirit that many wonderful arts such as music, dancing and fine arts, came about. Music can be used as an inducement to help your mind become harmonious with your body. Gentle movements such as T'ai Chi can also serve the same purpose. By your movement you have shown me whether your spirit is happy or uneasy. Movement is a non-verbal language, a kind of spiritual or energy expression.

Almost all of you could make some improvements in your spiritual condition. I can tell you this with certainty. If you have good energy, you will show good energy. Good movement just follows nature.

If there is any design or thought put into your movements, it belongs to the after-Heaven stage. The best kind of movement is pure, free and spontaneous; that kind of movement we would say comes from pre-Heaven energy. Pre-Heaven energy manifests without any thought or design. What you do when you move like that manifests the purest spirit, with wonderful language and wonderful spiritual expression.

It is interesting as a teacher to observe how some of you are growing, changing and improving. The change has come because you have changed your focus in life. Some of you concentrate your energy on one part of the body, some on another. This same energy is the energy with which you can live your life or leave your body. If you nurture and control your energy to become a subtle form, you can have that experience. This class is for you to start learning how to focus your energy.

When you practice sitting cultivation or sitting meditation, it is important to sit correctly, especially in the very beginning stages. You will want to sit upright, with an attitude of calm relaxation. The tailbone must be straight, but not stiff. If any of you have back pain when you sit, it is because you do not sit well. If you have too much sex, the lower section of the spine becomes weak, thus it will be painful. Too much sex also causes a color change in the bone because it causes it to have a different structure. This can be seen by spiritual vision.

If you sit all hunched over and form a kind of hollow, it means your middle is already empty. If you straighten it, the energy will rise.

The neck and its position is also important. In this spiritual tradition, we call it "the Jade Pillar." It is the pathway or means of communication between the brain and the body. The chin must not stick out.

Typically, a weak man has a big Adam's apple. If you sit correctly, the hormones will circulate correctly throughout all the channels of the body. You may think that hormones can only be found in the lower part of the body, but in the saliva there are also many important hormones. Scientists have found more than fifty kinds of hormones in saliva. Surely, hormones are a type of energy. If not, how can they be produced by organs and circulate through the channels?

In our practice, for generations we have tried to tell people not to spit, but always swallow the saliva. Saliva is a kind of nourishment. We have an illustration that proves how important saliva is to one's well being. Oxen help till the fields in China, so we are friendly to them. Oxen salivate a lot in the summertime. Someone tried to suction out the saliva from some oxen for the purpose of testing, but after 27 sessions of suctioning, the oxen fell down and died. This was proof of how important saliva is.

In most Chinese families, the daughters are encouraged to stay at home and not be social. In a way, it is almost like keeping the daughters in hiding. Thus, typically the young girls do not have any social life, so the parents allow them to have small pets such as singing birds or goldfish. One young girl who had a goldfish liked to spit in the fish bowl and watch the fish eat the saliva. After several years of doing this, the girl died of weakness; the spitting exhausted her. Each person's internal energy transforms itself into saliva. What happened in the case of the young girl was that she transferred her energy to the fish every day, and the fish got stronger and she got weaker. It is an obvious illustration.

When you sit in meditation, and also in general sitting, make a communication between the head and the body and always swallow your saliva. By making a communication between the head and the body, I mean to maintain the body in one piece. Also, do not waste your saliva on envelopes, stamps, or spitting. This is important.

Also, do not oversleep. If you sleep too much, less oxygen comes into the body; your body becomes stiff and your eyes become dry. The energy movement slows down and is not as generating. It is better to sleep just enough, but not to oversleep.

Internal energy movement is important. There are four principles of internal energy movement: ascending, descending, floating and sinking. When your energy is floating or ungrounded, you are not peaceful, you are restless. When your energy is low or sinking or depressed, you feel weak or sluggish and have no motivation to do anything. On these occasions, you can attune your own energy by mental conducting or physical posture or movements using the key points of bodily energy. You may refer to the *Workbook for Spiritual Development* to learn the postures to move energy.

Q: What is the difference between sinking and descending energy?

Master Ni: Sinking energy makes your emotions low. Descending energy is a natural internal energy movement. Your energy always ascends in the morning, from midnight to noon, and always descends in the afternoon and evening, from noon to midnight.

Your body possesses good natural knowledge about the postures and your own energy. People are used to trusting the mind only, but if they listened to their bodies they might do better. Mental dominance makes people believe that the body needs some kind of separate care from "doctors." Doctors are only valuable if they have a knowledge of nature and of the body's nature, which has a healing power that is greater than any medicine or external knowledge.

Today, I would like to give you another four principles of energy in the body. They are hot, cold, warm and cool. When the weather changes, the body's energy also changes. In the summertime, when it is hot, your energy transforms into sweat. When it is cold, you tend to urinate more. Regardless of whether you drink a lot of liquids or not, you will still sweat more in summer and urinate more in winter. So try to supply your body with sufficient water during both times of heat and cold, or your own bodily energy will be transformed into water and you will lose it.

How can you control your energy when it is hot or cold outside? In the human body, there is a system of "air conditioning" in the extensive breathing system called the skin. When it is cold, the pores of your skin close, and you become warm. When it is hot, the pores of your skin open, and the heat is dispersed. In prehistory, people did not have air conditioning, of course, but they knew the secrets of the body. Spiritually developed individuals did many kinds of breathing that served to control the body's temperature. Thus, they relied upon their bodies to maintain the proper temperature. This important knowledge has been passed down from master to master over the generations.

When it is cold outside, it is a good time to study, because a person's energy gathers in the brain. When the energy is in the brain, the lower part of the body is cold, which causes frequent urination, so you need to keep the body warm and drink warm, not hot, liquids. If, for example, you are a writer and you wish to harmonize yourself with the natural energies to produce more, plan to do more writing work in the wintertime or in a cool place. Also, winter is an excellent time for spiritual cultivation because the energy is concentrated in the brain. On the other hand, when it is hot outside, the external heat causes the energy to comes out of the four limbs; this makes you lazy and makes you tire easily. Hot weather is not a good time for cultivation unless you have a cool place to stay. To cultivate in an air conditioned place is not ideal because the air is not fresh.

If you do not follow the natural way, and if you study or force yourself to concentrate on hot days, you will disorder yourself and hurt yourself. This is important physical knowledge. In this tradition, in the summertime, you need to become less active and not study or cultivate if it is hot. Winter is the most important time for people to cultivate themselves. Please do not let winter pass without cultivating yourself; if you do not do it, you will be missing a good opportunity.

In winter, people usually have a lot of dreams and can probably remember them. In summertime, you might also have a lot of dreams, but usually you cannot remember them. Dreams are affected by the internal and external environments. They are also connected with the attraction of the sun and moon, as well as by the food you eat.

In warm climates, everything grows faster. In Thailand, where the weather is hot, people just sow the rice; they hardly have to work, and they might not even need to use fertilizer, because the rice just grows. In cold places, crops do not grow easily and people have to struggle more for survival. The energetic function of struggling causes them to have a hard mentality. By hard, I mean that they tends toward stubbornness, closed-mindedness and conservatism.

A place that is very cold or very hot never engenders or produces a civilization or culture which is well balanced. Places with balanced or even temperatures grow cultural flowers. Also, a day with a temperature that is not too hot or too cold is a correct time to accomplish many things. Someone wished me to give approximate temperatures for what is not too hot and not too cold, but I cannot do this because temperature, time and distance are all relative. You do not need Einstein to tell you that; it is all built into your natural system.

A good weather pattern is a suitable time to accomplish good things. Spring and autumn are wonderful times. Summer is too hot and winter is too cold.

I would like to give you some instruction about how to control your body. If you stay too cold, your personality will be come hard or condensed. This means you will become a little mean. If you stay too hot, your personality will become diluted or scattered; this means you will have no center.

Whether the temperature where you live tends to be too hot or too cold, or an alternation of each, you can learn to adapt to your environment by adjusting your food and clothing. You can also arrange a good internal environment for yourself by how you use your body. How can you make yourself warm? How can you make yourself cold? One way to make yourself warm is to practice T'ai Chi. T'ai Chi can make every muscle in your body warm. After you have practiced T'ai Chi over a period of months or years, you can do it and not sweat. If you practice it and you feel itchy, it is because the pores of the skin are blocked and the perspiration cannot come out properly. To help that, a person can take a bath and adjust the temperature of water to the right condition so that you sweat and let the internal water out. If you practice T'ai Chi Chuan well, then you have learned the best adjustment for temperature, which is even better than hot baths. When you do the exercise, the energy can come and go beautifully.

Also, do not wear synthetic material. If you do, the pores of your skin are blocked from breathing. A lot of the body's breathing occurs through the skin.

All bodies create heat, especially young ones. Heat is created from food and activity, especially activity like exercise or work. Argument can also create heat. A certain amount of heat is necessary to life, but an excess of heat causes tension, congestion and constipation, sleeplessness, high blood pressure, etc. It is important to maintain the right balance or right amount of heat in the body.

Most people only have three ways to adjust the amount of heat in their bodies: sweating, urination and sex. These three things, suitably done, can be considered adjustments for body heat. This is respected knowledge and part of the art of learning spirituality. If these things are not suitably done, especially if they are overdone, a person weakens himself. Too much sweating, drinking too much liquid which causes excessive urination, and too much sex all cause one to lose energy and heat. For example, after some people have sex, they easily catch cold, because the sex has created a bodily imbalance.

In learning spiritual reality, the key word or principle of "balance" is applied to all apparent and subtle spheres and aspects of life. Balancing the amount of your body heat is almost like balancing a checkbook. Your level of body heat has an apparent effect or immediate influence upon your health condition on the subtle level. One important discovery in the learning of spirit is the different breathing techniques which can help adjust the amount of heat in the body.

Activity, movement or exercise is one thing that generates more heat in the body. By the way, the word "energy" could also be substituted for "heat." Generally, only athletic types of people do lots of physical movement. Unathletic people tend not to do anything at all. Both express extremes. In spiritual culture, through many generations, we have developed all kinds of gentle movement, called physical energy conducting, which can help increase one's body heat: Dao-In, Chi Gong and T'ai Chi, etc. The movements of these exercises encourage athletic people to appreciate the artistic aspect of physical movement. They can also find the value of systematic physical activity with natural rhythm and meet the spiritual balancing point. These movements are one way to change scattering types of competitive physical sports into graceful, controlled and gentle exercise.

Because those movements are gentle, they encourage unathletic people to use their bodies and find enjoyment, happiness and emotional communication through body movement. We promote this kind of activity so that people will not become too extreme either one way or the other.

The basic purpose of spiritual cultivation is to aid human health on the three levels of body, mind and spirit. If a person has not attuned one's body to be in the range of health, or if one's body heat is not adjusted, there will be trouble. In modern times, many people suffer the risk of high blood pressure which is caused by too much body heat. If people so afflicted knew how to sweat in a suitable way and knew the right amount of water to drink for the purpose of urination, they could decrease their blood pressure naturally rather than relying upon medication. It is always better to use natural means to balance the body rather than the "poison" of artificial medication.

The subject of aging, as well as the hardening of blood vessels, could be considered part of the subject of spirituality in this tradition. We are not religious Taoists; we focus upon the natural way of life. We consider ourselves students of natural universal life. Learning about the natural way of life is the way to attain the essence of millions of years of human experience and knowledge of life. In other words, using this knowledge to live a natural life actually maintains the essential wisdom of a million years of human life experience. We use the help of herbs, acupuncture and other natural approaches to keep ourselves balanced so that we do not need to look for external help. This is much better than the modern trend of using mechanical means which keep a body alive but kill the spirit.

As mentioned above, seasonal heat and cold are factors in regard to the body's heat. In the summertime, people usually eat lots of ice cream with the wish to cool down their bodies. A little bit of ice cream is fun and not really harmful. However, if you eat too much, you actually cause more heat to be created. Although the ice creams cools down the stomach, the material that ice cream is made of contains a lot of heat. This eventually results in creating heat inside of a person. On a hot day, it is not suitable to eat too much or foods that are too rich. For instance, winter types of food are overly nutritious and can cause you to generate too much heat in a warmer season.

When young people who tend to have a lot of body heat do not find the right way to release it or use it, they join gangs and consider vandalism to be fun. Many types of mischief and many irresponsible things are done because of poor management of internal heat.

It is important to have sufficient daytime activity to disperse some of your body heat. Never give up opportunities such as gardening, cleaning or any other physical activities which are not too vigorous. If your internal heat does not disperse but collects during the daytime, you will tend to think too much. This will not necessarily be positive. It's interesting that people tend to do well riding horses or driving cars because there are external standards with which they can compare their performance, but they tend to do poorly at managing and correcting their own thoughts, because they cannot see them. The mind is much more subtle than the body or other physical things, thus it allows more freedom for personal projection or roaming. Philosophers make thinking their way of life, but I do not recommend that profession for most people; instead, I recommend a balanced life.

If your body heat is not dispersed or released through physical movement or work, then you will not sleep well at night. Too much heat causes insomnia. Once insomnia becomes serious, many people rely on sleeping pills. These are dangerous, not only because of a possible overdose, but also because of the chemical substances they contain which are harmful to the body.

Many physical problems can be adjusted by watching the internal water condition and heat condition of the body. At some level, your body is your house or your vehicle, therefore it is important to care for it properly and learn to drive it well. Actually, for most people, the physical body is much more than just a house or vehicle, it is life itself. Well, you are the one who lives the life. You are the one responsible for keeping the house comfortable by adjusting the temperature.

During each summer, the sun is close to the earth. At noon, and during the afternoon, the effect or attraction of the sun on your energy is strong. These times are not suitable for outdoor activity, except for when absolutely necessary. The strong attraction of the sun and moon are a natural reason why it is harder for people to manage themselves in a rational way or with rational behavior during the heat of summer. This is why during the summer, people easily express anger or cause a fight and then rush out of the house, speed in their cars and cause traffic accidents, etc.

In general, people who live in the northern hemisphere tend to be more creative than those who live in tropical zones, close to the equator, although people in the tropics engage in artistic creation or religious activity more easily than other forms of development because their environment has a stronger influence from the sun.

In the southern hemisphere, cultural achievements and the progress of life is usually not as noticeable as in the northern hemisphere. Some people think there is a natural difference in intelligence between people of the different zones of the earth. I think that the difference is caused by the relationship of the sun and moon to the earth, especially that of the sun and its magnetic influences, which are so dramatically experienced by human people.

Among all the influences that affect human life and personality, one of the most important is the weather and its effect upon culture. A warm place produces a different culture than a cold place. We can also notice a different effect between warm and hot, cold and very cold. Very cold and very hot climates do not bring about any cultural contributions which influence the entirety of the earth.

Dry heat and humid heat, and dry cold and wet cold, also produce mental and physical differences in people. Generally speaking, in a place or region with cooler weather, people have better mental concentration and thus can easily produce mental achievements or expressions. A hot place surrounded by water could become an enclave for the creation of poetry, fine arts and religious development.

In spiritual cultivation, if you are seeking enlightenment, it is suitable to live in a slightly cooler place or in the high mountains. If you wish to achieve other types of spiritual development, different climates offer different experiences to help your development and understanding. Although your individuality plays a large part in the expression of your thoughts, life attitudes and personal achievement, your natural surroundings are also an important factor.

Mountain people tend to be more conservative than people who live in a place with a harbor and who have lots of foreign contact. Geographical and climatic aspects of countries and cities, as a singular, noticeable factor which can determine the kind of people or personality produced, will also form a particular type of leader or leadership. This suggests that if the influence of the climate is negative, then perhaps a leader needs to work out all sorts of negative influences, whether physical, mental or spiritual before he or she can give the best service.

If, as a spiritual student, you wish to nurture your spiritual baby, it is not suitable to stay in a place that is too cold or too hot, where you need to expend a lot of energy struggling with the weather. However, wherever people live, it is their responsibility to maintain a balanced vision, life and financial support.

We learn a lot by going to school and reading on our own. We have numerous libraries across this nation, but the most useful knowledge for life is this simple type of thing that I am discussing here. This is fundamental knowledge for a healthy, happy life which, in turn, helps society.

On warm summer nights, young people tend to gather together. Because they do not understand how to manage their internal heat, they eat lots of ice cream and probably drink beer, too. Both beer and ice cream tend to increase body heat. Drinking too much and becoming drunk is a manifestation of too much body heat. All kinds of internal heat, no matter what the source, will cause you to lose your balance. This is exactly the same effect on the body caused by drugs and alcohol. Too many people with too much internal heat create the type of urban culture characterized by fighting, criminal behavior and other wasteful, meaningless social activities. I call this "the modern subnormal culture of heat."

The cultural trend itself causes a lack of knowledge about one's own body by overly externalizing the focus of life. The basic cause of bad cultural or social trends is so simple: people do not know how to manage their heat. Heat is one expression of valuable physical energy. It is body heat or body energy that enables people to write, teach, talk, treat patients and fulfill their duties in life. This heat is the body's source of energy. It takes this kind of activity to drain the body's source of energy and thus balance a person's nature and guide him or her toward socially acceptable behavior. Lawbreakers, adult criminals or mobsters do not know how to conduct the heat of their bodies correctly. This results in the game of war on a small or a big scale. Therefore, I sincerely request social leaders and people of knowledge to thoroughly understand the problem and help find a good way to guide people to use their own body heat in constructive ways. I especially request that they avoid big wars, improper behavior and the type of small war that can occur within a family. All of these activities are related to the improper conduction of heat inside a person's body.

Overweight people who have too much water retention will find that vigorous exercise regularly causes them to sweat a lot. This can be helpful in order to get rid of water poison and evil heat. Natural medicine refers to too much water as "water poison" and too much heat as "evil heat." Excess water or heat can both cause internal organ problems which, when not relieved, can cause failure of an organ and thus the entire body. Therefore, it is best to live a natural life which includes physical movement and sweat to bring about a self-adjustment of the physical functions and body heat. People who are already weak need to maintain their energy by gentle exercise and avoid heavy sweating. Gentle exercise and light sweating will not cause a loss of energy.

This is all important knowledge for your physical condition. Basically, life is a salvation for life itself. I mean, the correct way of life contains health and produces energy which will produce a kind of natural joy of life in all kinds of decent activities. Learning spirituality, by intellectual standards, sometimes is cause for laughter, because it teaches things that are related to bodily functions. It is general, common knowledge, but most people do not respect it. Worldly people tend to respect and make a big deal of fancy things which stimulate their emotions. However, those things and the emotions they cause can both cause problems. Although things that are unusual and strange easily attract people's attention, they do not tend to serve your life as well as small, general matters of everyday life which you might ignore.

I have seen people who are doing immortal practice control their bodily heat. In the winter they do not need warm clothes to protect themselves from the cold weather. I have seen people who did not need to eat for many days or months because they had developed special breathing and meditative skills that would sustain them. I have even seen people sit in big sealed jars, with no air holes, survive for a long time. Also, there are some people who can dive under the water and stay there for a number of days. Some ancient people could do these kinds of thing. Many people marvel over such things, but to me it is believable that one could achieve such a high level of self-control. Realistically, this type of thing is not suitable for people because such feats or practices do not indicate that a person has achieved oneself spiritually. At most, they prove the potential of one's divine body. I would call them strange practices rather than immortal practice. They are only of value if they save one's life in a special circumstance or extend a person's longevity. I think such things are just as crazy as some of the practices done by religious people. However, in self-cultivation, or in cultivating your spiritual immortality, the knowledge and the skill of controlling the heat and the water inside the body are still very important.

What I hope you would conclude from this talk is to learn to regulate your body naturally rather than do unusual things or follow a cultural trend. A natural life is a balanced life, so be natural. A natural life has the potential for divine energy to enter. If we keep open to higher energy with sincerity, the divine energy comes to our body. Divine energy is good energy. Divine energy is natural energy. Natural energy is good energy.

Perhaps some people think individuals who live a natural life are less spiritual than religious people, but I say those who follow the natural way of life are superspiritual. People think that religious people who attend church and say prayers are spiritual. I say they are not, because they are not even themselves. God is not external; culture is external. External performance such as formalized ritual or prayer does not necessarily have internal meaning or show spiritual substance. Only when internal meaning or internal spirit expresses itself naturally can we say that something is truthful and right. God is not a big man out there who takes pity on people and gives them things. God is an energy that responds to energy of a similar nature. God is within you. Universal nature is connected with you.

Universal nature can transform all kinds of energy into beings, so we trust the universal nature as good life energy. It responds correctly and transforms where necessary according to its nature, if not too much damage has been already made. With or without your trust, the universal nature brings every thing and every energy into being. Everything was born with divine energy, but there are two conditions for divine energy. The first is that of the person who lives to reach the deep nature. The second is that of the person who can only live on the surface of nature. This second person experiences life, death and struggle without ever enjoying the deep level of life which can enable one to adjust to or enhance what life offers. You develop your self-awareness, then self-control, then try to be equal to the universe with its complete or wonderful functions. In general, people only live with part of nature, not the whole-ness of nature. To learn spiritual science is to know the secret universal functions in life.

All of you must know the reality of universal nature and the reality of your own energy or your own nature. Your nature and universal nature are one, not two. This is helpful to know. Do you find that you have troubles in your life instead of having universal nature in your life? When you live in the narrow environment of modern society, you forget that you are part of the big universal nature, because your small environment gives you false information and false impressions. You produce false knowledge; then, when you try to apply this to your life, many kinds of contorted, distorted troubles and disasters come.

This is why the first thing we do in this class is self-release; to give up the bad mental structure formed by your narrow social environment. After you achieve a kind of clear-mindedness, you can follow the teachings of our spiritually achieved ancestors who also had clear minds and left their instructions on how to return to a natural life and return to the subtle origin. Their minds were highly developed and their spirits were nurtured because they lived in cool places, not in hot or cold places. Their energy arrangement was balanced. Because they did not have to fight with extreme heat or cold, they had no obstacles and could easily offer a balanced teaching based on their personal experiences. To follow the teaching of the Integral Way is not to follow an outside teaching, but to follow the internal truth.

What was the method they used? What was the inner experience they had? They did not experience or use faith, they experienced and used self-development. If you follow the same way and have the same experiences, then you will have the same development as they did. Then you can achieve the same level of being they did, with form or without form.

Today we have this opportunity to discuss these important things. I have shown you a simple principle. I hope that all of you who are listening can understand, at least superficially. To reach the high level, you still need to penetrate, study and explore it for yourself.

Are there any questions?

Q: Would you repeat what you said about hot and cold again?

Master Ni: I will teach you a breathing exercise to help regulate your internal temperature. When you are too cold, make your mouth round and blow two or three times in short puffs. When you are too hot, open your mouth widely and say "Kau" for 7, 21 or 36 times etc., depending on the situation.

Q: In the big cities, when it is very hot, there is much killing and fighting going on. Is this inevitable?

Master Ni: Ordinarily it is natural for people living in cold countries to like to fight; in hot countries, people tend to be lazy. It is different now because of cultural developments and because people live so close to each other due to over-population. It is common knowledge in big cities that heat makes people violent and that in hot, dry deserts, like Iran and Iraq, people are known for their warlike tendencies.

We need to avoid being over-active in summer. Let us control our temperature all the time. Let us adjust the hot and cold of our personality.

Q: Did you say that sweating is a way that a person loses energy?

Master Ni: Yes, if you sweat too much.

Q: Then isn't sweating a good way to get rid of some bad energy?

Master Ni: When you sweat to the extent that you leave yourself without energy, you become open and vulnerable to invasions of the worst energies, like viruses. Some sweating is okay, but not too much; dry the body carefully, then protect it by wearing proper clothing. If you sweat too much, you will catch colds easily. Water, if retained in the body, can be a poison. Sweating and urination are two ways to naturally adjust the amount of water that is in your body. Urinating too much can cause you to be weak, too.

Q: If you have a full bladder during the night, is it not correct to go and urinate?

Master Ni: If your bladder is full, surely you must go to the bathroom to urinate. Have you noticed that if you have a full bladder, in your dreams you always go looking for a toilet? It is caused by your internal pressure. The key to water control is how much you drink, what you drink and when you drink it.

Q: What is the best way to sleep at night?

Master Ni: When you sleep, do not sleep in one position only. If you do not change your position, it is bad for your muscles and causes stagnation in your internal system too. Young people sleep soundly, so this change of position is automatically done by the body. They do not even know that they have moved.

How do you sleep? Do you lay down like a bump on a log? Do you collapse exhausted? If you do, you will not sleep well and it will be hard to get up early the next day. Before you go to sleep, do not stuff yourself with a big meal or snack. Relax completely before you go to sleep. If you spend some time relaxing before you sleep, you will also not have any bad dreams.

The basic principle of learning spiritual reality is to cultivate your energy. Before doing anything, prepare yourself, but help yourself by relaxing. Gather good energy by reconnecting with the subtle source.

If you have good energy, then no matter what you do, it will be good. If you cook, the meal will be special. If you are a carpenter, then on high energy days your work will go smoothly. You will have good energy if you are well rested and if you eat properly and do not overdo things.

Q: Last night two energies came and tried to enter my body, or were close to my body right around my stomach. I was sleeping on my side. It woke me up and they left. I don't know who or what they were, but I vaguely, energetically perceived them as two balls each about 4 inches in diameter.

Master Ni: There are some spiritual practices suitable to be done in bed before sleep. Some invocations are useful which are in the Yellow Book (please refer to the *Workbook for the Spiritual Development for All People.*)

Q: Can you make suggestions on how I can get myself up earlier in the morning?

Master Ni: First, practice the helpful way of sleeping that I mentioned above. Perhaps you formed bad sleeping habits a long time ago. If you believe in your divine body and begin to cultivate yourself, you can begin to nurture spiritual energy; then your personal spirits will wake you up early in the morning when the energy is strong.

Q: What direction should one sleep in? Where should the head be?

Master Ni: Always South or East, but never North. This is because of the magnetic field. Magnetic activity can disorder your mind, so if you sleep in the wrong direction, you violate your order. At worst, you become crazy.

Q: How should a person breathe? I am wondering if I should breathe differently in the mornings and in the afternoons.

Master Ni: It is helpful to breathe according to yin/yang, which means, breathing upward and moving the bodily energy upwardly from the feet from midnight to noon, and breathing downward and moving the bodily energy downward from the head down to the feet from noon to midnight.

Q: Master Ni, you have said in a different class that the energy can be stored in the tan tiens. How is this done? Does a person want to store the energy rather than let it go? Or sometimes store it, and other times let it go?

Master Ni: If you assign your mind to command the body, the result will be limited because the mind is busy with something else all the time. If you allow your body to function naturally, there is one secret to the storing of energy: do not let the mind move away from the body too much or for too long. With the cooperation of the mind and body, plus your spiritual energy, these three partners bring you a happy and long life and help you achieve oneness with the subtle origin. All other knowledge or practices can be considered auxiliary measures.

II

People have many kinds of experiences, but most of them are ordinary ones which are related to common daily life and are easily understood. Some are unusual but are nothing more than the performance of an active subconscious mind. When I was young, I came across this story several times in old storybooks. A man who lived a thousand years ago had a really uncommon and unusual spiritual experience. I would like to relate his experience to you.

During the Tang Dynasty (618-906 A.D.), life was good in China because many religions were accepted and people could still enjoy a natural life. This was also a period when cultural glory was shared by all neighboring countries near and far. One day, during the fall of the year 759, in a town some distance from the capital, the officials of a certain magistrate's court had finished their morning duties and were passing time outside the main official's residence while waiting for their lunch. Two officials were sitting out in the courtyard playing a game of Chinese chess. They both looked up when a servant came in through the gate to cross the courtyard.

"That's a nice-looking fish, Chahng Pi," one of the officials said to the servant, expressing his approval of the fish the man had bought for their lunch. It was a tempting fat carp of exceptional size, which Chahng Pi carried by a string threaded through its gills. Chahng Pi held up the fish so they could take a look at it. One of the officials said, "That fish is so large, although there are five of us here, we will each get three or four pounds of fish meat in our soup!"

The other official smiled in agreement, and Chahng Pi began to walk toward the kitchen. Then the second official said, "Did you notice something curious about that fish? I think that fish knows what is going to happen to it! Look, there are tears running down its eyes, and its mouth is moving. It looks like it is trying to say something. Maybe it is praying to us!" He called Chahng Pi to bring the fish back over so they could look at it again.

Then he called the other officials who were waiting inside the residence to come look at the praying fish. One officer was eating peaches and two others were playing a game of dice as they sat in the hall. They left what they were doing and came out to the courtyard. When they saw the fish, they all agreed that it was unusual for a fish to look sad and also move its mouth in such a way. Chahng Pi thought they were all talking nonsense and as soon as they finished examining the fish, he took it to the kitchen and gave it to the cook, who immediately prepared it for the noon meal.

The officers had just returned to their pastimes when suddenly they heard a loud sigh coming from one of the rooms on the first floor by the main hall. In this room was a high ranking official, lieutenant-magistrate Shueh Wei, who had been ill for almost a month. For the first seven days, he had suffered from a sudden fever, which was very high and caused him to have delirious tremors. After the seven-day fever, he laid unconscious on his bed, pale and exhausted. His doctors and nurses could do nothing for him, but because his heart was still warm and sometimes he would turn over, they did not give up. Thus, for twenty days, he laid there and was carefully monitored by his attendants. Suddenly this great, loud sigh had come from his mouth. All of his colleagues were startled and rushed into the room. Tears of joy streamed down their cheeks as they saw him sitting up in bed, looking a bit weak, but in good health and good spirits.

"How long have I laid here and not joined all of you?" asked Shueh Wei.

"Almost a month," was the reply.

His next question surprised them: "Did you eat fish soup for lunch today?"

"We haven't eaten yet," his colleagues answered, "but fish soup is on the menu for today. How did you know that?"

"Did Chahng Pi go to buy the fish today?"

Startled and surprised, his companions confirmed what he asked. Then, Shueh Wei turned to the servant and said, "You went to buy a fish from the fisherman Chah Kan. He had caught a large carp, but he hid it in the reeds and tried to sell you a small fish instead. Then you found the big carp in the reeds, so he had to sell it to you, and he charged you two pieces of money. When you came in the door, these two gentlemen were out in the courtyard playing Chinese chess, these two gentlemen were inside the main hall playing dice and that gentleman was eating peaches. All of them were interested in the fish and came to look at it. Then you delivered the carp to the cook, who was delighted with it and killed it immediately. All this is true, is it not?"

Everyone agreed that Shueh Wei had described exactly what had happened, but they were bewildered at how he could have known all of this.

"How do you know this?" they asked him. "You were in bed all this time."

"That carp," said Shueh Wei, "was me. Let me tell you my story."

"When I became ill, I had a scorching fever," he said. "I was so hot, I could hardly stand it. I was wishing for anything to obtain some relief from the heat. After several days of discomfort, I took my walking stick and went outside to take a walk in the coolness of the early morning."

His companions looked at him in disbelief, because he had been under 24 hour care. Shueh continued, "It did not seem like a dream, and yet I suppose it must have been. Anyway, I walked right through town and went toward the foothills of Hua mountain, where the weather is cooler. However, I did not feel much cooler up there, so I descended down toward the valley where the headwaters of the Blue River flows in many streams. The water was crystal clear and sparkled beautifully in the sunlight, and since it came down from the tallest peaks, it brought a cooling air with it. I walked along the side of the river, until eventually I came to a natural pool formed by the widening of the stream. There the water was still and deep, cool and tempting. I could not resist because I was still very hot, and after a short while, I took off my clothes and plunged in.

"I have not swum since I was a boy, and although I was good at it then, as I glided through the water, I felt like I was swimming quite awkwardly, but I realized that this swim was just what I had been longing for. I felt cool and refreshed by the waters. I began to regret that I was not a fish, so that I could swim with perfect ease. 'If only I could become a fish!' I said to myself.

"Immediately a trout which was swimming close by said to me, "Do you really want to be a fish? I know someone who can help you."

"The fish swam away; and before long, a strange large creature appeared. It had the head of a fish and the body of a man, and it rode toward me on the back of a giant crocodile. Several dozen fish swam to help escort it. This creature told me of a proclamation that had been recently given by the Lord of All Waters. The proclamation stated that any land creatures who entered the water must immediately return to their native terrain. There was only one exception to this rule, which was that those creatures who wished to live underwater and join the ranks of the fish could be transformed. "Thus," the creature said, "I can fulfill your desire and transform you into a golden carp. However," he warned, "You must be careful neither to cause damage by stirring up the waves and overturning boats, nor to risk your safety by swallowing bait. It is necessary to avoid those things, or else disgrace will be caused to the fish kingdom."

"I looked down and discovered that I had been given the form of a handsome golden carp. I swam swiftly and gracefully through the water with ease. I was so delighted. I played with the waves and dove into the depths. I explored everywhere. I met all kinds of fish and other creatures as I journeyed throughout the water network of rivers and lakes. Each night I had to return to that one pool since that was my assigned home.

"One day I suddenly began to feel very hungry, but I couldn't find anything to eat. I was looking around everywhere for food, but to no avail. Suddenly, I saw a delicious morsel floating in the water and looked up to see a boat overhead. Chah Kan, the fisherman, was sitting in the boat reading his newspaper as he fished. Although I clearly remembered that I must not take bait, I wandered over by it and began to look at it closely. It smelled delicious.

Then I said to myself, "I am a man, not a fish. I must not eat this bait, even though I am hungry, because I know that there is a hook in the middle of it." And so I swam away a little.

However, I was hungrier than ever. I began to reason with myself, 'I am not really a fish, I am a man. Not only am I a man, I am also a high official of the court, and Chah Kan will surely recognize me and take me home where I belong. We have purchased many fish from him."

"I convinced myself that Chah Kan would arrange for me to be taken back to the residence, so I swam up to the bait again and swallowed it, hook and all. Chah Kan, who is quite a skillful fisherman, pulled me up into his boat with ease. I called out to him, telling him who I was, but strangely, he did not seem to hear me. As soon as he caught me, he put me with some smaller fish and went back to the shore where he keeps his boat. After he docked, he threaded a cord through my gill - that is to say, my cheek - and tied the other end to a clump of reeds.

"Then Chahng Pi showed up, and said, 'The court officials would like a fish, and they want a big one.'

"I haven't caught any big ones," Chah Kan lied. "You can have several small ones. Here are some nice ones that are about three pounds or so."

"It has to be a big one - what use is a little one?" said Chahng Pi. He wandered about the place where the fish were set out, and suddenly he saw the line tying me to the reeds, and pulled me out of the water. "This one's better. Here's two pieces of silver." He paid for me and then started to walk back to the residence, dragging my tail a little on the ground.

"I am the lieutenant magistrate, Shueh Wei," I said to Chahng Pi. "I have changed myself into a carp for the time being so I could swim about more easily. Why don't you treat me with the proper respect? After all, I am your superior!"

"Chahng Pi didn't pay any attention at all. I began to shout, but he totally ignored me. He did bring me back to the residence. As we entered the courtyard, I saw two of you sitting there, playing Chinese chess. I called out to both of you as loud as I could, but neither one of you paid any attention. One of you turned to the other and said, "There'll be three or four pounds of fish meat for each of us from that tempting fish!" Then, the two of you left your dice game, and you left your peaches and all came out and looked at me. All of you had hungry looks on your faces. Chahng Pi told you how Chah Kan had kept me hidden in the reeds and tried to substitute some smaller fish, and you ordered that he be warned that he would be punished if he did that again.

"By this time I was desperate, fearing that I would be killed. I shouted to you, "I am Shueh Wei, your colleague. How could you kill me?" I wept and sobbed, but it was of no use. Chahng Pi took me to the kitchen and gave me to the cook, who laid me on the butcher block and picked up his knife. I was pleading with him to spare my life, but down came the knife and off came my head. I made one dash back into my own body - and here I am."

All the officials and the servants remembered how they had noticed the fish's mouth moving, yet none of them had heard a sound. Now they knew why there had been something so unusual about the fish.

None of them ate lunch that day, and whenever any of them were served fish soup for the rest of their lives, they always remembered that unusual event.

As for Shueh Wei himself, he was profoundly affected by his experience. He kept thinking that such an experience was meant to teach him that there was more to his existence than the easy, courtly life of a government official. He also had a strong belief that there was more to a person besides just being a body. Thus, he became very religious. I am not sure he learned from the right teacher; perhaps it was someone who was less developed.

Many people have experiences which they believe relate to the spiritual world. It seems that during the last 1,400 years since this story was written, no one has been able to understand it or solve the riddle of its meaning. Once I offered an analysis to a friend of my father. I said, this experience relates to body connection and life connection, not to the spiritual world. When the person was attacked by a high fever, the heat caused his subconscious mind to think of being cold. Cold or coolness is associated with water. Water is associated with swimming; swimming with fish, fish with bait, and bait with being caught and eaten.

By the time the fish was brought through the gate to the courtyard, Shueh Wei had already recovered from the fever but was still unconscious due to weakness. In his weakened state, his subconscious mind was aware of the general activity. He knew who was the one that usually gave suggestions for punishment and how the cook usually handled the fish. Because he associated himself with the fish, when he thought about how the fish would be killed, the picture horrified him, thus from the subconscious mind he slipped back to his conscious mind.

The only thing worthy of admiration and marvel is that even after 20 days of trauma, he was able to survive his physical illness. The second interesting thing is that his subconscious mind seemed to have special vision to know the details of the events around him without the witness of his physical eyes. The whole story was his perception in the last few short minutes before wholly regaining his consciousness. There are many similar phenomena related by people who have "near death" experiences, although they usually do not identify themselves with an animate object.

This seemed to be a reasonable explanation and an effective way to solve the riddle. My father's friend smiled in approval and encouraged me, saying, "To be a spiritual student, it is important not to be confused by partial or incomplete spiritual experiences. Some people only experience their own minds but take such an event for a spiritual experience. Most people do not know the difference between what is spiritual and what is mental."

I would like all of you to have the correct understanding about spiritual teaching. True spiritual growth does not mean that you become something other than what you are; it means you see what you are as clearly as you see things in the bright daytime. Then after you see what you are, you put yourself on the right track and work to improve your own spiritual quality in order to attain truthful spiritual achievement. That is called attainment.

Q: Master Ni, this explanation is really helpful, but it does not answer one question: If the man was actually not in the fish body, then why did the fish eyes cry and why did the fish mouth move?

Master Ni: Almost all live fish leave the water with an open mouth like praying. As for the tears, usually a fish's eyes weep blood because of the change of air pressure. I have seen carp after they were caught and brought to market in my home town.

My conclusion is that the true student of spiritual learning simplifies one's life and stays with the body rather than separating oneself into pieces and allowing the mind to wander about. There is nothing worse than to allow your soul out of your body. The study of internal alchemy teaches refinement of one's own soul with real life. That is the true path to spiritual achievement.

Tonight's class will soon be over. I have told you this story to emphasize the point that the way to achieve spiritual unity or spiritual integrity is to unite body and mind, mind and spirit, and spirit and body. The body is the foundation; the spirit is the energy. The three need to be suitably linked together at all times.

Q: Are near death experiences real?

Master Ni: I was asked to talk about some people's experience of momentary death and then coming back to the world. They see some light energy and swim in light energy, and then the light energy itself transforms into different levels of light. This cannot be truly recognized as an experience of death. Those people who come back from such an experience, mostly still have an active mind. The light they see is the experience of stimulation caused by light upon the pupil of the eye. Also, near-death experiences such as leaving the body and floating up to the ceiling and watching the doctors work on oneself, etc. are still related to the feeling of body.

At the time of real death, a person will pay attention to one's accumulated experiences of the lifetime. This is known because of mediumship that has been done to communicate with people who have passed away. The soul of the departed described the experience of death. A certain folk practice or process took forty-nine days to make the soul come back to visit people. At the beginning, when this practice was first performed, it was genuine and truthful.

After forty-nine days, the practitioner asks the family to put the dead people's clothes on or over a child. Then they invite the dead person's soul into one of the children to give the communication. However, doing this is not as reliable as turning on a faucet; sometimes it works and sometimes it does not. Also, there are some impostors who do not really have the power to do it at all, or other reasons.

Later, folk Taoism continued this practice. Typically, once a religion becomes promoted, the original genuineness is lost or the practice became nothing more than an occupational skill. Surely some elements of falseness become mixed in with it.

If you are serious about looking for spiritual reality, it is worth your time and attention to objectively gather some information about the soul after death. A soul approaching death lives on a different sphere of existence than a soul living an ordinary life. Because the soul of a dying person is in the yin sphere, when the dying person is around other people there is an energy conflict between the yin of death and the yang of the living. People had better stay away from a person who is dead or from contact with the soul after physical death unless it is absolutely necessary. People can receive a message from them after they die. Sometimes children can communicate or act as a medium for sending and receiving information.

After someone passes away, the soul of that person goes through a forty-nine day process called "delivering the soul from suffering to become a normal soul." The relatives of that soul can help by doing a certain practice. When I was in China, I experienced that the children of the family of the deceased or the neighbor children could sometimes see the person who passed away. Some people doubt whether children can see the soul of one who has crossed over, but this has been proven by children who came from a different village or who were too young to have a strong memory of what someone looked like.

Also, the one who passed over can sometimes communicate through "magic writing" which is usually done by a child writing in a plate of sand. The soul attaches itself to the child's hand and gives the message. Usually such a thing is not done with the purpose of teaching, and often it is impostors who just use their minds. However, if a question is asked, the soul can answer questions or tell something such as where to find the missing key, where are the important documents or money, who owed money to the deceased, or who the deceased owed money to, etc.

Some channels or mediums are real, but others just play on the psychology of the family of the departed. It can be true or not true, but there is no way to verify it; professional people need to be paid, because that is how they make a living. Children are not professional, nor are they making a living, so you can get more trustworthy information, after you filter through what they say. If you let them talk too much, their minds become wild and they start telling all kinds of fictitious stories. Religions are also the product of wild or fictitious stories, especially when a religion is based upon the channeling of a ghost. Ghosts can lie. They know that people's minds are afraid of death, so they talk wildly about god, about a different world. You cannot trust that.

There are several levels of energy. The soul of a deceased person responds to the call or summons of living person. Living people have both yin and yang energy. Those with strong energy are able to contact a soul if it has not sunk into the ground. If a soul is above the earth level, the energy of the soul is already much different from living people. If a soul is above the earth level, the soul is achieved spiritually and will not sink into the ground. An example of a soul which has sunk into the ground is a soul that stays in the tomb with its body. Staying with one's body is to keep one's left-over energy with the body. When the bones of a skeleton are disturbed, sometimes it causes a response on a different level. That means the death energy can be felt or the image of the death can be seen.

This is why if a person opens a tomb, the energy that is there can cause a person to become sick or something. Such an influence would not last long, but it is a bad influence. This is why I always say it is not a good idea to visit tombs or pyramids and make a disturbance. People should only go where there are people and sunshine, where you can see the sun, moon and the North Star. If you are alive and you cannot see the sun, moon and stars, then you are in a different world.

The truth is that death is the disintegration of a person's energy; this is the common experience of death, unless a person is achieved. Each part of the person's spiritual existence goes to a different level. The soul is not like a person who is still put together and has all kinds of functions; there is no more function.

Typically, the transition to a different sphere of living is called disintegration. Some souls can maintain themselves safely in one piece during this time and not disintegrate, but other souls suffer from all kinds of trouble. That trouble is the result of bad experiences caused by the person. By bad life experiences, I do not mean suffering from poverty or physical trouble; that is different. By bad life experience, I am describing a person who only sees profit or takes benefit from worldly life. This type of person schemes and does all kinds of evil. Such a person does not see the bad effect of one's actions until the time of transition. Especially during the first forty-nine days after death, a person is still associated with worldly life experience. For example, even if a person murders, wrongs, hurts, takes advantage of, slights or plays schemes on some people, he will not be bothered by his actions at the time. When a person is integrated with all kinds of energy, he feels safe and believes that he can do whatever he wishes. Once the person is disintegrated, the protection leaves. At that time the person is equal in strength with the person who was murdered, wronged or damaged. The revenge, suffering and payback all happen during those 49 days.

If the trouble is too bad, the revenge or retribution will last a long time, because there is no way to dissolve one's harmful behavior. Many people do not care about their actions; they do not know the force of natural retribution because they are still alive. They misunderstand retribution, thinking that it means that just as long as the policeman does not see them, they can do whatever they want. They have forgotten the subtle sphere. Do not darken your soul by dark behavior. Basically, the only insurance or power, the only way to enjoy respect or protection, is through righteousness. A righteous soul is respected by the spirits, and so they will not allow anything to happen to such a person at the time of death.

Once someone told me that whenever he travels, he always mentions to the hotel people or other servers that he is a doctor. By doing that, he found that he got better treatment from them. However, after death, in the other world, your social position is of no use, because the only thing that is real there is the quality of your energy. Whether you have a strong or weak soul can be seen by your energy. If you have committed many faults, you will suffer attack from different sources or relatives. If you are an upright person, even if you are poor, you will receive benefit at that time. When you live, even if you do not have a high position, if you have an upright soul, you will enjoy much more protection and power than a soul who has been in high position and enjoyed lots of material success from non-upright means.

During the last 2,500 years there have been many different records giving evidence of such things. China was a natural society, and spiritual evidence was profuse. Spiritual communication happened spontaneously to children or women, and the information that was gathered was natural and deep. What I am talking about is different from someone who makes a living out of such things or does them as a profession. I am talking about occasional spiritual phenomenon, something that might happen to somebody once in a lifetime.

In the ancient culture of Chinese society, the key words are faithful love to the parents, although perhaps the words used may not be accurate. Family life was the center of Chinese society before communism destroyed the natural society. A family centered life was a kind of heavy moral education, but it was also true relationship. The Chinese people were devoted to their parents and their children. No father or mother talked about their personal freedom or enjoyment. Their life goal was to raise their children to be decent people and to be happy. Unfortunately, the negative side of this was that there was too much concern and interference on the part of the parents. This kind of spiritual influence made the Chinese people care about the dead soul of their father, mother or relatives, so this is why that kind of practice existed. It made people crazy about finding out how their parents lived after death. Naturally, there was lots of cheating by religious people, who told them that their parents had come to communicate with them.

I would like to tell you a humorous story which will contrast with all this serious talk and give you an example of how people can so easily be misled. When I was in Taiwan, some one told me that their friend was following a group of religious people who did magic writing. The father who had died recently, had come and begun to communicate with the son. He said, "Son, I am not really happy about being over here. You know our lousy neighbor who was so arrogant? His father died a month before I did and has become mayor of the shadow world. I have become a small worker under him and am really unhappy about it." His son felt bad about his father being subject to the neighbor's old man who passed away, so the man gathered some money to pay the priests to do something. The next time the father communicated he said, "Son, I got a promotion. Now I have become one of the chiefs of the bureaucracy. I am so much happier, but I am still under him." So the son paid more money to get another promotion for his father.

This kind of thing happens to some people who believe that money is not as important as their parents' souls. They let religious people take advantage of them. Do you think that the religious people know the reality of the soul? They do not. At the beginning they learned from a teacher, but the teacher was an impostor who was cheating people. Thus, the impostors also have a tradition, and pass down their knowledge through generations.

In the world, the only way to guard yourself is to develop yourself instead of depending upon other people's information or service. If you learn spiritual cultivation, you can help your father's soul in reality, because you have a flesh relationship. How can a person truly help his parents' souls? Your thoughts can cause a response from your parent's souls, because now the spirits do not have the physical bodies which maintained them as independent entities. If your relatives sink too deeply, it is harder for you to help. Some time, your thought also creates a disturbance to the soul. Only good souls can support other souls. In general, to remain in peace seems the best policy. That gives no harm or benefit to the souls.

You may wonder if the living soul is also afraid of disturbance. Yes; people of spiritual sensitivity will experience internal restlessness but may not know the source or cause of the disturbance. A person with higher achievement will know the source. In general, the ancient spiritual way of living is very different from today. They like to have more privacy and do not like to relate to people too much. The practices suggested in the *Workbook for Spiritual Development* can at least provide spiritual protection to shield yourself from general disturbance or black magic.

The truth is that your spiritual power can absorb the spirit of your parents. If you so choose, your achievement can even encompass nine generations.

Each of us received physical life from our father and mother; if possible, you need to forgive them for the mistakes they made when you were young. They did not know better because they were not experts. No parent is an expert. You have to forgive them. Once you achieve your own soul, you can spiritually support the poor condition of your parents' souls. Sometimes it is hard to use the intellectual mind to communicate to each other, but on a spiritual level, instinctively they can be helped. This is truthful information.

For a person living in the world, it is better to take the part of one who suffers a little bit, rather than taking advantage of anyone else by scheming, through evil doing or wrong doing. Some religious people or priests do all kinds of inappropriate things because they have not attained the truth. It is not hard to learn to speak in public, it is hard to achieve the reality which exists beyond the seeable or durable level.

Eleventh Class

January 20, 1978

Good evening everyone. As I listened to you all share your experiences with each other, I noticed that some of you were proud of your progress and some were disappointed. Some of you try hard to have order in your lives and others just yield to whatever comes to you. Your experiences are similar to mine when I was a beginning student, so I can understand and relate to you all.

In learning spiritual reality, we do not emphasize the kind of music a person makes as much as the silence or stillness of one's mind before composing the music. By using the word "music," I am referring to your disposition, temperament, personality and your external and internal lives. In other words, it is how you express yourself. Your peaceful mind, or the origin of your music, is more important than the music itself. It does not matter whether your music is happy or sad, loud or soft; it all comes from silence.

Just as music comes from silence, the entirety of your psychological life comes from your peaceful mind. Any day that goes by without any mental disturbance can be considered a good day. It is not necessary to seek excitement or expect wondrous things to happen to you. If you need excitement or adventure to be happy, then you are in a pitiful state because all types of stimulation and fun carry side effects or trouble. It is not necessarily true that you are not making any progress if nothing exciting or adventurous is happening on the outside. In fact, sometimes there is more spiritual progress if your life is kind of boring.

Some of you feel that if you are not agitated, then your lives are empty! I would say, on the contrary, if your mind is pure and still, then that is great. Remember, if you lose the calmness of your pure mind, then you have lost your balance. Please do not misunderstand me, I am not talking about the stillness that a dead person experiences. You can be thinking and still have a calm mind. You can be in motion and still have a calm body. You can be creative and dynamic and still have a calm spirit. Just be sure that your thinking is not doing the opposite of what your real being is doing; then you will truly have a good day, whether anything exciting happens or not. When your body, mind and spirit are all engaged in the same activity, it is called congruency. This is keeping in harmony with spiritual law.

Most people fall into one of two categories. On the one hand, there are materialistic people who are too restless and need physical excitement all the time, and then there are the spiritually inclined who overdo their spiritual disciplines and try to deny themselves everything. Both of these extremes are abnormal.

Let me tell you this: when your mind is peaceful, your energy is beautifully arranged. If you expect more than this from your spiritual cultivation, then you are totally missing the point. Peacefulness, sweetness and mellowness are the real fruits of life. Do not be foolish and throw them away while looking for what you call a "spiritual experience," whatever that is! Your fanatic search for a spiritual experience is just more sickness.

Some of you mentioned feeling energy coming into you and manifesting through you in certain ways. This is a more practical subject than looking for bizarre spiritual experiences. The energy flowing through you is changing the foundation of your life. You know, if you eat too much or have too much sex, your energy manifestations will become unhealthy, so restrain yourself and do not overdo anything. Then your energy will be subtle and manifest itself in a beautiful, harmonious way.

Some of you showed good energy that did not demonstrate any psychological imbalance. For those of you who keep learning about energy and working on improving yourself, good things will happen to you in this class. However, I do not want to hear anyone boasting about all the shiens that come to you and ask you to go to Heaven with them.

You are all making progress and this experience is valuable to you. Just be sure to avoid any psychological or emotional exaggerations. Some of you are digging a big hole and burying yourself in it by not using it correctly. Then you complain about living in darkness! Exaggeration is not the learning of spiritual reality; that is not what this class is all about. When you do your cultivations regularly and seriously, then the need or desire for exaggeration will not arise, and the result will be healthy and beautiful. If you overdo your cultivation, I mean to use your spiritual cultivation to evade other important activities or obligations, even by one "fen" (a small unit of measure in China), then the results will not be so good.

Another thing I would like to mention is that most of you are too tense. You have allowed the pressure of the outside world to affect your nerves. When you are overly tense, you cannot react appropriately to any situation. Do not let external circumstances affect your mind so easily and cause you such tension. We Chinese have a saying: "Shen mang, shin shi," which means, "Keep your body active and your mind relaxed." It is helpful to keep the body active because this keeps the energy from becoming stagnant, but always keep the mind unattached and free. This may seem difficult when you have to be on the job all day, but if you want to achieve that state of calmness within activity, and you try to find a way to do it, it can be done.

Your American minds are more busy than your bodies. You have a lot of leisure time but your minds are never at rest. You ruin your minds by overworking them, just as I ruined my eyes when I was young. I was given the assignment to read 20,000 books by the time I was 16. Because of that, my eyes are near-sighted now. It is good to read, but one needs to practice moderation in everything.

Anyhow, it takes a lot of energy to overwork and abuse your mind like the modern intellectuals do. You could save all that energy and use it to strengthen the substance of your life. You are always talking about gathering and refining energy, etc., but the first thing you can do for yourself is to stop wasting the energy you already have. You have no idea how much energy you waste. For example, there is a constant dialogue going on in your minds all day and all night. You also exaggerate your emotions most of the time. Do you know how much energy is needed to keep your muscles tense all the time? An enormous amount!

Almost everybody does these things constantly without being aware of it.

I hope you take a long, scientific look at your energy wastage and stop all your unnecessary activities. The next time you catch yourself thinking about unnecessary things or going out every night to this place or that, or putting food into your mouth that you do not need, exercise a little restraint. These kinds of habits exhaust your energy and create imbalance in your life.

You will find that if you stop such wasteful activities, your mind will become clear. When your mind is crystal clear, then you will no longer be deceived by external appearances and you will know the deep nature of everything that comes to you. You will know whether to truly embrace something or reject it. This is a practical ability to have.

To recognize the real nature of things or people is only one kind of energy, and to be able to effectively deal with them is another kind of energy. Many of you already know when something is not beneficial to your lives but you still go ahead and get involved with it, because your energy to resist harmful things is not strong enough. There is nothing as important in life as having strong energy or energy which is both high and strong. From now on, make the focus of your lives the saving, gathering and refining of your energy. If you do this, your lives will be smooth and worry-free.

Are there any questions?

Q: You mentioned that behavior which is motivated by emotional need is a waste of energy. Is there no such thing as positive emotional need?

Master Ni: Not really, except perhaps for eagerness in learning. Generally speaking, we are much more emotional when we are younger than when we are adults. My son, for instance, is about 13 years old. He recently asked me to buy him a radio. He expected me to immediately stop everything I was doing to go get one for him. This is an unreasonable emotion caused by ignorance. As adults, you never demand that of anyone because your awareness has grown.   Your understanding and powers of reason are greater.

I hope you can see that all emotional needs and demands are based upon ignorance of a total situation. I am not talking about needs that arise, for example, when you are in danger. If that causes you to be emotional, perhaps your emotion is the force that will help take you away from such a situation. However, a spiritually achieved one prefers not to get in a situation of danger to begin with, thus I reiterate the point that emotional needs are based on ignorance.

There is another kind of emotion that can come to a person who is spiritually sensitive. It is a result of internal or external energy changes, particularly sudden ones. Sometimes when one is open spiritually, he or she will be vulnerable to the energies of all things and people. If this is the case, you must not only protect yourself but must also learn how to deal with the emotions that arise.

What happens to most people is that their minds have expectations that are not fulfilled as envisioned, so unreasonable emotions arise. Why do you think I have you do quiet sitting everyday? It is so you will overcome your ignorance and expand your awareness. If your energy is scattered and floating, you are easily influenced by external pressures and you cannot effectively deal with people and circumstances when you are busy. If you allow yourself some quiet time every day, you will be able to concentrate your energy rather than scatter it. You will be able to see a total situation much more clearly than when you are caught up in the middle of it. Also, you will see yourself more clearly and will be better able to handle things.

Many times, the real nature of an event is quite different than what it appears to be. When you are scattered and busy, you often deal only with the outer manifestations of a situation and never even know its real nature. The real nature of a situation is its energy manifestation. After you change your floating energy to be more calm, you will intuitively respond to the deep nature of the situation.

Two people may have the same potential for intelligence but one of them does better than the other. Can you tell me why one always seems more intelligent than the other? It is because one keeps his personal energy calm and the other one does not. One person is clear-minded and the other is not. You can make more reasonable decisions when you are calm than when you are scattered and disturbed.

When the monkey mind spends so much time making emotional circus shows, your perceptions and understanding are much shallower and your responses are more immature. You must learn the correct way to upgrade or improve the way you respond to things. It is not easy, and it takes time. For instance, I cannot just recommend a book for my young son to read which will suddenly make him mature. He must develop his subtle mind so that it will tell him when to make demands of people and when not to. This, of course, does not only apply to my son. Some of you, even though you have adult bodies, have minds like children. The outside world is crucial and you still have not learned how to deal with it.

Some of you are like trees that have serious defects in your roots which have caused poor growth. However, the past is the past, and now you have come to me because you are looking for some guidance so that you can correct your own defects. People say that the herb tea I prescribe to cure their physical illnesses tastes bitter. Sometimes my teachings are like my herbs, not particularly tasty but very useful.

Q: Are you saying that when a person develops spiritually, he or she will spontaneously do the right thing at the right time?

Master Ni: Certainly. Undeveloped people say: "I want to do this or that," and then they follow their desires without knowing whether what they want is beneficial for them or not. As your intuition develops, you will be able to see the total picture and know for sure if your actions are beneficial to yourself and harmonious with the people in your life.

Now, my good students, I would like to return to the chart I introduced to you on a different occasion. It is the chart of the great universal energy manifestation.

Global/Annual/Monthly/Diurnal Chart

1 Universal Energy Rotation Equals: 129,600 Time Units
1/12 Rotation Equals: 10,800 Time Units
1/24 Rotation equals: 5,400 Time Units

The universe is energy, and it is always in a state of transformation. We have drawn up this chart to show you the twelve major stages.

As you can see, the universe takes 129,600 time units (yung nyan) to complete one rotation. This is one year. Each of the 12 sections or twelve months is 10,800 time units and then half of that leaves 5,400 time units for the 24 dimensions (two week period). Thus, this chart represents the yearly, monthly and also the daily cycles.

As you all know, this is the Year of the Horse. This particular horse year is at the top of our chart under the heading Wu. This Wu year is a yang fire year and is coupled with another yang fire symbol from the 10 Heavenly stems.

As I mentioned last week, the universe and the year and month and day all have their origin in the Tzu (beaver) section. The bottom quadrant is like the dark time when pregnancy is just beginning; nothing is born yet, but there are the stirrings of life. The energy has the reproductive qualities of the rat and the nourishing quality of a cow, etc.

The quadrant on the left is the time of birth and growth. During this time, yin and yang separate and the earth condenses. In the earthly sense, this stage gave birth to trees, animals and people.

The upper quadrant, beginning with the Shr (snake) section, is the time when the energy flourishes and grows to maturity. The ancient Chinese believe that some snakes can cause fire. I believe the image of the fire snake came from the observation of lightning striking trees in the forest. Lightning looks like a snake, and that may be the connection that the ancient people made in their minds.

Anyway, after the energy reaches the Wu (horse) stage, it begins to devolve. Up to this point, the energy has been evolving. It is impossible for evolution to exist separately from devolution.

Starting with the shen (monkey) section, the right quadrant is the time of decomposition. The time of the monkey is a time of changes and ignorant destruction. Sometimes humanity seems like it is rapidly approaching the time of destruction. After the monkey stage, the energy becomes like a brooding hen and then like a lazy dog.

Finally in the lower quadrant, the energy goes into hibernation beginning with the qualities of a pig, which are inactive, desirous and sleepy. This is followed by the faint stirrings of life in the Tzu section.

This great universal cycle goes on eternally. This is the energy cycle of all material things. Everything must change; nothing remains the same. If you spiritualize yourself, you do not need to be a slave to this cycle. Physically you are still influenced by it but spiritually you are not.

If you think you are still partially under the influence of this cycle, you must not do anything abnormal or go against the natural transformation. For instance, if you sleep all day and work all night, you will hurt your energy.

Q: From the chart, it seems like everyone should go to bed at 9 p.m. Who can do that?

Master Ni: That is the ideal time, but it is not practical for all people. I suggest that my serious students are in bed before 10 p.m., but no later than 11 p.m. Never be up at midnight. To a student of spirituality, the old saying, "Early to bed and early to rise" is useful. Instead of staying up late organizing oneself for the next day, some people find it helpful to get up early to do the same.

Some of this depends on what time of day a person was born. People born in early morning usually have better yang (working energy) during the day and yin (thinking energy) at night. People born at night usually have better thinking energy in the day and more physical energy at night.

Q: Why does the Chinese New Year start at the beginning of the wood section (the left quadrant) instead of at the time when the yang energy begins to grow at Tzu?

Master Ni: Energywise, for the purpose of self-cultivation, the new cycle begins at the Winter Solstice. The New Year cycle was adopted by the Great Yu over four thousand years ago when agriculture became the dominant force in human life. It is at the time of the New Year that the solar cycle begins to generate vegetation. The energy during this time is represented by the image of wood, or vegetation.

Q: Could you please explain the movement of energy through the organs as indicated in this chart? Or does the energy move only through the meridian related to the organ and not through the organ itself? Does having the gall bladder in the bottom quadrant mean that it is a yin organ and having the heart in the top quadrant mean that it is a yang organ?

Master Ni: A diagram or a table will help you; here it is.

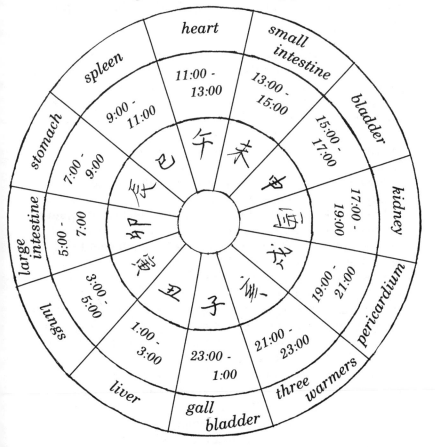

Q: All the great cycles don't come back to the same place, do they? Don't they spiral upward?

Master Ni: It is as you described, yet big patterns such as those of whole civilizations reach their peak and then decline. The following civilizations reach the same or higher peaks. New civilizations are not exactly the same as the old.

What is certain is that we need to achieve or develop our lives consistently.

Q: I work with 5-year olds all day long. Is this a good year for them?

Master Ni: Well, let's look at the chart. Since this is the year of the horse, then they must have been born in the year of the cow. The cow's energy is Earth and the horse's energy is Fire. According to the five element correspondences, Fire is the mother of Earth, so this must be a good year for them. Unless, of course, their monthly, daily or hourly energies conflict with their yearly energy. This is usually the case. Typically, the monthly, daily or hourly energies are experienced more strongly in a human individual, and the yearly energies are less strong.

Very seldom is anyone's energy completely harmonious. Each child's complete energy pattern could be looked at individually to see how they will react in each year but that is usually not as important as just responding to them appropriately in daily life. Generally, the signs are favorable for people born in the year of the oxen.

People's cycles, as well as the natural cycles, are so subtle that they can only be observed by the subtlety of the mind. External formalities create examples and illustrations of this reality. This is important understanding. Anyone who identifies with their physical body and who thinks they live in a material world cannot escape the influences of the cyclic nature of the earth. Jesus died on the cross because his personal energy was in conflict with the five element influences in that year, month and day. In other words, he was experiencing a low cycle and should have been more careful! During a low cycle, it is better to stay quiet and keep a low profile.

Q: Are you saying that if he had knowledge of this energy system he would have altered his life?

Master Ni: Yes. Some years and days are good to expand and express yourself and some years are unfavorable. During those unfavorable years, just keep to yourself and wait for a better year. Much more important than learning how to accommodate ourselves to different energies is the development of the supernatural side of our nature. If we do that, then we do not have to worry about the gross physical energy and drama of bodily life. If you succeed in transcending the material plane, safely speaking, whatever happens to you externally is of less concern.

A person who is happily married and raises a lot of children and then retires in old age may feel fortunate, but another may think that kind of life is boring and hard. So you see, what happens to you on the physical plane is not nearly as important as how you regard it. However your life drama is playing itself out, you can still cultivate yourself to achieve spiritually.

Q: What do you see for us in this year of the Horse?

Master Ni: It is my understanding that two years from now, the Year of the Monkey will be a time of great change. Thus, during the Year of the Goat, one needs to practice being less stubborn. In the Year of the Monkey, one needs to practice being less restless. Intense cultivation and preparation for that year is to know the energy and remind oneself of the tendency of the natural cycle through different energy expression. The basic energy of this year is good, but I do not want you to become lazy. So prepare yourselves for the coming changes and remember to put the emphasis on developing your spirit so that you will no longer be a slave to the forces of the physical cycles. See the chart. This is the real message I want to tell you today.

12-YEAR CYCLE ENERGY VIBRATION	SYMBOL	WESTERN EQUIVALENT BY SYMBOL OR MEANING	YANG OR YIN	NATURE OF THE ENERGY	ADJUSTMENT OF THE ENERGY
Tze	beaver or rat	*Aquarius*	YANG	active	*less active*
Chiu	cow, oxen or buffalo	*Capricorn*	YIN	submissive; toiling	*guide the energy in the right direction*
Ein	tiger	*Sagittarius*	YANG	rising	*less aggressive; guard against being trapped*
Mao	hare or rabbit	*Scorpio*	YIN	submissive	*make good use of energy*
Chen	dragon	*Libra*	YANG	impulsive	*harmonizing with external circumstance*
Sze	snake or serpent	*Virgo*	YIN	hiding	*make correct use of energy*
Wu	horse	*Leo*	YANG	dashing	*guard against wrong direction of energy use*
Wei	goat, sheep or antelope	*Cancer*	YIN	resistent	*less stubborn*
Shen	monkey	*Gemini*	YANG	restless	*less restless*
Yu	hen, bird, rooster or phoenix	*Taurus*	YIN	submissive	*hold onto principles*
Shu	dog, sled dog or hound	*Aries*	YANG	alert	*be defensive*
Hai	hog or hippo	*Pisces*	YIN	reposeful	*do not be greedy*

The solar monthly cyclic order is read from the bottom upward.

Note: How to use this chart.[1] Find your sun sign (e.g. in the Western system, Aries) and find your sign of the 12-year cycle (e.g., were you born in the year of the Horse?) These describe two important factors that determine your natural tendency and the two most important adjustments you need to make. Then, look for the year and the month of the present time. That will give you guidance for how to discipline yourself in order to harmonize yourself with the current external energies.

Q: Can a person change one's personal energy configuration while cultivating oneself to be a supernatural being and thus change one's physical destiny, too? For example, a person might wish to escape having a difficult old age. It seems more practical to be able to use that time to be of service to others or to cultivate rather than having scattered energy or other difficulties.

Master Ni: Yes, at least relatively, your achievement will reduce the difficulty. It depends upon how well you achieve yourself.

Q: If we are born in the year of the Monkey, does that mean we will have the disposition of a monkey?

Master Ni: Yes, especially if you are born in the 7th month on a metal day at 4 p.m. However, if the month, day and hour are different from that kind of energy, then the yearly effect will be much less.

---

[1]This chart was given by Master Ni when this book was edited and prepared for publication in August 1991. This chart corrects and replaces the chart entitled "Similarities of Yearly Cyclic Phases with Western Terms" in the *Book of Changes and the Unchanging Truth*. It is Figure 67 in the First Edition and Figure 87 in the Second Edition. It will be corrected according to this chart in future printings of the book.

Q: Do I understand correctly that every 12 years there is a Horse year, but not all Horse years are the same? It depends upon which of the ten Heavenly influences it is coupled with, right?

Master Ni: Right. This year is Mu Wu. It is a year of yang energy with strong fire. A strong fire year can either help or hurt you depending upon your five element composition.

Everything in the universe is composed of these five phases of energy transformation. We are lucky there are not more of them or life would be intolerably complicated! With only five, they act together like the five harmonious Chinese tones to create a kind of beautiful music of their own.

One day someone told one of the students that we should use Indian music in our self-release class because he thinks their music is more spiritual. However, their music only has three tones, so how could it be complete? Your music, like your lives, must be complete and well rounded. I never told you to give up sex or leave your families and jobs to cultivate yourselves in the mountains. You must be well balanced, not like the Hindus and Buddhists who leave everything to hide in the mountains. Surely there are circumstances of life for people to do that.

Here, I am not seriously talking about music. The division of tones, in popular music, are eight. I am talking about using five natural sounds to cause the correspondence of the five main organs inside of the body.

Buddhism, which was the officially adopted religion of China, blended with Chinese culture, thus serving new generations by expressing the richness of cultural life with two other elements: Confucianism and Taoism. None of these three ever really replaced the others as the central influence in the Chinese life. Why? Because the focus of each is different. The Buddhist culture emphasizes only partial development of life. It serves the emotions. Confucianism and folk Taoism are also partial and have a different focus. Confucianism serves the orderliness of the family and society. Folk Taoism in its essence serves physical health, while the Integral Way as I received it is to serve the entirety of life. It developed earlier than any of the religions or ideologies. It is the broad spiritual teaching, while the three main religions in China elucidate only one part of spiritual reality. However, spiritual reality cannot be partially elucidated because the truth of life is one with three spheres: body, mind and spirit.

Just as the Chinese say that technology and a materialistic way of life are incomplete, we also say it is wrong to overemphasize the spiritual aspect by denying the physical aspect of life. Unfortunately, India and Tibet are so poor and the people have such hard lives that all that is left for them is the spiritual aspect. However, it is not a balanced life. Both aspects of life, spiritual and material, must be positively developed in order to have a balanced life and spiritual achievement.

Even the Buddha made the mistake of being too ascetic or denying the physical side early in his life. I would not call it a mistake, because he learned something from it and changed his way. As you may know, he gave up his enthronement and ran away to the "Big Snow Mountains" (Himalayas) to cultivate himself. Actually he had strong competition from his uncle for the throne, so instead of fighting his uncle, he decided to become a "sage king" instead of an ordinary king. Thus, he gave up the throne.

His background is interesting. Sakyamuni was a prince who had the best education possible at that time. When he gave up his throne he went to the mountains to educate, cultivate and prove to himself that the methods for achieving immortality that he had learned were correct. He was taught that ego and the physical body were no good, and that the more you were able to deny and punish them, the more spiritual you could be. It took him many years to realize that those ideas were not right.

Sakyamuni was a strict ascetic for a long time until one night, while sitting under a tree in the full moon, he was awakened. The same moon and stars were there for everyone but for him they were special that night. He suddenly realized that to attain self-delivery, the life of self-punishment was unnecessary. It was there that he first formulated his "middle path."

Because of his enlightenment, the next day he did what seemed strange to the other ascetics. He got up from his tree and went looking for something to eat. His famous ten disciples were with him then, and they were amazed at what he was doing. You see, a Hindu yogi does not take food first thing in the morning. Sakyamuni not only had some milk and cheese that the shepherds gave him, but he also decided to sleep with one of the shepherdesses. All his disciples were there to witness this shameful act. After he was done shocking everyone, he then began teaching his new doctrine of the pathway of moderation. He taught that the extremes of both materialism and asceticism were not right or natural. So you see, even Buddha did not believe in denying physical life after he learned that lesson through his experience of self-denial.

Many Christian sects deny the fleshly life also. It is a helpful discipline for a while, but ultimately, it is not the way to a healthy life. In the Vatican, there is a record of a pope raping one hundred nuns. This is true. The Catholics do not allow their priests or high officials to ever have sex, so that kind of thing happens. They must learn to regulate that aspect of life instead of trying to stop it completely.

In Chinese literature, we have a drama written by the famous writer Shr Wen Tsang. He wrote about a famous Buddhist master who was influential with the emperor. Because the master was knowledgeable in spiritual matters and was a strict ascetic, he was respected by everyone in the country. However, he flaunted his virtue in front of the emperor a little too much, so one night the emperor decided to make him look bad. The emperor was a vicious and practical man. So he decided to bribe a beautiful prostitute to go to the master's cave when it was raining and to use the rain as an excuse to get into the cave and try to seduce him.

Well, the woman, Lotus Leaves, did her job well. She used her charms to get into the cave and, because the master was basically a kind and trustful person, he did not suspect anything. She then complained about how wet and cold her clothes were and asked him if he had any dry ones for her, etc. The poor master had no experience in such matters so he naively did everything she requested. By now,

Lotus Leaves was getting aggressive because the master still did not do anything. She rolled around on the floor of the cave and complained about a pain in her stomach. The master said he was not a doctor and could do nothing for her. She said that the only way to ease her old problem was for a man to rub his navel against hers. He said that he was a Buddhist master and could not. She argued that if he was a true master he must have compassion for human suffering. This was good logic, so he tried it with her.

The next morning she was gone and he was again sitting in a quiet meditation when a messenger of the king arrived with a letter. In the envelope was a short poem with her dirty underpants and when the master saw all this he immediately hanged himself in the cave.

All of this was done in the name of spirituality! I always teach my students that if a king tries to trick you in this manner, you tell the king to send his daughters and mother next time! Anytime you overly develop one side of your nature, you can be tricked and cheated on the other side. You must be mature and develop all aspects of your being.

Sometimes I ask some of you to keep your chastity, but there is no such law about that in this tradition.

Q: Then why do you tell us that?

Master Ni: Because some of you have gone too far the other way. You have no discrimination. Another reason is because if you sleep with too many partners, you lose your sincerity. The same thing happens if you practice twenty different spiritual methods. You cannot be truly involved in that many disciplines, so the result is that you benefit from none. Can you be seriously interested in fifty different women? No. The subtle universal energy responds to this lack of sincerity and the result is that you find that other people will not take you seriously. This is the real tragedy.

Some people have sex with a heart of pure love and the energy response to those people is much different from the ones who do it out of psychological need. So even if you sleep with someone, it is better to remain chaste. Even though you give birth to babies, you can still be a virgin. My mother was a virgin because she remained pure in spirit. If you do not purify your heart, mind and body, you will never achieve the birth of a spiritual baby, nor will you ever be highly achieved in a broad spiritual sense. So never compromise your chaste virtue for any reason.

Today, what I wanted to share with you was the universal energy chart so you could see how the energy transforms itself. Please remember that this is only a chart of the physical level. If you develop yourself spiritually, then you can transcend all that stuff and become an immortal.

Also remember to develop yourself fully as a well-rounded human being. Do not neglect any aspect of your lives or you will not be well balanced. I am not telling you to rush out and do many things at once, because people can basically learn things only a little at a time. Keep to a normal, regular, harmonious way. If you do this, you too can join me in drinking the pure water from Heaven.

Twelfth Class

January 27, 1978

Many spiritual people say there is a Heavenly place in the universe where only good energy exists. This is true, but what most of them do not know is that there are also places in our bodies that have the same kind of energy Heaven has. You can easily access this wonderful energy if you can learn how to handle your body and your energy. If your energy is gross or coarse, it will only travel around such areas as old wounds, troubles and emotions without ever being able to pass through them. After you refine and sublimate your energy, it can then flow into those spots where Heaven is located in your body and you will have an experience of enlightenment.

This kind of experience is possible for anyone. It can happen for you if you continue to eliminate your post-natal ego. However, if you always let your ego control you, you will never have the opportunity to refine your energy and make the connection with Heavenly energy. Your ego is that sense of yourself as an individual self that exists separately from the influences of the universe.

For some of you, the possibility of having that kind of experience of Heavenly energy is something that will take longer. What can you do to help yourself? First, do not worry about it, because such things take time. I do not want to tell you what to expect because that might encourage you to overlook some other experience that might be valuable to you. Any specific advice I might give you might make you anxious and encourage you to try to hurry things along. Sometimes people become foolish if they feel inadequate or if they feel that they need success. It is like the story I told you about the farmer who became anxious when he saw how quickly and beautifully his neighbor's vegetables were growing. He became apprehensive because he thought that his were not doing as well, so he decided to pull on his vegetables so they would grow faster! You can imagine the outcome of his action: they all died.

I do not want anything like that to happen to you. You cannot expect to accomplish in one night what could possibly take ten years to accomplish. I only mention the destination so you will know that the freeing of your soul is possible through energy refinement. You must refine your impure energy to become subtle. By using the word "impure," I do not mean anything in a moral sense. You are all more or less moral people. It is just that through years of bad habits, you have become a little too self-centered. This is a common spiritual defect and although we must overcome it, I do not want to emphasize that tonight. Let us talk about energy refinement.

Now, you have begun the refinement of your energy and the spiritualization of your being. When it is complete, you will have made a spiritual connection with the energy of the Mysterious Mother. The reason you have not been able to do it until now is that you have not put into practice the first principle of learning spirituality, which is to simplify your life. This means to simplify your mind as well as your activities. The complete spiritualization of your life can only come about after you do this.

Why does a student of spiritual reality need to simplify one's life? There is a practical reason. If you are spending all your energy on unimportant or needless things, then you will not have any energy left to refine. Most of the things people consider important do not support their lives at all, but actually take away their life force, their energy.

Tonight, as I observe you, I can see that you are all making some progress, but many of you still cannot control your energy well. Your uncontrolled energy is like a yo-yo. It is constantly going up and down and up and down. There is no smoothness or balance. The goal is to be calm and steady in life, not to alternate between having outbursts and becoming withdrawn. You might be wondering how you can do this. It is simple: first, become aware of what your energy is doing. Can you even tell when you are having an outburst? Many cannot. Can you tell when you are withdrawing? Most people do it without thinking about it. The second thing to do is to learn to control your energy with your mind. Controlling it with your mind means to think about what else you can do that is more calming instead of having an emotional outburst. In other words, you find a substitute for your anger or emotion. Simplifying your lives can help greatly in this undertaking. One way to do this is to examine your desires and motives to see if they are really necessary or not - if not, then do not indulge in them. The more desires you pursue, the more complicated and painful your lives become.

Keeping your lives simple means to keep them straight. Your energy should go directly to your spiritual center. By this I mean, remain spiritually centered. Your energy should not take any detours but stay directly on target all the time. In a way, spiritual cultivation is just like the sport of archery. If you put too much pressure on the bow, the arrow goes past the target. If you use too little pressure, the arrow falls short.

In your personal cultivation, the reason you always miss the target is because of egotistical ways of thinking and behaving. This means, your focus is upon material benefit. Temptations and hesitations and desires make your way crooked and filled with detours. Many of your desires just dissipate your energy. Your mad pursuit of power gets you into all kinds of trouble. If you only knew that your spiritual center, while being gentle and subtle, is at the same time the most powerful force of all, you would not bother pursuing petty desires.

One of the women students told me that she would like to have a baby. I wonder if she has ever really considered why she wants one. Some women have a reason which is no more profound than wanting another doll to play with. Some women are conditioned as a child to play with dolls, and even though they are in their thirties or older, they are still programmed with that desire. They do not understand that having a child is a big responsibility. I can assure you, however, that having children is not at all like playing with dolls. Children are an enormous detour from the straightness of your spirit, so you need to seriously ask yourselves why you think you want one. I only use this example to illustrate how great an impact your unconscious urges can have on your lives. It is helpful to question and examine the real reasons behind why we want to have things or do things. It is all right to have children for the right reason and if the right support will be constantly available.

You might be wondering, "If I do not listen to the desires of my ego, then what or who do I listen to? Isn't it important to protect myself, take care of myself, accumulate enough money for financial security?" The answer to this is to listen to the deeper part of your being, which is sometimes called the conscience. It does not only have a voice when you do wrong, it talks to you constantly about all things if you choose to listen. It will guide you correctly in your spiritual growth. In other words, you take care of yourself, protect yourself and become frugal, but you do so in a correct way, not in an incorrect way.

All the so-called troubles, accidents, failings and misadventures of your lives are just different manifestations or detours of your energy that did not go straight toward your spiritual target, which is life itself. If you live simply, you can live a whole and complete life. By living simply, I do not mean you must live in a cave and do nothing. I do mean fewer material luxuries, but I also I mean that your minds must be clear and unattached in all circumstances. When your mind is clear, then your energy will go straight to the target.

At this stage of your lives - most of you are in your thirties - many of you just wander around the edge of life and do not really go directly to the heart of life. Wandering only makes you weak. Certainly, some people need to go through a stage where they wander about to find out what is available in the world, but if a person does not eventually settle down somewhere, in a steady job or profession, it will be difficult to accomplish any spiritual growth. Excessive wandering may be only staying on the surface of life.

For example, some of you have looked into our different classes but you only study the Integral Way in order to teach it to earn money or to impress your friends. You do not really take the teachings into the center of your being and make them part of yourselves. You know, my verbal teachings are only for beginners; the real, deep teaching is non-verbal, so do not just play around the perimeter of my teaching by only studying spirituality with your minds. Try to absorb the deep, silent teachings into your being, then you will be truly benefitted.

Please try not to be dogmatic about my teachings. This means, do not take them word for word. It is bad enough that you have already been molded into a life shape that someone else designed for you; do not add to your own misery by further enslaving yourselves with rigid doctrines. Any kind of mold or form or pattern you create for yourself is a pitfall. Be careful every time you say "I don't want this and I don't want that," or whenever you strongly express a personal preference. Usually, you are only setting a trap to catch yourself, because there is no permanency anywhere. When you try to hold onto something, or when you always try to keep something away from you, you are asking for trouble.

People form their personalities at a young age by imitating their parents and friends. For example, when my two boys first arrived in America, they saw everyone on skateboards, so they immediately had to learn how to use a skateboard. At that age - they were about 12 at the time - a child is not mature enough to know whether he or she is imitating a good thing or not. Of course, all children live with and learn from their parents and accept what they learn at home because they do not know anything else. If the parent's habits are not all good, the child will not learn that until later. Also, when the child faces the outside world, he or she will come across many different things and influences, good and bad.

Because we are all children who have grown up, we have the most beneficial opportunity to evaluate the habits we have picked up. We can use our new learning to see whether what we are doing is helpful to our lives or harmful. Now it is your job to undo all the rigid patterns you have created for yourself. This may sound like an impossible task but this is one of the standards of discipline in my tradition. It can be done; many people have done it.

I was trained in spiritual truth by the traditional methods. My training was severe and the standards of our tradition are very high, yet it is the most valuable thing I have encountered in my life on earth. Such standards make it difficult for some people to remain as students of my tradition. After all of you have worked on yourselves some more, you may qualify. What typically keeps people from being a true student is being too self-centered. This makes a person stumble on the pathway. However, please understand that it is not I who determine whether you "qualify" or not. My job is to give you the information with which you can achieve yourselves, not to judge you. How far you progress depends solely upon your own relationship with the subtle law and the divine energy of the universe.

Do you know what? In past centuries, a kind master would scold you, beat you or kick you every time you made a mistake. In modern times, he would scold you or insult your dignity by calmly telling you your error. He helps you see what you are doing wrong; but some impatient masters who are not so kind will just tell you to forget it and go away. They will not bother to teach you or to show you how you can improve yourself. Or they may just let you continue to superficially touch the lesser teachings of the Integral Way but never get to the heart of it. It is not the master who prevents you from going further, however, it is you who limit yourself. Even when a person has access to the deepest teachings, unless the basic teachings have been understood and learned, the higher teachings are useless. It is kind of like handing a calculus book to a third grader who still has not learned simple multiplication. This is why I encourage you all to work on step A so that you can go to step B.

Typically, it takes a certain amount of life experience and maturity to learn the deeper teachings. All of you are young. You have been around for years now and you still feel isolated living in this world. You all have looked sincerely for, and have invested a lot of time and money in searching for what your spirit needs. However, the more you search, the farther you wander from the spiritual center.

Now I would like to share a verse with you that may help you understand how to learn spirit.

Those of you who are wondering
    why you have not made much progress yet,
    it is because you do not have any faithfulness
    or loyalty to your own spiritual reality.
Why? You are too interested in your own individual self.
Your limited self blocks your vast spiritual light.
You might be paying more attention to mental games
    of "Can I win?" or "Am I doing all right?"
    rather than relaxing into the moment
    and experiencing the life energy.
If you wish to succeed in your spiritual learning,
    you must resolutely take that leap into the unknown.
You must make yourself an incarnation of spiritual truth.
Take a good long look at yourself.
Do you manifest the subtle truth in everything you do?
Or are you person of scattered energy?

I am not trying to change you or me into philosophers.
You are already too philosophical.
You already think too much and differentiate too much.

What knowledge of yours is based on your own reality?
Most of it comes from books and television.
So many people are only the products of mixed cultural
    conditioning.
Your slow progress in spirit is all a result of your thinking.
Your thinking is not your thinking;
    it is society's thinking.
Modern society has cut itself off from its roots,
    which are the kindness and mercy
    of the deep life nature.

If you suffer from depression, anxiety, weakness and fear,
    do not dwell on it.
Instead, find a positive expression for your life.
The most important reason people feel that way
    is that they do not have a really positive
    and whole-minded attitude toward life.
By that I mean, while part of you wants to succeed,
    another part wants you to fail.

One part desires and the other part is afraid.
People act without being clear-minded.
They look like a hungry dog
  chasing the shadow of a piece of meat.
Find a simple task that you can do well,
  and make it the positive focus of your life.

Here is another refrain from this same verse.

When living a spiritual life,
  self-inspection is very important.
Have you asked yourself,
  "What kind of life am I?
Can I accept what I am and bring out my positive aspects?"
Have you asked yourself,
  "Am I manifesting the natural truth
  in everything I do?
Am I a person of confused and scattered energy?"

You do not want a verbal answer.
You do not need to be philosophical
  to answer the question.

If you only use thinking,
  you might become very judgmental.
Judgement is only a relative standard.
It is a comparison,
  not the truth.
Do we trust the judgements of our human companions
  as the truth of life?
It is up to you to decide what is truthful knowledge
  and what is reality.
Your thoughts could be the product
  of the mixed cultural condition,
  something you picked up from someone else.
They could all be the result of your insistence.
People of the world have cut off the root -
  the kindness and mercy of the deep life nature.
How can they know the truth?

Look in the mirror at your face.
Do you see depression, anxiety, weakness or fear?
What did you do to yourself?
Who asked you to do that to yourself?
Did someone encourage you to chase
*   money, power, fame and vanity?*
Do you expect that you can control
*   all the people and events in your world?*
It could be only your expectation that has caused
*   you to feel unhappy.*
Depression, fear, anxiety and worry come when
*   you have looked outside of yourself*
*   for your happiness.*
The most important reason
*   you were pushed to feel those things*
*   is your lack of a positive and whole-minded attitude*
*   toward life.*
That means, part of you wants to succeed,
*   part of you wants you to fail.*
One part desires someone
*   and the other part is afraid.*
You go on and on like this
*   instead of finding a simple, positive goal*
*   for your life.*
You look like a hungry dog
*   chasing the shadow of a piece of meat.*
Please look at the reality of your life.

What do I mean when I talk about a shadow? Most people chase shadows. Some want a degree, others want property, others want to write books or are looking for the perfect mate, etc. Let me ask you this: Even if you accomplish these things, will you be satisfied? No, because these things have no real substance. That is why I say that they are like shadows. Your real hunger is for eternity, not for temporary, material things. That is why they can never truly satisfy you for long. They can only satisfy part of your nature. Your spiritual nature will remain unsatisfied.

The world is bright and people are bright. In the perspective of learning spirituality, we say that if you cultivate and raise your own internal subtle energy, all the good things of life will come to you naturally without your having to chase after them. Even if you chose to live a plain, ordinary, normal life, it will still be on a higher level than that of people who do not cultivate themselves. It is an interesting and important spiritual truth that only after you give up wanting something does it come to you.

This is an encouragement, not a scolding. I wish that all of you can become fully enlightened. If I could do it for you, I would, but that is not the way it is set up. You all have to figure it out for yourselves.

It is time for you to share your experiences or to ask questions. Do you have any questions?

Q: What was your impression of that strange man who came to the house earlier who said he was Jehovah and was visiting all the great masters of the planet and wanted your picture, etc.?

Master Ni: He was a man full of knowledge that he had not learned yet. I listened to him calling me a great master with deep regret because, you see, if I was not playing this role, I could be doing something else. I could just sit around all day exchanging pleasant stories with you instead of reminding you over and over again to work on yourselves.

Q: When you refer to the spiritual realms, is that the same thing as Heaven?

Master Ni: No, the spiritual realms have many levels. Heaven is just the realm of highest yang energy. The realms go from yin to yang in degrees. I will tell you a little bit about them. The realms of yin/yang energy are lower than the spiritual realms. The spiritual realms have many levels ranging from the connection with the range of yin to yang by degrees. In general, the pure yang realm is called Heaven to differentiate it from the physical sphere, which is pure yin energy.

In the spiritual range, spirits belong to the yang category, while in the lower realms, ghosts result when people's gross physical bodies die. It is like when you burn wood and the only thing that remains is some smoke. This is what the lower yin realms are like.

In between the lower yin realms and the high yang realms of Heaven are the starry sky and the realm of natural deities. These realms belong to the yang sphere by virtue of their energy. The realms that are purer are the Heavenly Realms.

Heaven is where the pure subtle beings reside. It is not necessarily a place, it is a high level of energy and can be anywhere. The beings that cultivate and refine themselves on that level of energy can reside there even if they still have a physical body. They are able to see and hear subtle and exquisite things that ordinary people are not aware of. When their bodies eventually dissolve, they make an effortless change to that realm as easily as going out of one room into another. They have already formed their diamond body, so no matter where they reside, it is Heaven. Wherever they go, there is only brightness and joy.

The Heavenly realms of high yang energy are called the Heavenly realms of Great Purity, Crystal Purity, and Ultimate Purity. The absolute highest level of yang is the Subtle Origin. The Subtle Origin is pure yang energy, even more so than the Heavenly realms.

I hope you see that in order to experience Heaven it is only necessary to change your energy. If you do not change your energy to become more subtle, there can be no Heaven for you, no matter whether you are here in a physical body or in the spiritual realms without one.

The lower realms of yin energy are sometimes called hell. Hell is a place of yin energy and is characterized by suffering and limitations. Hell not only exists for ghosts and demons with no bodies, but it even exists here in the earthly realm. I think modern hospitals are a kind of hell and some fundamentalist churches too, because whenever you go there all you hear about is that place.

Q: How can you recognize a Heavenly being since they seldom show themselves outwardly?

Master Ni: The best way to know them is intuitively, but that can only be done if you are already one yourself. Another way is to observe how affected a person is by circumstances. A truly spiritual person will remain basically unaffected even by bad situations. Another thing is that misfortune usually never comes to them; their lives tend to be quieter. When you are highly achieved, you do not attract negative energy, nor are you attracted to it.

Q: How is it possible to reside in Heaven?

Master Ni: When you cultivate your energy, or in other words refine it, your vibrations change. Your mind becomes crystal clear and is able to resonate with the refined Heavenly energy. Again, I repeat: Heaven is not a place or a location that you go to, it is an energy field that exists within you. It is you who decides what kind of energy stays with you as you go through your day. No matter where you are, you could be in a state of Heaven if you wished. However, some of you are so unaccustomed to Heavenly energy that it will take a little work to learn how to stay with it again.

Q: When you talk about spirit, are you referring to ghosts?

Master Ni: Not at all. When I refer to your spirit, I mean the essential energy of the universe or the extended spiritual energy. Your spirit is an extension of Heavenly energy, just as your hand is an extension of your body.

I would also like to make the distinction between spirits and spirit. There are individual spirits which exist in the universe. They are the natural deities and, although their form is subtle, they still have form. There is also the spirit of the universe, which is the larger energy field of divine energy that has no form but can move into all forms which are receptive.

Q: When we finish this class, will we be able to retain the level of awareness we gain from it?

Master Ni: That depends on you. If you go back to thinking about mundane things all the time, the higher energies will dissipate unless you continue your daily cultivation. Your other activities all have the tendency to cloud your minds and scatter your energy. Any person will slowly take on contamination and gross energy if they do not constantly renew, invigorate, store and refine their subtle energy. This is why it is so important to keep up your practices or you will slowly lose what you gain here. It is kind of like sounding a gong; when you stop hitting it, the sound will fade away.

Q: How is it possible to go out into the world every day and not be influenced by it?

Master Ni: The key is to do your cultivation without fail and keep your level of energy vibration very strong. If your energy is high enough and strong enough, you will not have anything to worry about.

Having strong energy is like the story of the two masters who were invited to dinner by a rich landowner who gave a lot of money to their temple. Because there happened to be a prostitute at the dinner, one Master never looked up from his plate. The other master was friendly and even accepted a toast from the prostitute. When they returned to the temple, the one who kept his head bowed told the other one he should be ashamed of himself. However, the friendly one said that the prostitute only existed in the other master's mind and all he saw was a friendly person who honored them. Similarly, when you do your cultivation every day without fail, you do not see the darkness in the world just as this person did not see the prostitute in the woman.

When you refine your energy, everything becomes sacred and your whole perspective changes. I realize some of you must go to work in smoke-filled rooms, mix with unspiritual people and breathe polluted air, etc. However, if you do these things and you let them worry you, then you have double trouble. If you can keep calm about it and have a clear mind, then that actually helps to reduce the bad influence. Again I repeat: you can have a state of Heaven inside of you no matter where you are. Your mind, mental attitudes and beliefs are very important.

One day when I was young, I just finished practicing Kung Fu and was very thirsty, so I rushed into the kitchen and quickly gulped down a cup of water that was sitting on the table. I thought it tasted a little strange but I did not think too much about it. The next day, my mother asked what had happened to the cup of gasoline she had sitting on the table. As soon as I heard that, I started getting nauseous. You see, the mind has a powerful influence on us, so the more calm and peaceful it is, the better your life will be.

I knew a general in the army who got shot in his arm with a poisoned arrow. Because his mental powers of concentration were so strong, he allowed the doctors to remove the arrow and cut away the poisoned flesh without any anesthesia. Do you know what he concentrated on? Chinese chess. He played chess the whole time they operated on him and he never felt any pain. This power of the mind is available to everyone but most people never learn to utilize it. If you could use just a little bit of that kind of power in your daily lives and in your cultivation, you would be amazed to see the result of how different your life can be and the high quality it can have.

It is a tradition in folk Taoism that when disciples graduate from a certain level of training, they must demonstrate their power of concentration by walking on hot coals or sharp nails, or by holding a hot cauldron of boiling oil. This demonstrates that their mind is above the physical world. This kind of test is totally unnecessary to prove one's spirituality. It was used for martial arts training, and here we are learning spirituality so that type of thing is not relevant. However, it could be done by them as proof of their level of concentration.

Actually, the mind is capable of much greater things than just making a person numb to pain. Good concentration is a useful power but more important than that is the power of your deep calm mind. At the center of your being, there is a place of calm inactivity. This is the true unlimited source of power. The more you think and use your mind in a rational, discriminating way, the less power the calm center has.

A good example of the power of a calm mind was demonstrated by a master who liked to meditate on a certain rock at the edge of the ocean. For the first several years, whenever the tide came in, he would retreat further inland because his favorite rock would be under the water. One day, he was in deep meditation and all his energy had gone out of his limbs, so he could not escape the arrival of the tide. He thought to himself that if he died there at that time it would be okay, so he just relaxed. After he surrendered to that notion, a deep calm came over him. To his surprise, when he returned to consciousness in his body, he realized that the water had not touched him, even though everywhere else was wet. After that, he was able to meditate there any time he wanted and never had to worry about the water drowning him. However, do not go try this, because it is not a situation of normal life.

Let us apply this principle of working with the mind in daily life. It is just as great a power not to be upset if someone insults you, intentionally or unintentionally, as it is to keep from drowning by the tide.

This is just one small example of the power of the deep mind. If you let every little thing that comes along disturb your mind, you will never know this kind of peace and power. Please practice non-attachment and do not let things influence you so much. Give this deep calmness a chance to grow in your life.

February 2 1978

I

There are many books about the history of the ancient ones who achieved themselves spiritually. If you spoke of them in religious terms, you might call them "holy people." In the Integral Way, we do not use the term holy people, but simply call them "true people" or "shiens." What is the difference between a holy person and a true person? The notion of holiness is an artificial standard. Also, the definition of holiness differs among religions. It implies someone whose conduct is special or unusual, but a true person is a simple, natural person and is not necessarily unusual in any way. A person does not have to be unusual to express true achievement. Using my definition from a different class, a true person is a person who has Heavenly energy, even though all that person's behavior might be totally ordinary.

In another sense, we all have the same spiritual essence and our lives are already holy even if we do not do anything special. By a true being we just mean someone whose mind is not spoiled. What do I mean by that? Most people's minds have been greatly influenced and conditioned by society and by their religion. Many of you still hold the beliefs you had as children. In spiritual learning, all rigid beliefs and dogmas are given up. In the Integral Way, we do not have any formalized religion, so we have less to unlearn.

Most people do not realize how much they are bound by their society. For instance, when I was a young boy in China, all the young women in our town wore high collars around their necks. They did not think there was anything strange about it, but the truth was, they could not even turn their head and they also had trouble breathing because those collars were so tight. Western friends with those ties around their necks also look strange to me, and they seem as confining as those collars. If the necktie got caught on something, a man would hang himself. This is a straightforward example of how society suffocates us. Why are people so willing to go along with such madness? All illnesses are a result of how people have formed their minds to fit society, so people must learn to detoxify themselves.

Anyway, back to the books about the ancient achieved ones. There are many levels of achievement. The service or function provided by these books depends upon what and how much you have achieved by yourself. There are books about the lives of the true beings which have not yet been translated into modern Chinese. Maybe you do not realize that we have a modern and an ancient style of writing. Most modern Chinese people cannot read the old style of writing, so the important books are hard to understand now. Those are the ones which tell about the spiritual practices of ancient Chinese people.

The lifestyle of the ancient developed beings was very different than ours today. Today, everyone goes to school so they can earn a big paycheck and have a nice home, a fancy car and several TVs, etc., but in ancient times, the true beings never concerned themselves with those things. They just wanted to develop their lives in a way that would enable them to achieve immortality.

Let us now open one of these old books to a random page and see which of the ancient beings is described there. This man was named Wang Ren Lai. As a scholar, he did not seek an official position because he was more interested in developing himself further to have wealth, power and fame, but he was strongly recommended by a friend to the government, so he took a position as an official. He was soon promoted to the position of administrator to the emperor. His job was to investigate any shortcomings in the government and then report it to the top authorities along with his suggestions about what to do.

Wang was unlike most of the political people around the emperor; he was a man of truth and dignity. Although he was a Confucian scholar, he was interested in the studies of the Yellow Emperor and Lao Tzu. Because he was so broadminded, a master was attracted to him and gave him one of his daughters in marriage. He also taught him some secret magic.

After some time, Wang was assigned to Ching Jyeo county, far from home. He went there alone because his wife had to stay and take care of his old mother and father. However, he learned the ancient magic of instant travel, so every night he would appear to his wife and then disappear in the early morning. One night, one of the servants of the house heard his wife laughing and talking with a man and the next day reported it to Master Wang's parents.

That was a serious charge in those days. When his parents questioned her about it, she told them the truth. They did not believe her, of course, but she insisted it was true. She said they had to keep the magic a secret or the magic power would not support him to perform such practice. However, she could offer no proof of her story.

That night, when Wang showed up and learned what had happened, he decided to appear before his parents and straighten everything out. After he showed himself to them, he went out into the courtyard and broke off a piece of bamboo. He then said an incantation and the bamboo became a dragon and he then flew back to his office.

This story also says that later, his father also went to study with his Master, and one day Wang, his parents and wife all flew away together to the East.

This was an actual story written about a thousand years ago. All the people described in the book, including Master Wang, actually lived.

You may wonder why Wang did not teach his secrets to some students. Perhaps some people would appreciate him more if he had started a new religion and promised to be everyone's savior. Before he flew away, he could have promised to return and to be the light of people's lives, etc., but he did not make such a promise.

It is not necessary to have any saviors at all, because each of us can save oneself. It is necessary for us to be our own light in the world. Even if you have a master teacher right in front of you, it is still necessary to save yourself.

Q: Does a spiritual student need to go through a lot of difficult spiritual experiences?

Master Ni: There are several conditions which are important to know if you want to avoid bad experiences. First, you need to truly recognize the authority of the mind. Your mind is what invites both good and bad fortune, a peaceful life or disturbing experiences. The safest way to learn spiritually is to start by learning about the mind. Then, you can use your original life spirit to guide your mind to unite with the natural life being. In that way, you will live your life in a range of normalcy. That will be safe.

Many people learn religion or become religious believers. Sometimes they are just looking for spiritual protection. Let me tell you how a religion can protect you. Although it is not the truth, it presents one way or another to help you to gather the scatteredness of the mind. Once you learn the structure of a religion, then you can channel your mind so that your experiences fit that structure. Thus, you mentally unify all your experiences. However, never fasten your developable mind to any religion; if you do, you will become prejudicial and that will start to harm your true growth. It is still a fact that the mind tells itself a religious story to make itself feel protected. Basically, a person engages in religious practice because of a weakness of the mind, spirit and body to start with. Under this situation of feeling vulnerable, a person will accept anything they think works to protect him or her. This is a psychological game and does not actually bring protection. It is not real spiritual development, but if it helps someone temporarily, it is all right. If a person is really developed spiritually and has a higher spirit, then the spirits understand your mind. Once you develop your spirits, whatever your mind does not understand, the developed spirits understand and will assist the inadequate capability of the mind. However, if you do not develop your spirit, then the mind is the authority. Some minds are good and some minds are not.

Your mind is subtle, but your spiritual energy is even more subtle. Spiritual energy has two sources, your body and your mind. Generally the spirits of the mind establish another level of being, then the trinity of mind, spirit and physics are established. Although all people have the foundation of a partnership between these three, because we live on the level of worldly life, we rely on our minds very much. We habitually trust the mind to take charge of our lives. Development of the mind is important.

In spiritual development, there is actually not much to do. In contrast, the development of the mind is never ending. Each person experiences both the natural truth and the world with its bad tendencies caused by time, leaders, society and customs. Both the natural truth and the world are right in front of you. Some of you are interested in the natural truth, but others are annoyed by it. If you do not develop your mind through spiritual learning, your mind will explain the floating and sinking of the emotions as being caused by the drama of daily life. Learning religion is one of the psychological ways for people who are looking for a thought, system, belief or insurance to be their protection, but, at the same time, it blocks real growth. Although your experience of everyday life does not change, you have new religious rationalizations to explain why things happen. Therefore, you achieve no growth.

During many generations of human history, people recorded their experiences through written language and left them as teachings for others. Not all experiences are accurate reactions to what actually happened to the person. By this I mean, not all the people who wrote down teachings based on their experiences really understood what was happening to them. Not all teachings are good conclusions of their experiences. You might wonder, if I am interested in a certain teaching, how can I judge what is a true experience, whether or not the person understood the experience correctly, and whether they came to a useful conclusion in their teaching? Personally, I believe that your own spiritual development will lead you to the right decision. Only through examining the teaching by your own experiences will you know accurately.

When you accept spiritual cultivation and development as a way of life, please understand that it requires more effort than just listening to one religion or one teacher. During my own learning, I kept open to all possible experiences and broke all the prohibitions. Also, if a person would truly like to restore their own spiritual sensitivity, it becomes a natural tendency to withdraw somewhat and avoid the complication of the confused, mixed crowds. In other words, you could not totally stay involved with crowds of people. That means, however, that you cannot help large groups of people and also you lose touch with what the crowds of common people are doing. You cannot stay too far away from the crowd, otherwise, you could not help people at all. When you do choose to stay and give service, or give partial service or intermittent service, you still have contact and transactions with the undeveloped crowds. You have to pay the price; at least, you need lots of patience to stand such a situation. This is quite unnecessary for people who are already achieved. You create no public teaching but you teach yourself and thus further withdraw. That is the negativity or weakness of the sensitive mind, it is not a positive achievement. You need to learn the real spiritual practice that can fortify your spiritual energy, and then you can selectively face and choose the pressures you would like to take. Otherwise, nobody gives any service or help at all, and the world is not a place for a developed person to live.

Even if, as a developed person, you decide to withdraw totally from worldly contact, it is difficult to maintain a decent and peaceful minimum condition for survival without exercising your spiritual strength. Basically, whatever you do, it is your spiritual strength which supports you for a normal, decent life.

It is beneficial to understand these things deeply. The benefit is that you do not blame the world because you understand the world, and you do not blame people because you understand people. You selectively take some trouble; I am not saying that you can totally live without trouble. The most important part of a spiritual life is for you to attain the spiritual power which has nothing to do with magic, but the power of a decent, upright, righteous life. With that type of life, you can withstand all possible pressures and disturbances. If trouble happens, it is not from your own wrongdoing. An oversensitive mind might think that life is a mistake, sin or wrongdoing. That sensitivity does not help.

I study spiritual truth. Spiritual reality is a subtle power. It is health, uprightness, righteousness, kindness

and harmlessness. At the same time, it does not accept
harm from any sphere because it is a subtle power that
always practices yielding. You do not experience confrontation or conflict because when you learn spirit, you also learn
to lower yourself and learn to yield to a situation. To
achieve your spiritual virtue and morality, you need to
exercise great capacity of the mind. Spiritual narrowness or
steepness is no longer of service to you. Most selfish people
cannot find happiness in the world or in themselves. Thus
what they hold all turns out to be self-poison or becomes an
enemy or rival in their lives.

For political leaders, it is not hard to create new powers
and ways to find strength from the mob. They always say,
"Lets turn the world around to let people of no money, no
education and no creation become the leaders of the world.
We will all enjoy special privileges and special treatment
after we have successfully seized authority." This kind of
motivation comes from narrowness. It creates and uses
confrontation to establish a one-sided social strength. It
does not guide people to work toward and to achieve what
each person can achieve in a reasonable way.

What is the end product of these leaders of narrow
mindedness? Once they have gained acceptance by the
common people, and have robbed everything they could
from the upper class, they discover that they have destroyed
the natural, organic condition of the world. Their narrow
thoughts have only caused trouble. It is for this reason that
I ask you, the developing ones, to use your patience, virtue
and tolerance to live with and help the world. You will find
that it also serves your own life because it creates happy
relationships with others.

Not many people, have created as large a mess as
political leaders. In our everyday lives, if you become
jealous or envious of others, if you place expectations or
demands upon people that they cannot meet, if your own
communication is not clear, then you might consider the
opposite side to be your enemy and try to harm them.
However, fruit is only healthy when it is eaten by the person
who has planted the fruit tree, not when it is eaten by a
thief. The new trend of the world makes people overly

strong and unable to recognize these important disciplines and personal virtues. They tend to act like bullies by stealing and robbing from others, but these people are weak in personality and morality and, surely, sick in spiritual reality. To cultivate oneself is to live a healthy life, physically, mentally and spiritually. To live healthily is not selfish. On the contrary, being sick is selfish, because you make people serve you, pay a price for you and suffer for you. This is why spiritual development, including the development of the mind, is everybody's business. When all people develop themselves, then a healthy world can be reached without the need for a desperate hope that there is a Heavenly paradise somewhere else. A Heavenly paradise somewhere else is the carrot on the stick which is offered by general religion. This does not encourage people to work for further development and thus gain the moral strength and power of virtue that they are looking for. In the worldly structure of the modern church, the Heavenly door is only open to those who make the biggest donation. They do not guide people to improve their real personalities and life condition. This is the difference between my teaching and other religious promotions.

Q: *Master Ni, stories of demons and evil spirits, and fairy tales exist in all cultures. Are these stories true? Is it necessary that a spiritual student encounter such things in their spiritual experience?*

Master Ni: My personal learning and experience is that there are wild spirits. At least, they are semi-spiritual. They are semi-spiritual because they can be known with the shape of particles like a thin thread or a bee sting. Yet, they are individually responsive. Thus, they are semi-spiritual. Demons or evil spirits are human concepts. In reality, there are different spheres and levels of the universe. We have observed and studied two levels: the physical level and the life level. Life level means vegetation and animals, including human life. Now, the new frontier for the sciences is to study the energy formation of stars, nebulas, etc., but they still use a physical approach to understand such things.

Let us come back to the reality of the living world, not society, but the basic life condition.

In our natural surroundings, there are subtle particles that we call spirits. Some of them are stronger than others. Some are more developed, and some are more powerful. They are just a natural level of energy. If you apply the concept of demons, devils, evil spirits, or good and holy spirits, you are only drawing an unnatural, mechanical conclusion. Then what is the objective conclusion? The objective conclusion is that we have a concrete body, and with spiritual practice and development, you discover yourself to be a composite of many types of energy. The smallest forms of life are like particles. I do not mean the cells at the physical level. Any tangible level I leave to modern scientists.

What I learned is the knowledge and true experiences of the spiritual realm. This practice can be taught to anyone who is a ready student. It is possible to do a "spiritual disassembly" which can make you understand and see that your life being consists of thousands of spiritual particles, all organized at different levels. These particles are the materials with which an individual can achieve a subtle life of immortality. From this practice, you gain the truthful knowledge that you know yourself as a world. Your life consists of a big group of different spirits on different levels. Because the spiritual level is unknown to most of you and to scientists, I feel it is my obligation to offer help through my teaching. I offer a special service to qualified scientists who wish to devote themselves to the new frontier of spiritual discovery in nature.

Let me come back to your question. Your question talks about demons, devils, evil spirits on one hand, and on the other hand, angels and holy spirits. Dualistic thinking which divides things into good and bad is just a mental structure or habit pattern which lacks truth or reality. Western movies and soap operas do the same thing; they teach people that there is a good guy and bad guy, and then demonstrate how the bad guy makes trouble and how the good guy suffers. How they tackle the task of triumph and defeat makes people identify with the development of the stories. This becomes the basic pattern of the knowledge of your mind. But with a really objective attitude, things which oppose each other actually accomplish each other in the deep sphere. My personal experience is that all spirits can become your friend. It is only when you do not understand them that you fear them. They do have different spiritual energies; some of them you are at the ghost level. They might cause you to have a body sensation of coldness or stiffness. That is different from natural spirits; that is the level of ghosts.

The ancient spiritually achieved ones and the modern ones too are able to bring about great things such as useful inventions to the world. They are supported or inspired by different spirits, internally or externally. In general, people who have not learned a spiritual practice will feel scared. In truth, it may not be somebody's ghost; possibly it is their own ghost. Fear often arises when you contact a different energy. It may not be as pleasant as you wish, but to use the word "evil" to define it is not proper. In the process of spiritual cultivation, many evil things appear to you, but the real trouble is the undeveloped or semi-developed mind. It can create harm, but it can not guard you from harm, because it associates with harm. It is not necessarily your own, it can be someone you listen to who is at this level.

I would like to give you some practical guidance. Maintain yourself well-centered spiritually during any situation where there are lots of things or beings starting to become active and surround you. That is the first principle. Second, you have to learn some spiritual protection which is contained in *The Workbook for Spiritual Development for All People.*

Now I would like to tell you about someone's real experience. Once someone took a sightseeing trip to some South Pacific islands. One night, he was tired after riding in a motorboat to visit one island after another. After eating a good dinner, he went back to his hotel. When he arrived at the hotel, he felt a sensation right above the upper lip, in the little hollow under the nostril. We call that spot the middle of the person or body. It is a sensitive spot for spiritual communication between one's own spirit and one's own mind. He frequently received a signal in that place, but this time, he did not know what the message was about, so he just went to bed and went to sleep. Suddenly, he felt he was controlled by a piece of white energy which snuck in through the partly opened window. That piece of energy laid down at the person's side because it wished to steal energy from my friend. Fortunately, he knew it was a spiritual attack from what you might call demons or evil spirits. He immediately used one of the invocations from the *Workbook for Spiritual Development* to make the spirit go away. Later he told me he regretted not have been more alert. His body had already given him a signal about having a different energy around. If he had heeded that signal and done his spiritual practice, it would not have waited until he undressed himself and laid down on the bed, thus allowing something else to lie down on the bed with him at the same time. When he had that warning from his body, he could have done something to handle the situation before the event actually happened.

My impression is that in the spiritual world, there are rascals and villains. If you are alert you can ward them off, for example, by simply sitting upright in good meditation or just by continuing to bite your teeth together. We call that "Beating the Heavenly Drum," and that is used to keep your spirit alert, so you will be safe. This knowledge is something which can help you in a spiritual emergency, but in general, spiritual practice is most helpful if you do it all the time. I hope you respect it and when necessary, you can make use of these suggestions to guard your good energy.

Sometimes, if you have a nightmare, you might feel like something is pressing over you that makes it impossible for you to move or even yell. It could be a black energy or a white energy. On these occasions, you might not know whether the cause is spiritual or physical. It could be physical: if you lie down in one position too long, and your heart muscle becomes numb, you could also feel that way. This is why we suggest you do not sleep on your back or use a heavy comforter. It is better to sleep on your right side. Sleep on the left side only for short adjustments. Also, learn one or two invocations from the *Workbook For Spiritual*

Development and recite them frequently. Those simple English words, which I translated from Chinese, will work to help you.

If your physical structure is strong and tight, you do not need to learn any of this but can ignore it and live like a regular person. Do you know that? To know nothing about spiritual matters, like a childlike mind, is also a kind of service. Because such things will not happen to ordinary people who are in a healthy condition or live in a healthy environment. Unless you are already spiritually sensitive, you do not need to learn about such things.

I am not afraid of spirits, but it is important to be cautious about different energies. The real value of spiritual learning is to assist us in living a healthy, normal life. I would like to add here, since we are talking about demons, devils and evil spirits, that those words might be applied to narrow-minded people or political leaders who are transformed demon energy, devil energy or evil spirits in human life. They cause so much trouble in the human world. They are proud and stubborn; they never listen to a single word from the world of light. They are so powerful and dominant that they consider whatever they think to be right without considering the consequences of their actions. In general, people who have not yet developed themselves spiritually could do bad things too. Some misguided actions are due to the tension of life, some from bad education or bad influence. Some people need lessons or experiences which might help them develop their spiritual awareness to know their mistake and learn to be better people.

Normal life is the best protection from the spiritual world. Normal life, however, is not enough to protect you from undeveloped people who might make trouble or annoy you unless you guard yourself correctly and avoid creating any opportunity for them to be close to you. You may ask me how to best guard yourself. In all honesty, I must say that I have not become totally proficient at that yet. When I learn it, you will be the first ones I will tell. However, in general, we should not have the intention to harm anyone. Instead, we need to be alert to prevent people of inferior virtue from harming or taking advantage of our nice nature.

Sometimes you can accept the problem, sometimes you cannot accept it; it all depends on the situation.

There is one thing I want to mention before you go home tonight. Do not fear any ghosts. Most people have both yin and yang energy, and if you keep your energy balanced and at a high level, no ghost can possibly influence you. When your energy is balanced, your mind will be calm and strong. It is only when you weaken yourself or let your imagination run wild that you can be influenced. Also, some of you who are developing your sensitivity, do not let any bad psychic disturbance in your environment disturb you. Just keep centered and ignore it, and it will go away.

If you have a bad dream, sometimes there is a bad spirit influencing you. Most people are more vulnerable when they are dreaming than when they are awake. Whenever you start to have a bad dream, just wake yourself up. I am not joking; when you are awake, you can program yourself to avoid bad dreams. Why do you think most cultivators sleep sitting up? It is because it is much easier to return to the body and the waking state if you are sitting up. When you lie down flat, especially on your stomach or back, you sleep deeper and are more exposed to bad influences. Your physical body is your protection in this case.

Many bad dreams are just your imagination or are the result of too many hot spices in your dinner. Some dreams can be an important message, but there truly are beings who take people's energy when they are asleep, so you must be careful. Some of you are cultivating good energy so you will be a target for this, but do not worry about it. Remember that good energy can dispel bad energy. Continue your meditations and cultivations, and make friends with the shiens and you will have nothing to fear. This is all for tonight. Have good dreams tonight.

II

The following is a metaphoric story related to internal alchemy. It was written during the Tang Dynasty when the influence of spiritual learning was at its peak in Chinese society. You can arrive at your own understanding about the meaning of the story and apply it to your cultivation.

"The Squanderer and the Alchemist"

Du Tsi-chun, who lived during the end of the Northern Chou dynasty (557-581 A.D.) and the beginning of the Sui Dynasty (581-618 A.D.) was an extravagant young man who neglected the fortune left to him by his parents. Corrupt and fond of drinking and low pleasures, he soon squandered his entire fortune. Then he went to his relatives and asked them to take him in. However, all of them turned him away because he refused to work. One cold winter day, with an empty stomach and threadbare clothing, not knowing where to go, he wandered about by the West gate of the East Market. Miserable, he looked up at the Heavens and sighed.

An old man carrying a stick came up to him and asked, "Why are you sighing?"

Du poured out his resentment and indignation at his relatives' lack of sensitivity. His face mirrored his feelings.

"How much money do you think you need?" asked the old man.

"I think that thirty or forty thousand would suffice," said Du.

"That's not enough," said the old man. "Think again."

"A hundred thousand?"

"That's not enough."

"Five hundred thousand?"

"Still not enough."

"A million? Two million?"

"That sounds more like it," said the old man. He took some money from his wallet hidden in his big sleeve and gave it to Du, saying, "This small amount is for tonight. Tomorrow I will be at the Singapore Grand Hotel in the West Market. Meet me there at one o'clock, and don't be late."

Du went to the hotel on time the next day, and the old man gave him two million in cash, but then left without even telling his name.

Now that he was rich, Du, confident that his experience as a tramp was over, returned to all his bad habits. He bought expensive horses and tailored suits. He went to live in the aristocratic section of town, and gathered a group of people who enjoyed music and dancing. Not even once did it occur to him that he could invest his newfound wealth. Instead, he spent as though he did not have a care in the world. After several years, however, he had no money left. Then he sold his expensive clothing, carriages and fine horses to buy cheaper ones. Eventually, he sold his last horse and bought a donkey, then sold his donkey to go on foot. Soon he was as destitute as before.

Once again, he did not know what to do or where to go, and returned to the market gate and wandered about. Shortly, the old man appeared, grasped his hand and said, "What! Are you reduced to this sorry state again? How much do you need this time?"

Du was ashamed to answer, and although the old man pressed him, he would not accept. At last, the old man told him, "Meet me tomorrow at the hotel at one o'clock."

Despite his shame, Du went to meet the old man and accepted five million in cash. He spent the night thinking about how he would change himself and go into business so he would not run into the same trouble again. However, once he had some money in his pocket, he forgot his good resolution and returned to his bad habits of pursuing wine, women and song. Thus, again, after three or four years, wearing rags and with an empty stomach, he sat down in front of the West gate. The old man appeared in front of him. Overcome with shame, Du hid his face and tried to leave, but the old man took hold of his coat and stopped him, saying, "How badly you manage!" With that, he gave him ten million on the spot and said, "If this does not cure you, there is no hope for you."

Du thought, "I have lead a shameful life, having squandered several fortunes and wasted my life. None of my relatives helped me, but this old man has given me money three times. I must find a way to repay him."

So he said to the old man, "I am deeply grateful to you. With this money I will take care of my worldly affairs, provide for my poor relatives and pay all my obligations. After everything has been settled, I shall do whatever you tell me."

"That is what I wish," was the old man's reply. "After you have taken care of everything, meet me next year on the fifteenth day of the seventh month under the two juniper trees in front of the Taoist temple. Be there at one o'clock."

Most of Du's poor relatives lived in the Hwai river valley, near the valley's central city. He bought two thousand acres of fertile land, and built villas, mansions and highways. After he settled all his poor relations there, he arranged marriages for his nephews and nieces and moved back to the ancestral burial place all members of the family who had been buried outside. He settled things with his old enemies and repaid all those who had offered some kindness to him. Everything being accomplished, he went to meet the old man at the temple at the appointed time and date.

When he arrived, he found the old man sitting on a stump, singing in the shade of the two juniper trees. Together, they set out for the Peak of Cloud Terrace on Hua Mountain. After they walked about fifteen miles and were close to the peak, they came to an immense mansion which was obviously not the dwelling of any common man. Bright clouds hovered over it and phoenixes and storks perched in the garden. They entered the building, and Du looked around. He saw that in the central hall there was a cauldron over nine feet high in which herbal teas were being brewed. It was suspended over a fire with purple flame which cast a bright light on all the windows of the room. Around the cauldron were statues of some special spiritual symbols, the Jade Virgins, Green Dragons and White Tigers.

By now it was now nearly sunset, and the old man removed his overcoat, revealing himself to be a spiritual teacher wearing the typical yellow cap and red cape. He gave Du three white marble pills and a goblet of wine, which Du swallowed. Then the old spiritual teacher made him sit on a tiger skin by the West wall, facing East. "Be sure not to say a word!" he warned him. "Do not make a sound, even if you see deities, devils, vampires, wild beasts, the horrors of hell, or your relatives bound and in agony. It will all be an illusion. You must neither speak nor move. Do not be afraid, because no harm will come to you. Remember what I have said at all times." Then, the old man disappeared. When Du looked round the hall, he saw nothing but a huge jar filled with water. The cauldron was no longer to be seen, either.

The old spiritual teacher had no sooner gone than thousands of chariots and horsemen appeared with flags flying and weapons gleaming. Their battle cries were so loud that they shook Heaven and Earth. Their commander was over ten feet tall, and both he and his steed were dressed in gilded armor which dazzled Du's eyes. This giant led several hundred warriors straight into the hall, where they stopped right in front of Du and unsheathed their swords and stretched taught their bows. "Who are you?" the commander roared at Du. "How dare you confront me!" All the warriors rushed forward with drawn swords. The commander continued to demand Du's name and reason for being there. But he said not a word. This so enraged them that furious yells of "Shoot him! Kill him!" resounded through the hall like thunder. Still he uttered not a single word. Finally, the commander withdrew, fuming with rage, taking his warriors with him.

Then, suddenly, fierce tigers, deadly dragons, griffins, lions and tens of thousands of cobras rushed forward. Hissing and growling, they threatened to swallow Du or throw themselves on him to suffocate him. But not a single muscle of his face moved, and soon these monsters vanished too.

Then, a torrential rain fell and the sky grew dark. Intense lightning flashed around him until he could not open his eyes for the brightness and thunderbolts crashing beside him, shaking the ground until it seemed that everything was moving. The courtyard became more than ten feet deep in water which pressed against the big double doors. Suddenly, the doors broke and the water rushed in a deluge into the hall. In a flash the water reached up to chin height, but Du sat there and ignored it until finally the flood vanished too.

Then the commander returned, leading ox-headed jailers, horned monsters and other foul fiends from hell. They besieged Du and hemmed him in with their spears, knives, swords and prongs, and then set a boiling cauldron before him. "If he tells his name, let him go," ordered the commander. "Otherwise, run him through and throw him into the cauldron for our supper."

Still he said nothing.

Then they brought in his wife and threw her down at the foot of the steps leading to the hall. Pointing to her, they said to Du, "Speak, and we will spare her life."

Still he made no reply.

Then they whipped and beat her, shot and slashed her, burned and branded her, until she was in agony with her whole body streaming with blood.

"I know I am only a simple woman and not good enough for you," she cried desperately. "But I have served you faithfully for more than ten years. Now these devils have seized me and the pain is more than I can bear. I would not ask you to lower yourself to plead with them; but if you say just one word, my life will be spared. How can you be so heartless and begrudge me even one small word?" Tears poured down her cheeks as she began to reproach and curse him. Still, Du paid no attention and maintained silence.

"Do you think I cannot kill her?" roared the commander. Then he ordered the devils to fetch a chopper and chop off the woman's feet one inch at a time. Du's wife screamed with pain, but still he paid no attention.

"This scoundrel is well versed in the ways of magic," hissed the commander. "We cannot let him live; he is a threat to all of us." And he ordered his guards to kill Du without delay.

After Du had been killed, his spirit was hauled before the king of hell.

"Is this man the infamous wizard of the Peak of Cloud Terrace?" asked the king of hell. "Torture him."

Melted scalding copper was poured down his throat, he was beaten with cast iron rods, pounded with pestles, ground between millstones, thrown into a fiery pit, boiled in a cauldron and dashed against a forest of swords. But through all his sufferings he bore in mind what the old spiritual teacher had told him, and so he did not let even one groan escape from his lips. When the jailers announced that all the tortures had been tried and had failed, the king said, "This man is a scoundrel; we must get rid of him. However, I would not give him the satisfaction of being reborn a man. Let him be reborn as a woman to the family of Wangh Chin, the magistrate of Sanfurh County in Songchow."

So Du was reborn as a girl child to a family of moderate wealth. She was born premature and was weak, having some affliction to her health. As a child, she was delicate and often ill. Not for a single day was she free from painful medical treatment. Once she fell off the bed, and another time fell onto the stove. The pain was intense, but not a sound did she utter. She grew up to be a beautiful girl, but she never spoke a word, so her family came to believe that she had been born dumb, although she surely was not deaf. Her relatives insulted and taunted her in many ways, but she never retorted or reacted to the cruel things they said.

When she was in her teens, a scholar from the same county named Leu Gyei heard of the dumb girl's beauty and sent a match-maker to ask for her hand. When the family declined because she was dumb, Lu said, "She does not have to speak to be a good wife. And she will be a good example for women who talk too much." Then the family was convinced that his intentions were good and so they agreed, and Lu married Du in a proper ceremony. He was kind to her, and she was faithful, so they came to love each other, and after they had been married several years Du gave birth to a son. Soon the child was two years old, and amazingly bright.

However, Lu could not believe that his wife was really dumb. He wished to try to prompt her to speak. One day, holding the child in his arms, he asked Du about her silence, but she did not reply. Lu then tried various ways to trick his wife into speaking, but still Du did not make a sound. Then Lu flew into a rage and said, "In ancient times, Minister Chyia had a wife who despised him and would never smile, but after he proved to be a good hunter and brought her fine meats to eat, she changed her mind and smiled for him. Now I am not as bad as Chyia, and my literary talents are much superior to any man's skill in hunting; yet you refuse to speak to me. What use is it to have a son, when a husband is despised by his own wife?"

Then, seizing the child by its feet, he dashed his head against the brick wall. The little boy's skull was smashed, and blood spurted out several feet. Love for the child made Du forget the promise not to speak, and he give an exclamation of horror.

With the exclamation still on Du's lips, he found himself back on the tiger skin in the hall of the mansion, with the old spiritual teacher standing before him. It was dawn. Purple flames from the cauldron were shooting up through the roof to the sky, and fire was rising from all sides as the mansion began to burn to ashes.

"Look what you have done! You have spoilt all my work, you silly fellow!" exclaimed the man. Seizing Du by the hair, he picked him up and threw him into a huge jar of water.

"For a while, I had much hope in you. You succeeded in mastering joy, anger, sorrow, fear, hate and desire," said the old priest. "Love was the only thing that you could not overcome. If you had not cried out, my elixir would have been completed and you could have become immortal too. How hard it is to find a man who can attain the Godhead! However, I will go somewhere else to brew my elixir again, while you remain bound to earth as a mortal. Farewell!" Then he showed Du which road he could follow to go back to his home.

Du, bewildered, turned to look around. In the ruined cauldron was an iron rod as thick as a man's arm and several feet long. Taking off his outer garment, the priest began to cut this rod up with a knife.

After Du returned to the world, he felt ashamed that he had failed to repay the old man's kindness and swore to himself that he would make good his failure. But when he went back later to the Peak of Cloud Terrace, there was no one there and the mansion had disappeared. The only thing he could do was return sadly home.

February 10, 1978

These internal alchemy classes are special classes. Some of you still do not have any idea what these classes are all about. They are not just book learning classes that you forget in a year or two. This is your golden opportunity to reform your energy.

In other words:

Self-release and self-formation are special.
It is not book learning.
It is a golden opportunity to reform your energy.
Did you take the time to really understand
    what self-release and self-formation are all about?

If you would only open yourself up to the divine energy that is here, there would be no more obstacles. Some of you are self-conscious and stand in the corner so no one will see you. What are you holding on to? You will never touch the divine energy that way.

In other words:

Open yourself up to the divine energy
    that is right here with you.
When you do, there will be no more obstacles
    standing between you and the truth.
Do not stand intimidated in the corner
    trying to keep others from seeing you.
It will not keep you safe;
    your self cultivation will help you more.
Come out from hiding;
    touch the Divine Energy.

I also see that some of you have no intention of giving up your mental hold on fear. You are still strongly attached to this physical world and to the ego as your root of life, so what are you doing here? You are just wallowing in the mud of the mind. It is sad.

In other words:

Give up your fear.
It makes you fasten strongly
    to the physical shape and the ego.
Take steps to move toward good learning;
    try to keep a positive spirit.
One who remains entrapped in the repetitious
    patterns of one's own negative mind
    is truly lost.
Open up your mind to embrace the Light.

Some of you are growing like little sprouts coming up from the ground. Some even have little buds on their stems. Your growth depends entirely on your sincerity and willingness to change. The divine energy has come down from Heaven to help you. The source of such high energy is within you. May your life be the manifestation of Heavenly energy. Let your whole being respond to it, although there are others who cannot touch it at all.

You all come from Heaven and every one of you has a spark of divine light. However, some of you may have spun a hard cocoon around your Heavenly energy and will not let it out. Every one of your mental concepts and judgements adds to your shell. Some of you have created a living hell for yourselves, and your cocoon is getting thicker every day.

The good news is that your cocoon can be changed into a cradle for growing new divine energy inside of you if you wish to. The opportunity to remove your self-created cocoon is here and now. If you do not take advantage of it, you can always wait until later, but why wait?

The Heavenly selection is exact and fair. It is not I who decides who goes to Heaven and who does not; it is determined by your own efforts. The others will be left here to wander in the worldly mists.

Some of you are intelligent, but it means nothing because you only use your intelligence to gain small advantage in the world. You use a lot of energy to get what you want here while you completely ignore your divine nature. Some teachers would call that sickness. They would say some people who call themselves spiritual students are so sick that not even major spiritual surgery could save them.

If my words have made some of you uncomfortable, they are for you to remember. The things I say that are pleasant to listen to are sometimes more valuable if forgotten. Can you refuse to take advantage of this precious opportunity to mend your good energy? No. You cannot escape your spiritual consciousness, which is the angel living within you.

In other words:

Truthful words are not easily accepted.
If something makes you feel uneasy,
    it is because it is something that you
    need to examine in yourself.
Do not miss the opportunity
    that the sometimes painful truth
    gives you to resolve the problem
    that you will not admit to yourself.
Take advantage of the Divine Energy
    passed to you from your helpful teachers.
The teacher has a spiritual eye,
    which can see the truth.
Listen to all his words
    and work on yourself relentlessly
    yet still be kind to yourself.

At different times, new cultures are expressed. Now, people tend to be more complex. Nevertheless, whenever any person manifests one's energy, it comes from the source within that is untouched by culture. Therefore, anyone who has spiritual eyes can see how your energy manifests.

Some of you tell me you can speak five languages. Well, tonight, you are all speaking my language; it is the language of energy.

Q: What do you suggest we do who are still in the mud and dirt?

Master Ni: First of all, if you find that you are still in the mud and dirt, do not be too hard upon yourself, just realize the situation. Recognize that you need to improve and be open to see what kind of information, learning and help comes to you. Then, when you see your faults and you see the way to change and improve yourself, do it. Mostly, this means to find a way to keep your own positive energy manifesting.

In the case of the person who asked the question, I was not referring to you. Your problem is that you try too hard. Take it easy. In your case, just be open. Relax a little bit.

Q: I had what I thought was an experience of the energy in this room, but how do I know if it was real or just my imagination?

Master Ni: What makes you think it was not real? I tell you, the subtle realm is subtle, and this is why many people have experiences of subtle energy but think they are imagining things.

Getting someone to verify your experience one way or the other means nothing, because there will not always be someone around to tell you what is going on. I recommend that you expand your knowledge about spirit by reading good books.

Q: Do you approve of the macrobiotic diet?

Master Ni: For some people. It is an old diet with a new name. That diet was mostly used for overnourished or overweight people. It was never meant to be a diet for all people.

Eating balanced food is the best principle when talking about diet. It means not to eat too much of any one thing. It would be too rigid to categorize all food as yin or yang; that is not truly helpful. True distinctions between yin and yang are based on the food nature and the way of preparation, which also makes the food change its nature. The condition of ripeness of a fruit or vegetable changes its nature, too. Even among the same fruit and same vegetable, some could be put in yang divisions and others in yin divisions, just like people. Not all men are yang, and not all women are yin.

Knowing the nature of a food comes through developed spiritual discernment, not a rigid division of knowledge or using a pendulum to determine the different nature of each item.

Even a casual student of Chinese medicine knows that to strictly follow yin and yang in a diet is too shallow and will not bring health or balance.

Q: The Japanese teacher who developed the macrobiotic diet died from lung cancer because he smoked so much. However, there have been several deaths reported by students on that diet.

Master Ni: While we are discussing diets, I want to point out how the art of cooking reflects the depth of a culture. Chinese love to enjoy a wide variety of dishes. They eat meat with lots of vegetables. The cooking art is so refined that you may not even know what type of meat you are eating. If the food is a little too oily, they drink tea after the meal to take away the grease. Chinese tea is the best in the world for people who eat too much meat, because it helps them metabolize it. However, it is better still to eat less meat and drink less tea.

Also, when you are eating, do not accept any disturbance in your environment. If you are disturbed while eating, your stomach cannot do a good job. The Chinese have a saying that when you are eating, you are the same as a king, even if you are a beggar. No one has the right to disturb you, so do not disturb anyone else who is eating, either. This does not mean, however, that you can be hard with someone who has disturbed you; no long scoldings are necessary. If they are ignorant, do not complain.

About diet, people are so thirsty for truth that they will try anything that comes along. I had two women come to me who were both vegetarians and they both were suffering from malnutrition! That type of diet can be incomplete; you must be reasonable about everything. As a doctor I recommended to a pregnant woman who was on a vegetarian raw food diet to add some meat and bone broth to her meals. She refused the advice and years later wrote back to say that her daughter's leg bones were born misshapen and weak.   The child had to go through much therapy to strengthen itself. I wish her luck.

Your desire for truth is noble and loveable, but you must watch yourself closely. If something is not working for you, then abandon it before it gets too serious.

I would like to tell you the source of the macrobiotic diet. Monks and nuns in China who followed Zen Buddhism used this diet. The purpose of this diet is for self-control, especially for modern people who are over-nourished. Those people who have something to give up from their bodies might seriously consider using this diet for a short period of time. I have so many patients, men and women, who follow this diet, or run restaurants or centers based upon this diet. Some even publish magazines about it. When applied to the right case, I support it.

As a broad practice, I support a balanced diet which contains a little bit of everything. The principle of balance includes such things as good manners and not overeating or eating too little, in addition to following the dietary suggestions.   However, when you are losing weight or giving up something from your body, you can follow the macrobiotic diet with flexibility for a time. Then, keep your food intake at the levels suggested by the macrobiotics, but do not stick strictly to the categories of yin and yang, because those divisions are not absolute.

The macrobiotic diet also recommends avoiding tropical fruit. This recommendation is also not absolute. Papayas, for example, are healthy food for stomach conditions. When I visit southern lands, such as Mexico or Indonesia, I just buy and eat papayas, and do not eat the local food which might easily cause dysentery on a short trip because your body does not have time to adapt to local conditions. Pineapple is also good for digestion, if not overeaten, but if you have an acidic stomach, avoid it. Banana is a popular food in Japan. After a meal, upper class Japanese people eat a piece of banana. Banana can serve as part of a meal, but cannot replace an entire meal, unless you are a monkey.

Other kinds of valuable tropical fruits are known to Westerners such as dragon eyes, lychee, and many others. Mango is tasty. Mangoes with green skins that turn yellow when ripe are better than the bigger ones with green and red skins. Sensitive people may have a reaction of coughing when they eat mangoes. When I visited Thailand, I was served Western food, and the thing I enjoyed most was the dessert, which was mangoes sliced with glutinous rice. After several meals, I ordered it for each meal as my main dish. "Heaven" can be experienced by eating mango with sweet rice! However, trouble can be caused by overeating it, or overeating anything.

For people who wonder what to eat to improve the condition of their ordinary lives, here is a list organized by one of the helpers who prepared food for us:

"For people who want to begin to improve their diet without studying much, it can be a helpful general guideline to eat a balanced diet of approximately 40% grains and beans, 10% meat and fish, and 50% fruit and vegetables. Eat fresh food wherever possible and avoid processed foods such as sugar, canned foods, etc. Eat foods that are in season, such as light cooling foods in the summer and heavy warming foods in the winter.

"Avoid eating anything to extreme. This includes cold or hot foods any time of the year (cool and warm is all right but room temperature is best) and too much of any one thing at any time. Diet is individual according to health, physical constitution, geographical location and the type of work you do, so it is often helpful to learn some nutritional knowledge from books about healthy diet. These are some general guidelines which I learned from Master Ni."

Cooking is a beautiful art that I recommend to everyone. Food is important to life, and the proper meals make a big difference, even in how much a person enjoys each day and how well a person can perform in one's job.

For those of you ready to study more about food, I recommend my son Mao's book, *The Tao of Nutrition.*

Pregnant women or people feeding children need to plan the food to supply the right amount of everything to meet the needs of the young lives. There need not be any overly strict restraints. Another one of my principles is that when I am home, I eat clean and simple food and usually the way of cooking or preparing the food is also simple. When I'm traveling, I eat whatever is available in restaurants, I am not too picky. I have tasted MacDonalds, Kentucky Fried Chicken and Burger King. I do not recommend them, but when you are traveling there is not always much choice. I have also eaten many different types of food which high class American people are afraid of, including different levels of Chinese or Asian food from different countries. It is life. In life, sometimes you enjoy variety. If possible, choose the things which can best serve your life, but do not let your life serve those things. Eat and enjoy food, but do not let the food eat you. This principle still does not digress from my practice of a balanced diet, because if you eat clean food at home most of the time, your body can afford to eat a little bit of complicated or different food in other circumstances. If you are a person who already eats a lot of junk food, I recommend you spend from six months to three years on a macrobiotic or other cleansing diet. Or you might follow the simple list given by my helper.

Q: Would you discuss the mental images that come to us in our self-release?

Master Ni: Do not pay too much attention to them. Anything can happen in this kind of class, from the lowest emotional outburst to the highest experience of unity consciousness. The first step is the release of bad energy, so just let the images go.

Q: You mentioned divine selection. What is that?

Master Ni: Just as only certain animals and certain seeds survive a harsh winter, only certain immortal beings can retain their spiritual essence and survive the calamities of this worldly life.

Q: What is that spiritual essence?

Master Ni: It is a type of energy. People have different types of energy. You see, when most people die, they release a kind of heavy, worldly energy which is like the smoke given off after a piece of wood is all burned up. It sinks or eventually just disperses. However, when a Heavenly person dies, something different happens because his energy is the essential energy of the universe. The essence that a shien accumulates is the central energy of the universe and that is never lost. That person will rise. I am telling you this so that you understand that what you are and what happens to you is a matter of energy.

Divine selection is impersonal and impartial. In other words, the selection is made according to what kind of energy is contained in your body. Divine energy only responds to divine energy. It never considers a person's race or nationality - all nations are equally pure and equally corrupt! The difference between people is not their race, it is their energy. If you are a person of essential energy, you will be everlasting. If not, you will eventually disperse or sink. You have the capability to choose what kind of person you will be.

Q: *My experience is that my energy is always changing, always different. It seems hard to keep it constant.*

Master Ni: Keeping one's energy constant is not easy. Each of us needs to fight our own battles in order to develop internally and externally. Now I would like to tell you a story.

There was a young man whose family was in the profession of exorcism. Being an exorcist means chasing away ghosts or evil spirits. This family was quite popular and trusted as being powerful. As the father became older, the son slowly began to take his place and do all his father's work. One night, he came back after having given some service, happy about his success. The sick people recovered from an illness rapidly because he had been able to send away the evil spirits causing the disease, so he was treated by the patient's family with a good meal and wine and was walking home. At that time, in the countryside, people walked from place to place. On his way home on that dark night, because of his happy mood, he hummed some songs as he walked. After he had covered a certain distance, he felt an urgency in his bladder. It was a dark night, and there were no homes on this section of the road, so he just went over to the side of the road. He untied his trousers and started to release his tension. Then, suddenly, he felt a small stone hit him so he looked over the fence at somebody's vegetable garden. He saw a ghost with a head as big as a pumpkin, and another ghost with a small head and a big body. He hurried up and finished what he was doing, and then he started to use the invocations and postures he had learned to do something about the ghosts. At the same time, he started to walk away. It seemed that the exorcism technique his father taught him was of no use in that situation. The small group of ghosts followed and began to chase him; they would not let him go. After he tried the Tibetan mantra to make the ghosts go away, he had finished trying all the things he had learned, to no avail. By this time, he was really nervous and began to run, but the ghosts who followed were getting closer and closer. Finally, he started to yell, "Mother!" Then, the ghosts all disappeared.

Some time later, there was a big festival in town. He was in charge of performing the main role, which was to lead the spiritual ritual in front of the big abundant offering table. His performance attracted all the people to watch him, and he did well, so he felt happy. After the ceremony, someone approached him. It was one of his friends, who had a strange look on his face and said to him, "You know, the incantations and the magic power do not work to drive away the evil spirits." He paused a moment, then he continued, "And the Tibetan mantra does not work either." He paused again. Then he said, "Only calling 'Mother' really works." Then, the man suddenly understood that his friend had played a trick on him. Angrily, he grabbed him by the collar and held him up, wishing to punish him for the joke, but then he looked him in the eye and said, "Different type of ghost, different type of remedy." Then he put his friend down, and the two men laughed heartily.

In ancient times, the undeveloped majority accepted externalized religion. They believed that bad luck, troubles and problems of all kinds were related to evil spirits. Folk Taoism does not teach people to admit their own mistakes and bring about improvement by self-inspection, self-discipline and self-cultivation. Thus, chasing evil spirits became a professional service and business of the folk religion.

Dear friend, when you have fear, "mother" is the most powerful remedy. In all situations, she can chase away bad people and ghosts, too. By the way, in the last class, I recommended that you use the invocation from the *Workbook for Spiritual Development.* If that does not work, please just call your mom. This is the highest power. This great power is why the ancient wise ones developed the religion of the mother. I mean, the teaching of the universal mother, which is Tao, the source of all power.

Motherly energy is the strongest energy in the world. The lowly chicken gives us a strong example of that. In the countryside by my home in China, the hawks were always soaring over the sky. When a hawk saw a young chick on the ground, it would fly down to charge the little creatures and try to seize it with their sharp claws. When they did that, however, the mother hen would immediately run over to put the chick under her wing and fight the hawk. I respect this type of courage, even coming from a mother hen. The hen's motherly protection of all her youngsters is greatly impressive and unforgettable.

Good night. May the universal motherly energy protect you all.

February 17, 1978

A Simple History of Spiritual Teaching

I

It has always been interesting to me that the study of history can give a person some unique insight into his or her own nature. For example, the fundamentals of human life are all similar to what happened to ancient Chinese people. All people's experience is relevant to each other. Surely, the spiritual achievement of ancient people belongs to all people. I would like to take this opportunity to give you some important historical knowledge which relates to the learning of spiritual truth.

Since you have become my friends by taking this class, what I can share with you is the long-existing spirit of universal life. I have done this by giving you a few examples of the lives of some illustrious human beings. The universe lives outside of each one of us and the universe lives inside each of us. The universe is our life; our life is the universal life.

The history of people is sometimes the history of spiritual reality. There are two ways to define history. One is to consider it a continuous record of social activity. The other way is to record the good and bad times of people. During the good times, there are competent leaders, and people have more awareness and can manage their businesses and lives well. This produces good results. During bad times there are lousy, irresponsible leaders who create more problems and guide one group of people to suppress another group of people. This produces misfortune for everyone.

"Tao" means "the Way." Therefore, the Way is synonymous with history when human nature expresses normalcy, harmony and balance. This happens when people manage their own lives and the social relationship among all people meets that standard. Thus, the Way is the history of life.

When the Way prevails, there are good times. When the Way is absent, it is because the way of spiritual harmony and balance has been obstructed by over-ambitious people, poor leaders, and a misleading culture. During those times, history is interrupted. By this I mean, the health of human society is interrupted.

You might ask if the so-called bad times with bad leaders, etc. are just the yin side of Tao or spiritual energy. You might also wonder how there can be something that is not Tao. Well, anything either excessively positive or excessively negative, just as described here, is yin and yang. If one side suppresses the other side, bad times are caused. Tao, or the Integral Truth, means balance. Too much yin or too much yang does not represent Tao as symbolized by the Tai Chi diagram in which yin and yang fulfill their proper functions. At the same time as yin embraces yang, yang embraces yin with symmetry, equilibrium, mutual assistance and co-existence. Above all, a great time in history or life expresses cooperation.

In general, modern people consider those who were born a long time before them as primitive. We like to describe ourselves as civilized people. Generally people define civilization as having modern tools, such as a cigarette lighter in one's pocket. To me, turning one piece of wood around and around on another piece of wood to produce sparks and make fire is also civilization. It is just a different type of civilization.

A long time ago, at least several million years ago, people were civilized, but their civilization was different from modern civilization. Practically speaking, civilization can be defined as a way of earning a living and of living life. In modern times, we have made lots of technological progress, thus we call ourselves civilized. However, the basic shape of civilization also resided in the minds of ancient people whom we describe as externally primitive. You might agree with me in saying that ancient people had their own culture. They were not uncivilized. Although ancient people did not have the same cultural forms and customs we have now, they had the Way. The Way is the culture of the integral way of life.

You might ask me, what is culture? Culture is a complicated thing to describe because it has become conceptualized and segmented. I do not consider myself a scholar of external culture, but rather a student and a teacher of internal culture, of the integral truth.

The true way of life is not as complicated as external culture. Internal or integral culture arises when one person recognizes the privilege of another. Culture started when people began to recognize the natural rights of others. When this essence of culture is expressed, it is the Way. At any time in history, when this essence is lost, there is no true way, and also there is no true culture. Even the word the Way carries the meaning of the essence of culture. In ancient times, when there was not much superficial culture, the essence of recognizing another person's privilege still existed. Even before any sage was born, the essence of culture, which is called the Way, already existed.

How, then, can modern people say that ancient people had no culture? Even though people today have many types of religion, if you look at the facts, you will see that this religious culture is false. The teaching and existence of religions are also false. By this I mean, they are superficial, they are not the real essence of culture. They are external rather than internal and active within people's hearts.

Please allow me to repeat what real culture is: a person who is strong physically, socially or intellectually, recognizes the human rights of another who is not strong in anything. This person recognizes other people's right to live and considers their natural rights and privileges to be the same as those of the strongest people. That is true culture. That is the true teaching.

False religions use the concept of an overpowering god to try to tame people's behavior. However, this is not what spiritual learning and spiritual teaching are all about. The true teaching comes from the spiritual vision produced by sages from inside their life. Then this vision is described externally through writing or teaching, etc. This is truthful spiritual teaching.

If I have any pride at all, I am proud of the heritage of this tradition, which is the essence of culture. Spiritual culture has been brewed through millions of human lives, although not everyone and not every generation has followed it. It is okay that they did not, they are just different.

When spiritual awareness grows inside of you and you consider yourself a complete being, a whole person with all three aspects, physical, spiritual and mental, that is enough. That is enough to prove that the essence of culture exists within you and within me. Sometimes I say that the history of spiritual truth never dies. Even if there were only one person alive in the entire world, that person would still contain the potential for spiritual awareness within the physical body.

Religious Taoism does not carry the original spirit of the Subtle Source. During the Chin (248-207 B.C.) and Han dynasties (205 B.C.-219 A.D.), many people considered themselves to be the so-called "Scholars of Formulas." They declared that they had special formulas to do all kinds of things, such as treat people for sickness and help people live longer or become immortal. Although some of the Scholars of Formulas may have achieved themselves spiritually and carried the essence of the ancient culture, most of what they promoted or taught was different. Their teachings encouraged people to develop in a different direction from the basic recognition and promotion of human harmony.

The original spirit of the True Way is my personal tradition. I am not a religious Taoist whose only interest is personal benefit like the Scholars of Formulas. I am a person of the True Way who continues the ancient public spirit through making spiritual practice and Chinese medicine available to serve individual lives. The main thing I have to share with you, particularly in this class, is the essence of spiritual truth. Spirituality is the essence of all culture.

Religious Taoism first appeared at the end of the Han Dynasty (184 A.D), but the history of folk Taoism is comparatively much shorter than the pre-existing teaching of the Integral Way. History books only contain the activity of the masses of people. The history of the True Way is different than what the masses do, so it is not in most history books.

It is too long to be counted in years. Now, I would like to give you an outline of the history of the True Way.

History is a trace of the past. That is one way to describe the thick books written by historians. The knowledge that those thick books contain, however, is a narrow view of history. Fu Shi, Shen Nung, the Yellow Emperor, Niao, Shun and Lao Tzu were individuals who were the living history of spiritual achievement. I am the history of the True Way, too, and so are all people who live this eternal truth. They are the living spirit of the history of the True Way. What can be known about the depth of their lives is different from what history books describe, which is only skin deep.

Modern history digs in the ground to find the relics of the past. In China, historians and archaeologists keep digging and digging. I think their greatest achievement was to find the relics of a culture that is probably only around 3,500 to 4,000 years old. Records exist of the times before that, but since they did not dig up anything from before 4,000 years ago, modern historians have reservations about trusting any written historical records from before 2000 B.C.

As a spiritual student, I selectively trust the written histories of ancient times. The history of the True Way can be found inside of me and others who confirm this spirit of living. The True Way has been on Earth many millions of years; different people have discovered the True Way and carried the spirit of life in all times and all parts of the Earth through a long, long journey. Internally, I trust and believe the descriptions in the old records about the True Way because of the deep and profound knowledge I have of my own existence. There was no proof in the diggings that the spirit of the True Way existed and was experienced by people over the centuries. That is something that modern people cannot dig out of the ground. There are some records of the history of the True Way, but modern writers tend not to address them. In this period, Chinese scholars are busy making everything fit the frame of communism, which kills the natural truth. Fortunately, whether it is recorded or not, the Way and human life continue the true history, which is not limited to what people have recorded, written or created. Those recorded, written or created things are not the only things that count. Life is not a creation of modern people.

The True Way serves individual health in all aspects. At first, the True Way was recognized as the health of a society by the earliest people. People respected themselves as well as other people. The ancients saw that the True Way or the health of society is human social conscience. Later, governments and laws were structured in a way that differed from the natural social conscience of ancient society. The True Way is the foundation upon which the development of government, jurisdiction systems and religions are or were built, yet the True Way itself is much purer and cleaner than any of its creations.

I enjoy embracing the True Way as some of you do, too. The True Way reaches back millions of years and can even be traced to the beginning of the universe. With the True Way, ahead of us we can also see the boundless, far-reaching future.

II

Let's go back to the time in China which was recorded in ancient records that existed long before the time of artifacts found by digging. At the origin of time, Pang Gu was the first being. No dates can be given for his life. He was believed to be the first authority in the world.

After Pang Gu came the Emperor of Heaven, the Emperor of Earth and the Emperor of People, as they were called. It is also impossible to give dates for their reigns. It took a long time to recognize those imaged authorities of ancient human society in China.

In the earliest times, only god-people lived on earth. The fulfillment of life's obligation at that time was much simpler, of course. There was not much to be done. Then human history came to a new epoch, the time of Jui Ren Ssi. No date can be given for him, either. He was the man who discovered and used fire to cook food. For his contribution and virtue, in the Chinese way of thinking, he was recognized as the emperor. The people called him "Ti." Ti means center of society. He was considered the symbolic

center of society because of his contribution in making use
of fire. It took a long time in human history for the use of
fire to develop. Jui Ren Ssi represents the epoch of the use
of fire as well as the human who first used it. This particular epoch lasted a long time; it is not sure how long.

Then came the epoch represented by the man Ur Tzai
Ssi who built a nest or house instead of living in a cave.
This was called the epoch of housing. It, too, lasted a long
time, but there are no exact dates.

During all these epochs, natural disasters may have
happened, but there was never any indication that any
artificial disaster such as war was created by people. You
might think this was because people were less developed or
because they did not have the capability to make trouble.
People make trouble when they have external or internal
pressures, and few such pressures existed during those
early times. External pressures can be even stronger than
internal ones, but stress was not a problem of early human
society, nor were there demands to create religion for the
pacification of the mind. Religion happened much later, so
people just lived naturally and peacefully in the early times.

Then came a new epoch, the time of the famous Fu Shi,
who was successful in developing faster breeding cattle and
a superior quality of stock. There are still no accurate dates
available to describe this time. Fu Shi also developed the
system known as the *I Ching*. During this stage, ancient
natural intelligence reached its maturity. That intelligence
was the first harvest of real spiritual culture.

Fu Shi was naturally recognized by the people as the
symbolic center of society. After him came Shen Nung, who
lived from 3218 - 3078 B.C., and reigned for up to 140
years. Shen Nung, the initiator of agricultural life, wa also
recognized as a natural center of society.

Both Fu Shi's *I Ching* and Shen Nung's study of herbs
were important contributions to Chinese culture. Their
contributions to human society were natural, like the
blossoming of a flower. Their achievements came from
natural inspiration rather than artificial human creation.
Their contributions laid a strong foundation for the True
Way, which is different from religious or folk Taoism, which

believes that worship brings blessings in life. Folk Taoism and the belief in worship came much later.

After Shen Nung passed away, seven of his descendants or connections held the role of center of society, one after another. All of them together could be considered "the period of Shen Nung" covering a time span from approximately 3078-2677 B.C.

III

Then society took another step forward. Following the epoch which was called the time of Shen Nung came the time of the Yellow Emperor (reign 2678-2578 B.C.). The Yellow Emperor invented and designed clothing. Wearing clothing was a big step forward from wearing leaves in Summer and fur in Winter. The Yellow Emperor developed clothing after stopping the aggression of the nine cannibal tribes. In fact, the Yellow Emperor developed a whole new culture. He is considered the father of Chinese culture, because during his long life he was always a student. He went to visit many places in the mountains and wilderness and gathered the achievements of ancient times and created a new culture. In other words, he gathered the teaching of spiritual truth. In my work, I use the phrases "Integral Way" or "spiritual reality" etc. to distinguish real spiritual learning from folk or religious Taoism.

The learning that the Yellow Emperor gathered from the developed ones is of such practical value that it can benefit people of all times and all places. This timeless kind of knowledge and methods is what makes up the learning of spiritual reality. The Yellow Emperor was a diligent student. He continued Fu Shi's contribution of the *I Ching*, Shen Nung's herb book and other relevant materials, as well as producing a book about medicine called *The Yellow Emperor's Classic of Internal Medicine*.

During the time of the Yellow Emperor, many naturally achieved people existed on Earth. At that time, emperors were teachers or people who served other people. By teaching and serving people, they naturally gathered authority or recognition; their support or strength was not created by force. There were no people with great ambition trying to create something that did not really benefit their normal, good lives. By this I mean, there were no contests for authority or power such as kings, emperors, lords or generals fighting with each other.

There are one or two pictures of some of the Yellow Emperor's descendants still existing which show how they treated people's diseases and taught meditation as great servants and teachers of the people.

IV

Then came a special time which lasted through the time of Emperors Niao (reign 2357-2258 B.C.) and Shun (reign 2257-2208 B.C.). and continued through the time of the Great Yu (reign 2205-2197 B.C.). A deluge in China started during the time of Niao. The trouble got bigger and bigger. The Great Yu's father failed to solve the problem; he was eventually killed by lightning, so Yu was assigned to remedy the great flood. Yu and his large group of people were eventually successful in fighting the flood by digging canals to carry the water to the ocean. The Yellow River and other waterways were partly the achievement of manpower and partly formed by the powerful water flow through years. That original engineering work was done by those developed ancient people around 4,000 years ago.

At the time of the great flood, the Great Yu opened the Yellow River at a place called the Dragon Gate. Even with today's modern engineering, we could not imagine such a large task done without modern engineering, and he had only a few bare handed people to help him. If they were not god-people, how could they have accomplished such a great job? At the very least, it was unimaginably hard work.

After Yu achieved guiding the water into the sea, Shun gave him the position of emperor. This was similar to what emperor Niao did when he chose Shun to succeed him after recognizing Shun's capability and virtue. During these generations, the transfer of power was not accomplished by force or by personal preference, but by wise choice made upon the successor's virtue, capability and social merit. When Shun's reign was finished, Shun gave the position of emperor to Yu. Yu, in his later years, wished to give the throne to "I" (pronounced "ee"). After more than 116 years of fighting the water, he could no longer walk gracefully.

From the time of the Yellow Emperor until Yu, each emperor benefitted from the collection of knowledge gathered by the Yellow Emperor. They all achieved longevity and lived to be over 120 years old. Yu passed the position of emperor down to "I", who wrote a book called *The Book of Mountains and Seas* which consisted of the record he made following Yu as he traveled everywhere battling the flood. "I" saw different people, or just different types of beings, and recorded them in the book. At that time, the physical appearances of people or level of their evolution was not unified or similar. However, that book describes a totally different life experience than what we have now; the world and all its people have changed. Most scholars have reservations about the descriptions in that book, so in China, sometime we use that name, *The Book of Mountains and Seas*, to say that a person is talking nonsense. However, truthfully, that description of talking nonsense would more accurately describe people's own limited experience than the material in the book written by "I".

Yu wished "I" to be the next emperor; however, this met with resistance, because the people had developed a preference for Yu's son, Chi. Most people wished to follow Chi, the son of Yu, instead "I." And so they followed Chi. This started the custom of family inheritance in the political sense. Thus, Chi started the Shia dynasty, which lasted from 2207-1767 B.C. This dynasty lasted for 440 years, until Jiu, (reign 1818-1767 B.C.), the last emperor of Shia, could not maintain himself as a moral symbol for other people to follow, so he was abolished.

Then, a new dynasty started called the Sharng Dynasty (1766-1121 B.C.). It was started by Tang, who abolished the last, corrupt emperor of Shia. Tang dared not take the position for himself because he wished to avoid people's suspicion that he might have done this for his ambition. However, after more than 50 years, because there was no other person who was suitable to fill that position, he reluctantly accepted to be the new moral symbol of society. Thus, the Sharng Dynasty was started. It continued until

1154 B.C. with the enthronement of a new emperor. The last generation of the dynasty was the infamous corrupt emperor Jow (1154-1122 B.C.).

Emperor Jow was overconfident. He destroyed all the competent advisors appointed to help him by his father. Jow believed that he was smarter than all of them, but he was not. His reign was characterized by cruelty and ineptness. At this time, King Wen, one of the feudal princes, had a better reputation than Jow, and he quietly and naturally began to form a new social force against Jow's leadership. The revolution was eventually completed by his son, King Wu, and thus the Chou Dynasty began in 1121 B.C. At the end of the Chou dynasty came what we call The Warring Period from 722-256 B.C. During this time, again the central symbol of social morality could not function as expected, and rivalry for rulership started. The result of this rivalry, which lasted from 722 to 256 B.C., was a new, unified empire composed of all the feudal kingdoms together. The winner was the young emperor of Chin. Now the world as the people knew it was called China, the name obviously being derived from Chin.

Before the development of "China," there were many regional leaders of small areas and local societies. The regional leaders had always elected or recognized an emperor as the symbolic leader of the entire region of "China," but who did not actually control the territory. Now the young emperor of Chin had established his rule over the entire territory by a different way: military advantage.

By the way, the emperor of Chin was the one whose tomb was surrounded by several thousand life-size stone statues of his soldiers and horses. He is also the emperor who made China's culture known to the Arab tribes, who then brought Chinese culture to the West. Techniques of weaving, chemistry, etc., all went from China through the Arabic people to the West.

The period of intense rivalry just before the Emperor of Chin became leader of China was one of the worst times in Chinese history. It was called the Period of Spring and Autumn (started 722 B.C.), and the Period of Warring Kingdoms (beginning 402 B.C.). At this time, the rulers of the small regions used many inhumane controlling measures, systems and customs to try to consolidate and strengthen their rule. One such custom was that upon the death of a king, all his servants, concubines, wives, etc., were buried alive in the tomb with him. Certainly, they did their best to keep him alive and healthy!

During that dark time in human history, the ancient teaching was preserved and passed down through a few individuals to have an impact on future generations. For the benefit of the people of the future, some teachings were written down with the purpose of preserving them. This was how the most ancient books were produced. This new dark age presents a drastic challenge which these teachings meet through their elucidation of spiritual reality. All the sages, from Mo Tzu to Confucius to Lao Tzu and others gave teachings which were relevant to the dark time. Despite the restrictions upon writing which existed even in his day, Lao Tzu presented the deep essence of spiritual reality. However, despite the influences of the sages, people of ancient times and their descendants in modern times slowly became more self-centered. They turned away from the teachings and the original nature of humankind. They began to kill other forms of life in order to maintain and nourish their bodies. They learned that through war and force they could get whatever they thought they wanted, thus they extended themselves further into the physical sphere of the world.

The success of the first emperor of Chin (reign 248-207 B.C.) came about through force and cruelty. His new system of making laws abandoned the originally respected humanistic approach. Instead, a unified and cruel discipline was adopted, similar to what the hard-liners of today's Chinese communists proclaim; they inherited the spirit of that ancient school of ruling with cruel law. They believe this is the way to achieve social order, but they forget how a society makes progress.

The first emperor of Chin punished both his soldiers and the people strongly. Terror was how he finally unified the whole area. To consolidate his rule, he no longer recognized local feudal leaders, but appointed his own leaders for each region so that all magistrates, governors and mayors were under his control.

This type of absolute control was also a dream of the modern Chinese communist leader, Mao Tse Tung. He wished to do the same thing and enjoy the same kind of swollen personal glory.

In ancient times, until the later Han Dynasty around 200 A.D., spiritual law was a culture, a popularly recognized humanistic way of rule among all people.

After the emperor of Chin fulfilled his personal desire for control of the entire territory, he started to fear his own death. He forced many people into labor camps to build the Great Wall to protect his immortal safety on the throne. His personal search for immortality also commenced a search by the emperor to discover the activities of the so-called "Scholars of Formulas," who were one type of achieved one who had specific knowledge and skills.

The emperor of Chin adopted one formula that he learned from the Scholars of Formulas. He had heard that on one of the mountain islands of the ocean, some immortal medicine could be found growing, so he sent a man with a fleet of ships over to the island. In the fleet were 500 teenage boys and 500 teenage girls, quantities of seeds of important grains, beans and crops, and farming tools, all as a gift exchange for the medicine of the immortals who lived on the islands. However, the leader and the 1000 boys and girls became the ancestors of Japan, or at least part of it. That is to say, they went to Japan and colonized it instead of returning with the immortal medicine. Thus, a side effect of Emperor Chin's search for immortal medicine was one of the biggest immigration of people, seeds and grains that had ever occurred up to that time, which was around 220 B.C. Practically, the leader of the fleet wished to escape from the emperor's evil control, so he never returned to China. I believe he is a typical achieved one. This was, perhaps, a gentle way to fight an evil dictator or tyrant.

The first emperor of China then tried another formula for immortality. He heard that Tai Mountain, now in Santong province, was a sacred place. In ancient times, all rulers paid homage to Tai Mountain as an act of respect for the higher powers and to confirm their position.   The Emperor of Chin went there and followed the proper ceremony, but on his way home, he died of disease.   Practically, he received death as the result of his pilgrimage; one could say that Heaven did not bless him.   However, it is not actually Heaven that bestows blessings.   You must understand that blessings are more internal than external, which means that only a person of internal worth will receive Heavenly blessings.   In other words, he did not have enough good internal energy to attract any Heavenly energy.

He died in his thirties.   His ministers dared not tell the soldiers that the Emperor died, so they carried lots of strong smelling dead fish in the carriage of the emperor all the way back to the capital in Chinan, which is now called Shi-An.   This was to disguise the smell of the emperor's decaying body.   Thus, his dream of immortality was not fulfilled, but that did not stop the activity of the Scholars of Formulas.

V

Soon after the short-lived Chin dynasty ended with the death of the Emperor of Chin in 209 B.C., the Han Dynasty began (206 B.C.-219 A.D.)   The Han government wisely adopted the teaching of the *Tao Teh Ching,* which clearly describes the government of a natural society.   It was a great time for China because of the spiritual type of society existing most predominantly under the rulership of Emperors Wen (reign 179-156 B.C.) and Jing (156-140 B. C.).

The natural type of social philosophy that was implemented only lasted until the fourth generation ruler of the Han Dynasty.   Practically, he was the sixth political authority because the first emperor was succeeded by his queen and another emperor was succeeded by his brother, so he was the fourth generation.   The young Emperor Wu had a similar type of personality as the first Emperor of Chin.   The young man liked boundless authority, and because the spiritual teachings did not promote strong or tyrannical leaders, he adopted the teaching of Confucius as the philosophy of his rule.   Confucius' philosophy considered the emperor the supreme authority.   Confucius also confirmed the position of the emperor as the Son of Heaven, a special person who had the same authority as Heaven itself and therefore could not be disobeyed. Emperor Wu liked military adventures and expeditions, and he took advantage of the strength built up by his father and his grandfather through policies which followed spiritual law and which had helped people become rich and abundant.

Emperor Wu's ambition was not only to be the singular authority under Heaven but, just like the emperor of Chin, he also wished to live forever. One formula he adopted was to sleep with many, many women. He also adopted another formula, which was to build a tall terrace. Above the terrace, he built a statue of a woman holding what looked like a serving platter to receive the sweet dew from the sky. Someone would collect the dew and blend it with the powder of jade. It was said that by eating this combination, he would never die. He died in his 70s, but I do not ridicule him, and let me tell you why. Several years before his death, he began to complain about the untruthfulness of all the formulas. He realized that they were untruthful for bringing about physical immortality. However, after his death, each of the women he slept with in his palace testified that Emperor Wu still came to sleep with her every night. Also, a government officer caught a thief who was selling one of the items which was buried with Emperor Wu. This aroused the suspicion of the government, who believed he was a grave robber, but there was no trace of the tomb having been disturbed. When asked where the man obtained the item, he said that one evening a man brought it to him and exchanged it for some wine. In disbelief, the interrogator asked the man to describe what the person looked like. The man described his approximate age, appearance and physical characteristics. Then he described a certain mole in the middle of his chin. This made the regency suddenly aware that it was the emperor himself who had given the object to the man. Thus, he gave orders to different cities to bring 500 beautiful young women into the palace as an important offering to the emperor who no longer lived in the human world. However, these women did not have the same experience as the other women who had previously slept with the emperor. After that, there was no further trace of Emperor Wu.

The statue of the fairy lady looked similar to the Statue of Liberty, only the torch was replaced by a plate. It was a great work of art. That was the first great statue in Chinese history up to that time. She existed until the time of Buddhism, which is a religion that worships statues as spiritual symbols. About 367 years after the statue was constructed, Emperor Ming of Wei (reign 227-240 A.D.), the grandson of the usurper Tsao Tsao (192-232 A.D.), decided to move his capital to Lo Yan in Hunan province, about 1,000 miles east of the old capital. He sent an army to tear down the terrace and bring the statue to the new capital for his own use. It was really amazing that when the soldiers went there, the sky darkened, a strong wind blew up and an intense sandstorm beat the soldiers and pushed them into hiding. Afterwards, when the sky restored its clarity, and the whole army went to move the statue, they all saw tears falling from the eyes of the huge stone fairy lady. You can imagine a stone statue so tall and so majestic that could respond to people spiritually. She had been erected like a human being with the spiritual effect given by the spiritually achieved ones who helped to erect her.

Rather than leave the statue where it was, these events only made the emperor more interested in moving her than before. It took many people and animals to move the statue because she was so big. However, on the way to the capital, she disappeared. Nobody knows where she went. Of course there was an investigation, but the case was suspended because nothing was found. I do not know whether there was a mystical power at work or not, but because the record describing the event was made by scholars and not religious people, it seems that it could be trusted.

VII

People seek immortality in many ways. A woman of the Han Dynasty successfully preserved her body by using pieces of jade which were made like clothes sewn together with golden threads. Her body was thus protected and did not decay for 2,000 years. However, I do not think that has any value in the search for immortality. A dead body may be treated in a way that makes it last for a long time, but it is still not alive. Energy has different levels and frequencies; levels such as the physical or semi-physical levels are not everlasting. Only spiritual energy, high spiritual energy, is everlasting or immortal. At the stage of high spiritual energy, individual personality is unimportant. Thus, true immortality is not suitable for people who are strongly attached to ego or individuality. Usually such people do not have the patience to live for even a moment without stimulation.

For those who are interested in true immortality, the dissipation of the ego can be attained step by step. Also, the sublimation or evolution of physical energy into high subtle energy is done the same way. Do you have enough patience to slow down your process of living so that you can live a long life? Almost all modern people like to speed up the ripeness of life, which also hastens one's death.

In my work, I have not only given external proof of immortality, I also give the steps. No one before me has ever given such a complete picture. I am not proud of my work, but I am proud of the truthful achievable process that I received and can now pass down to you through the kindness of the achieved ones in the divine realms. They have allowed me to be a freestyle student of immortality with modern intellectual attitudes. Testing and experimenting is important to my spiritual studies.

Immortality is not for everybody. For some people, it is unnecessary or useless. Chuang Tzu described a person who spent many years learning the art of butchering dragons, only to find out later that there was no opportunity to apply the skills he had learned, or even to teach it. No one was as impractical as he was. Similarly, immortality is impractical for some people.

Spiritual learning is not only physical. Physical proof or physical improvement may increase your confidence, but it does not tell you that you have an immortal spirit. If you have an immortal spirit, then you are not bothered about living with a mortal body. In searching for immortality, it is not learning and being able to perform different, segmented immortal arts that is important. What is important is learning the arts to help the immortal spirit. All of my books describe the aspects of both the immortal arts and the immortal spirit.

I do not recognize any single religion as the authority of the total truth, because spiritual truth can only be defined one way or another conceptually. If religious leaders taught the truth, I do not think their religions would still exist, because they would have no business to do. The teaching of truth is not like teaching with a frame; general teachings only sell different frames. The subtle truth of the universe is too big and too long to be covered or put into a book. Its length of time and profundity cannot be measured. The subtle truth can be described, yet it cannot be presented as a controllable substance. This is why it is called the Integral Truth or spiritual reality. The words "Integral Truth" are my interpretation; they are the trademark of my teaching.

I am a religious person, but not in the way most people use the word religious. I am not religious in the sense of going to church. I am religious in the sense of being devoted to what is important. I am religious in my Chinese medicinal practice and religious in my life. I do not do anything wrong to people. I have a religious attitude toward my own learning, study and teaching. If the word religious means faithful, upright and diligent, I'm religious. Those of you with a similar attitude are also religious. However, established religions are just like different doors or walls that separate are from the integrity of the universal spiritual unity. In themselves, they are not the truth.

VIII

Religious Taoism was encouraged and fueled by the ambition of the first Emperor of Chin and Emperor Wu of the Han Dynasty, but basically it began around the end of the Han Dynasty around 184 A.D. Following that time, the activity of religious Taoism increased.

At this time, I would like to mention something related to the teaching of spiritual truth. At the end of the Chou dynasty, the teachings of the developed ones began to be offered through personal teaching and written works. This was how Confucius, Mo Tzu, Lao Tzu, Chuang Tzu and their associates began to bring about a new heritage.

In my tradition, Fu Shi's *I Ching*, Shen Nung's herb book, *The Yellow Emperor's Classic of Internal Medicine* and his collection of spiritual teachings and practices, plus Lao Tzu's book and Chuang Tzu's book are the source of my teaching. These five books represent what I stand for because of their true achievement and their true practice. Any other selected books on spiritual teachings are auxiliary. The later teaching turns the order upside down, making the root as the branches and the branches as the main teaching for people. This is the important difference I have with other teachers.

Personally, I reject the history of the mass movement of folk Taoism. They may adopt an ancient teaching, but their desires, ambition and will twist the true teaching.

If you study the history of the True Way, you cannot exclude the time of the Tang Dynasty (618-906 A.D.) During the Tang Dynasty, there was a new generation of leaders and teachers such as Master Chahng Ku Lou, etc. who responded to a new stage of culture or society. They have my respect and appreciation for their truthful achievement. I choose them as my friends and teachers because they taught self-cultivation, but never had an interest in the religious activities developed by leaders or teachers whose ambition and ignorance surpassed their truthful achievement of anything.

This is the historical background of my teaching which offers a broad spiritual education to all people instead of the narrow Taoism of Chinese folk religion.

In the China of ancient times, people respected spiritual truth because it is eternal truth. Anyone who knows this truth can learn to embody it. I am sure that in later times also, people who believed in the art of immortality respected spiritual truth as the eternal truth, although people such as emperors, officials, generals and scholars were almost always beings of desire rather than beings of eternal truth.

The immortal arts practiced as the pursuit of personal desire had become the royal privilege of the emperor of later generations. I do not believe that those emperors achieved anything. Ironically, those teachings of immortal arts shortened the lives of the emperors, because those emperors and other men used the teachings wrongly. They used the external "immortal medicine" as a love potion for sexual conquest rather than using it to help their immortality. If people could become immortal by drinking love potions alone, I would find the formulas and be the first one to open a shop and sell some. However, immortality does not happen that way, and as a follower of the immortal truth I cannot make money from something that shortens people's lives. People even use hormones to prolong or increase their sexual pleasure, but these have side effects, because they are not a natural response of the body.

IX

So far, we have covered the Han Dynasty (265-419 A.D.), then the Three Kingdoms, the northern and southern Jing Dynasties (420-556 A.D.), and the short-lived southern Chen Dynasty (557-588 A.D.) The last Emperor of Chen left the heritage of a new musical styled poem-making for China. He was excellent at writing poems. Unfortunately, he also initiated the custom of women binding their feet. Then, the Sui Dynasty (589-617 A.D.) ended with the emperor being fond of extreme luxury and vain glory. During the Tang Dynasty (618-906 A.D.), each emperor died one after another, much more so than during any of the other dynasties. What happened was that many of the emperors died quickly after ingesting too much external medicine trying to achieve immortality. Also, after the Tang Dynasty, there were many more short-lived dynasties. All those small emperors were quickly forgotten. The only people from that time who have been remembered are the spiritual teachers such as Master Lu, Tung Ping and Master Chen Tuan, both of whom lived during this period. They are the people who were concerned about the spiritual, mental and physical health of people, and who became immortals themselves.

After the Tang Dynasty came a period of five short-lived dynasties. Then came the Sung Dynasty, (960-1279 A.D.), a dynasty which utilized the Taoist religion to help control and rule the people. The emperors of the Sung Dynasty seemed to have true interest in religious Taoism, such as Emperor Hui Chun (reign 1101-1126 A.D.) However, he was captured by the Mongolians because he was too devoted to personal enjoyment and religious Taoism and neglected the need for national defense.

Then came the Yuan Dynasty, which was the Mongolian control of China (1280-1367 A.D.). Emperors of the Yuan Dynasty, the descendants of Genghis Kahn, enjoyed the sexual practices recommended by so-called esoteric Buddhism, which is also the sexual practice of Indian tantra. Tantra was originally based upon or similar to old Chinese sexual practices. The Mongolian dynasty thus ended because of weakened mental and physical functioning of the emperors who participated in such practice.

Next was the Ming Dynasty (1368-1643 A.D.), during which the emperors were interested in immortal practices. They actually made a contribution toward continuing the Taoist religion by compiling the *Taoist Canon*, which is a collection of hundreds of Taoist or spiritual books. A collection had been made previously during the Tang Dynasty, but it was lost or scattered at the end of that dynasty. I have examined the *Taoist Canon* and other collections and have understood what is of true value and what is not. I have incorporated the true development of natural spiritual teaching from it into my work and given up the unimportant chaff of the grain.

After the Ming Dynasty, the Manchurian rulership of the Ching Dynasty began (1644-1911 A.D.). Tibetan Buddhism was appreciated by the Ching royalty for political reasons. One of the emperors, Yung Chen (reign 1713-1736 A.D.), came to be quite an authority on the teaching of Zhan (Zen) Buddhism.

Following the demise of the Ching Dynasty in 1911 A.D. came the rise of the Republic of China. After fighting the Sino-Japanese war (1937-1946 A.D.), the Chinese communists used their new ideology to replace the traditional truth of life. They totally destroyed the ancient achievements without understanding what they were about. Fortunately, the ancient achievements were not lost. My work continues the work of my father and brings the ancient spiritual books to public awareness, and this work will be continued by those who learn the important spiritual practices and the practices of immortal arts from our teaching. We share it with our friends so that millions of years of achievement is not lost or forgotten. I believe that the main value of my life is in this work.

X

In this outline of Chinese history, my real purpose is to tell you that there are leaders and people who follow spiritual law, and there are leaders and people who are against it. Spiritual balance is a subtle standard; especially, it is a spiritual standard of being upright, not headstrong, but responsible in taking care of all aspects of your life correctly and suitably. You must pay your debts and be kind to others. In short, you must not be a harmful person; you must be a harmless person. You might wonder how spiritual achievement can be so simple; you already know those things. Yes, spiritual practice is simple because spirituality is what you already know, but if you know it but do not practice it, then you need my kind of teaching. I use the opposite fact, such as the mistake of religions, to teach the simple truth; this is how and why I have so much to say. I talk about the mistakes and troubles of doing different practices. You know, it does not matter if you are powerful as a dynasty or powerful as an individual; if you are with spirit, meeting the spiritual reality, although you are not special, you shall enjoy a long and happy, prosperous life. Typically, to stay with the truth of spiritual reality is too simple for leaders and people who wish to be successful too quickly or who wish to selfishly enjoy things by themselves. They deny spiritual law. They do whatever is for their own benefit, profit and advantage.

You must know that spiritual law is not external control; following spiritual law is the Way. It is internal truth. When we make it a teaching, then it becomes gentle advice. If you do not listen to it, if you overtrust your own power and capability to make everything go as you wish, you will fail in the end. This has been proven over and over through thousands of years of history. We have seen this happen to many conquerors and aggressive people in society. Being aggressive does not mean making progress by your own effort, but taking advantage of other people. Such people must fail in the end.

Under Heaven, there is nothing that does not change. Each dynasty in Chinese history represents a change, not necessarily of good or bad, but before the mechanical civilization, people expected that each dynasty would last forever. Ordinary people had pure minds and spirits, and their lives were much simpler than ours are today, even with our modern equipment and scientific devices. We think that those early people were less developed than we, but it is not true. Some real sages lived among them; they were less developed externally but more developed internally. Even in harsh times, they still knew that the best way to live was to restore their original nature. A few people strive for spirituality while most of the world strives to be more physical. The sages, who have always been few in number, knew that the way of physical power is degrading and always brings about the downfall of humanity, unless at the same time, the person develops his spirit.

In the world, demanding, aggressive people only look for material success and powerful social influence. They wish to command others as though they were commanding the wind and rain. We have seen emperors, evil ministers and general individuals who are just like that. Nevertheless, if they do not follow the subtle law, they must fail and their descendants must suffer or become extinct.

My own life experience and activity and that of most of you has been mostly in this twentieth century. There is an opportunity for all of us to see a better time of the world, with a better physical life also. It is our personal experience that so many wars were fought, such as the revolution to dethrone the Ching Dynasty in 1911, the warlords stealing the fruit of the revolution (1911-1928 A.D.), the civil war between the national party and the communist party (1934-1938 A.D.), the Sino-Japanese War (1938-1945 A.D.) and the civil war again between the national party and the communists (1934-1938 and 1944-1949 A.D.). This is not to mention all the wars that happened abroad in the period before 1949, while I lived in China. All these wars show that aggressive and evil people are finally defeated or collapse by themselves. The reason that they are aggressive in the first place is because they do not believe that there is a subtle law. They believe success can be attained by adventure and taking risks. They do not believe the subtle law and the eternal truth. The Sino-Japanese war and the communist control caused much suffering for the Chinese people and greatly damaged the organic condition of society.

In witnessing the devastation of the war at the side of my mother and father, as a young boy I concluded that power was everything. I believed that power could correct the world; surely I meant physical, political and military power. My father and mother always calmed me down. They said to me, "Violence and aggressive forces cannot last. People of virtue always survive and outlive the evil. The subtle law is not seen by many people, but it is here and there, it is everywhere and in each generation. There is no time when the subtle law is not there." As I became experienced, I came to see that my parents were right, and I gave up the illusions of my youth.

Unfortunately, people do not see that spiritual victory and spiritual success is more fundamental than any short-lived prosperity that is gained by evil means. If you have spiritual success, you enjoy your fruit. When success is brought about in a healthy, correct way, it is really beneficial. Any fruit you might enjoy which is obtained by evil means is poison. I teach you this; although spiritual truth is simple and it is not welcomed, it is the most fundamental truth and practice of life. The other things I teach are valuable, but they are auxiliary to the basics of your life.

The fundamentals are immortal; by this I mean, they always exist and never change. Strange practices, in whatever aspect, are short-lived. Learning the foundation of spiritual practice is much more advanced than the spiritual development of unachieved people, and it is independent from the teachings of general religions.

There is one question: without the threat of a strong religious image, can the average person still be virtuous? If you are, you are already spiritual and you have attained spiritual independence. Intellectuals get rid of religion, because religions do not make any logical, rational sense. Communists get rid of religion because without the moral influence of religion in society, they are more free to harm others.

In teaching spiritual reality, we put religion beneath us so we can go higher and work for our own spiritual development. If you are not ready for spiritual development, it is right to go back to church and follow what they teach. If you are devoted to learning spiritual truth, I refer to religion as a stepping stone to higher achievement. Old spiritual customs of religious practice are used as tools of communication to teach the profound subtle truth to help your progress. The teaching of spiritual truth aims at helping your spiritual development instead of mentally and emotionally controlling you in the name of religion.

Although religions are artificial, they affect you when you accept them as your spiritual expression or discipline. The Bible is part of the history of a race and partly a dramatized social promotion. However, if you put your hand over the Bible, or any book or thing, and make a vow, you are spiritually responsible for the vow you take. The vow will produce a spiritual effect on your soul. It is important to understand that any external establishment that is recognized or accepted by you influences you. Therefore, do not take any vow or make any commitment such as marriage unless you think you will not break it, or both sides later agree to forsake the original vow at the same time. If you bear false witness, you shall definitely have spiritual punishment on your precious soul. The same is true of taking public office; you must faithfully fulfill your duty.

My question is, again, can you still be nice and good without the existence of God? Once you have achieved God or the godly level, there is no more God above you. At that time, you are totally responsible for whatever you do. Can you admit your mistakes and correct yourself? If you discover that you are making an unrighteous action, can you stop doing it and withdraw after you become aware of it? If you do, you save your soul. If you do not, you will hold your excuse or misunderstanding as truth, and you will lose your soul, at least in that particular action and matter. It is important to straighten one's own life before expecting to go higher; otherwise belief will be unrealistic.

In spiritual learning, you must be more realistic and serious than anything else, because spiritual awareness happens subtly. I am telling you the subtle truth of life because I wish all of you to make appropriate use of it.

To be a spiritual student of the broad way, your goal is your spiritual development. You can ignore the promotions and stories of religious teachings and the rigid patterns of thought and behavior of your social background. Believers of religion are attracted to the psychological help provided by the social programs. It is valuable to respect and understand the value of some social discipline, personal discipline, ethics and morality with universal value that is offered by religious and other teachings. Never give up your self-discipline and personal virtuous fulfillment.

We cannot turn away from teachings and disciplines of universal value, because they are the basics of a good life. Openness and selective receptiveness toward all truthful, helpful teachings is an important positive sign of your spiritual development.

Spiritual development is different from intellectual development. In intellectual learning, you can find intellectual equality with some other people, freely exercise your intellectual judgement, make comments and express your personal ideas. Realistically, a devoted student of spiritual learning cannot do this. For example, 2,600 years ago, Sakyamuni withdrew from competition with his uncle for the throne. He decided to look for spiritual development rather than become attached to a position of worldly authority. If you were him, and your virtue were equal to his, you could do the same thing he did. If your virtue were less than his, spiritually you would still be a student, and to you, he would still be one of the early teachers who set a good example for your development.

In Judaism, when Moses brought down the ten commandments, he narrowed God down to being one name. However, he put aside the fact that God is also all names.

He set up guidance for a society that values spiritual strength above worldly attainment. However, he put aside the teachings of the correct way of providing for your worldly needs to support your spiritual achievement. Today, we choose spiritual broadness instead of a racially or tribally oriented approach. That has been adjusted by some Christian churches. I hope all Christians understand that Biblical descriptions of spirituality are metaphoric rather than literal descriptions of the truth. Narrowness of understanding and rigidity in explanation bring more harm than good to the common people.

The development of the teaching of spiritual reality was different than the development of religious teachings. The ordinary level of religious understanding is promoted in the folk religion which is called Taoism, but this level of Taoism is basically for people who have not yet attained spiritual development. To be a spiritual student, it is valuable and helpful to have good understanding about the development of religions. Religious guidance is given in a particular way to help people who have not yet developed. Thus, religious teaching is similar to a Chinese mother who tells her child not to use his chopsticks or spoons to hit his bowl or plate because that displeases the God of the kitchen. Or when she tells her child not to stand in the threshold of a door because he will not grow tall if he stays there. You must understand that educating children or giving a religious teaching is on a different level than what is taught to a mature person. Religious teaching is also not the same teaching given by a policeman or the government; they directly forbid certain things. Thus, religion serves a certain stage of growth, but hopefully, people will grow beyond them.

When the Buddhist religion came to China, it was restructured by the remaining influences of ancient Chinese culture. The five important precepts of Buddhism are no killing, no stealing money, no sex, no lying and no drinking alcohol. However, for the people who could not meet that standard, it was lowered to be no violence, no robbing or stealing, no raping people, no lying and no overdrinking.

These five precepts may be accepted by all people for the basic dignity of human life.

I hope that everyone who learns from me and reads my books understands that the comments I make about other religions are meant to constructively guide you to accept a broad practice. It is better to forsake the undeveloped aspects of all the religions and take the deep essence of all of them, which is spiritual reality. It takes great understanding to filter through all the lesser teachings to be able to understand the greater teachings. All old spiritual teachings, including the essential teaching of religions, serve one level of life. The highest level is spiritual unity which can be found in the innermost room of your life being. This is the teaching of spiritual reality.

I do not agree that once you learn spiritual truth, you can kick off all the time-tested valuable ethics and morals of human beings. If you choose to misunderstand this, it is a serious mistake. I hope you do not misunderstand all my discussions which are objective commentaries. Your correct understanding of what I say reflects the reality of your spiritual development.

If you are highly developed spiritually, I shall have the same respect toward you and accept you just as I do Sakyamuni, Moses, Jesus, Mohammed, Confucius and Lao Tzu and all achieved sages. I will have no less respect toward your achievement.

In this class, I have offered you information and discussions as an introduction which may possibly lead to your internal transformation and sublimation. The fulfillment of your self-realization can only come from you. The achievement is your own; therefore, if it is your choice, you truthfully need to work on yourself. I will give further guidance and instruction on the topic of achievement in internal alchemy and other spiritual arts in many different forms such as lectures, classes, seminars, books and videotapes. Thus, all the information you need will be made available to you. Practically, you have already made a good start by reading this book, which contains discussions about all aspects of life which affect your internal transformation and sublimation.

Basically, internal alchemy is accomplished by just withdrawing from extra or unnecessary activities of life and bringing that energy to the spiritual centers. By following the principles we have discussed in these classes, you will be better able to observe your own external and internal changes, and guide yourself subtly to reach your destination. All true meditation is the art of internal alchemy. The material in all the books aims at providing a complete picture of individual spiritual cultivation, so the instruction will be complete.[1] Your success depends upon your taking advantage of these instructions so that you obtain the best service for progress and personal achievement.

---

[1]This book functions as an introduction to the other important work of Master Ni, such as *Life and Teachings of Two Immortals, Volume I and II* and *Mysticism.*

Concluding Instruction

Each human individual is a small model of God. More precisely, this means that each human individual contains the potential to be a god.

Each person has three origins: sexual, mental and spiritual. Let us first talk about the sexual origin. The positive practice of sexual energy brings about human offspring, while the negative practice of sexual energy is transformed into uncontrollable sexual desire with countless sexual relationships which can bring harm to oneself and other people. In the ancient practice of spiritual science, the first requirement for self-awareness is to return your sexual strength to the sexual center of your life. This means to only engage in correct practice and to avoid uncontrolled sexual expression.

The center higher than the sexual center is the origin of the mind. The positive practice of using the mind brings about creations along with life activities in governing and serving oneself or in governing and serving other people in a gentle and reasonable way. The negative expansion of the mind brings about creations which turn out to be overly possessive, aggressive or dominant; they tend to harm one's own life and the lives of other people.

The practice of how to use the mind is called "learning the effective use of the mind." The mind also contains the level of emotion, such as joy, anger, sorrow, fear, shock, etc. When one's emotions are a natural response to a situation, expressed in due amount with good control, they can be healthy. If one's emotions are overexpressed in an uncontrollable way, they can easily turn out to be negative, selfish expressions. Sick emotions cause a sick mind, and a sick mind causes sick emotions. Thus, in following the original spiritual practice, return your mental energy to your mind to stop negative expansion and apply the mind only to positive, healthy creations which serve yourself and others.

Higher than the level of the mind is the center of the spirit. The growth of the spirit is the result of development. Although people who follow a natural lifestyle without spiritual training or education can also develop spiritually, for them the convergence of energy which brings life will be scattered. Spiritual achievement and development need correct practices.

The positive practice of spiritual energy or origin brings about the responsible sense of a healthy life. The negative practice of spiritual energy or origin brings about the darkness of life. People who do not have correct spiritual development have undeveloped spiritual energy, which would correlate with the mind to extend in a negative direction. Without correct spiritual education, the mind will misunderstand the natural experiences of internal, personal spirits or will support external religion or will create self-deception. You think you are serving God, but practically you are serving your misshapen ego.

Negative expansion of spiritual energy applies that energy incorrectly and forms a religion which correlates with the ignorance of the mind. Such a person will form a rigid, stiff teaching based on an imaginary spiritual world which is far removed from true spiritual reality. Such religions are obstacles to unity between different races and tribes because of different customs and concepts. If you are not a religious teacher, negative spiritual energy affects you by misforming you spiritually.

Spiritual energy and mental energy are especially prone to being scattered because they are less stable than physical energy. In your lifetime, if you scatter your energy, you will have an ignorant mind and will not know the existence of spirit, so the valuable mental and spiritual energies will not be of any help to you.

Spiritual practice returns your spiritual energy to the center of your own life and applies it in the correct direction; it brings about spiritual unity without allowing incomplete understanding to create psychological traps in your life.

Now let us look at these three origins of an individual in a slightly different way. We can line up the three practices as follows:

1. To return your overexpansive sexual energy to the sexual origin of your life being.

2. To return the overexpansive mental energy to the natural mind of your divine being.

3. To return your overexpansive religious ignorance, or misunderstanding of superstitious, unreasonable and partial beliefs to the pure spiritual center of your divine being.

The symbol for an energy field is ⊕ or 田 and is pronounced "dien."

The symbol for the origin of sexual energy is 由 or ⊕ and is pronounced "yu."

The symbol for the origin of one's mentality is 申 or ⊕ and is pronounced "shen."

The symbol for the origin of spiritual energy is 甲 or ⊕ and is pronounced "chia."

The symbol for immortal medicine is 丹 which is the integration of the two energies of yin and yang: 日 (sun) for yang and 月 (moon) for yin, which can be within oneself or within nature. The two energies of yin and yang are the integration of spiritual energy and sexual energy.

丹 is pronounced "tan"

日 is pronounced "erh"

月 is pronounced "yeh"

All three origins come from one origin. That origin is the formless, subtle origin:

By its nature, spiritual energy always moves upward. Because it moves away from the Earth, if it is too strong, it can easily cause divorce with worldly life. Thus, spiritual energy needs to be guided and conducted to descend to help the mind restrain the sexual center. The spiritual energy of a human being tends to move upward like 由 . In a good life, it is required to move downward to meet the mind, thus 甲 is the symbol. In other words, you keep the spiritual energy on the Earth by doing a useful job in the world and using that to discipline your sexual energy. This is how the symbol was determined.

By its nature, sexual energy tends to move lower. Because it moves away from Heaven or the spiritual center, it can easily cause divorce from the Heavenly spiritual energy. Thus, by its nature, it is like 圹 . In a good life, sexual energy needs to be guided and conducted to ascend to help the mind meet the spiritual energy. In other words, you keep the sexual energy from sinking into the earth and offer yourself to do a helpful job for the world, thereby disciplining your spiritual energy. Thus, the symbol of sexual energy is 由 .

Mental energy has its own tendency. It tends toward horizontal expansion, such as name, position, too much intellectual stimulation, influence over fellow people and the desire for possession of many things. Because it moves outward and away from the body, it can easily cause divorce from the sexual and spiritual energies, and from the body itself. By its nature, it is like this 刕 .

A different situation would cause the mental energy to become partial to the upward moving spiritual energy and thus enhances the spiritual energy, causing the further partiality of spiritual energy to become like 由 . Another situation would cause the mental energy to become partial to the downward moving sexual energy and enhances the sexual energy, causing the further partiality to sexual energy to become like 圹 . These situations would cause either the upward motion or the downward motion to become too strong, and would bring about an imbalance to the person.

Thus, mental energy is highly responsible for the well-being of one's life, because its job is to reach both above and below to connect the three partners. The mental energy brings about the enjoyment of unity of life. Its correct function should be like this 冉 . This is the meaning of the three energies represented by the three symbols.

Basically, in an individual human life and also on the big scale of nature, there are two types of energy, yin and yang. The interplay of these two energies establishes life. They establish the small human life and the big life of nature itself. These two types of energy are respectively symbolized by 日 or ⊙ which means sun, and 月 or 𝄃 which means moon. This does not mean the exact sun and moon, but merely describes two types of energy. The first type, sun energy, is the energy of being and doing. The second type, moon energy, is the energy produced by reflection or resistance to the first type of universal impetus. Finally, even though these two energies are superficially different, they are still one energy. When the two types of energy are integrated with each other, the one combined energy becomes 丹 which means medicine. The symbol 丹 is the combination of the symbols for sun and moon, 日 and 月 .

In an individual life, there are basically two types of energy as well: spiritual energy as yang, and physical or sexual energy as yin. The duty or function of the responsive mind, which is in the middle, is to integrate both to maintain the existence of life. In nature, just as in a human, the mind is not seen, although you can see the brain, which is not the mind. The deep nature of the mind is recognized as universal mind, universal potence or God. The universal mind is not seen as a tangible substance, but it does exist. One manifestation of the universal mind is the resilience of nature to recover its own healthy condition and return to a state of normalcy after a regional disaster.

Many times, I have mentioned that human life is a small model of this world, which consists of both Heaven and Earth. I say this because people contain both the creativity of the sky or Heaven and the receptivity of the Earth as formative energy. This discovery was made through the spiritual awareness of the forerunners of the ancient spiritually developed ones. They considered this as valuable guidance that a person could apply to practical life.

Besides following the above guidance about the three types of energies in your personal spiritual practice, there are five universal virtues that help you greatly when practiced in everyday life. Because we are living beings on Earth, we experience the five different energies which form a cycle or set of five phases. Each energy functions differently and affects our lives differently. Because each individual human life is a child of nature, spiritually the human mind was impressed by the constancy or virtue of nature, or the spiritual or subtle function of nature. This means that ancient people were impressed by these five energies or virtues which are the same for a single human life as well as for the entirety of universal life. Actually, the small life and the big life are the same except for their size. The ancients were impressed by the spiritual or subtle function of nature, which they called virtue.

If we talk a little bit about the solar system and how it works, we will be able to understand the five virtues that the ancients discovered. In general, there are three important cycles that affect the Earth: the yearly solar cycle, the daily Earth cycle and the monthly lunar cycle. These three cycles shape a specific natural environment which is also reflected inside a human individual.

The monthly lunar cycle, called by ancient people the White Route, was described by them as the 28 lodgings of the moon, because the moon would stay in a different constellation each night.

The daily earth cycle is caused by the rotation of the Earth which creates the appearance of the sun rising, moving across the sky and then sinking.

The yearly sun cycle is divided into five parts. Spring reflects the positive energy of regeneration. Summer is the time of full growth. Autumn expresses astringency or the retreat of heat. Winter is the time when heat from the surface sinks deeply into the earth and the life force is in a situation of storage. These four phases of the solar cycle are also expressive of any movement of life on earth. The fifth energy is the earth itself. The earth produces its own energy to harmonize the energy that comes from the sky. Thus, five types of energy exist and are expressed.

When these five energies become spiritualized in human nature, we have five virtues which express themselves exactly as the natural energy expresses itself.

The first of the virtues is kindness, or love. It is energy of Spring or vegetation (Wood). The second virtue is rite, manner or civilization. It is an expression of Summer energy or Fire. The third virtue is properness or uprightness; it is Autumn energy, which is also the energy of formable and reformable Metal. The fourth virtue is wisdom. It is Winter energy, the energy of Water. The fifth

virtue is the virtue of honesty and earnestness or faithfulness. It is the energy of the transition stage of the whole
cycle of four different energies, or the energy of Earth.

These five energies or virtues, if negatively or extremely
expressed, are as follows: kindness will become weakness;
rite or manner will become superficial; uprightness will
become no principle; wisdom will become cold-heartedness;
and the energy of faithfulness will become stubbornness or
inflexibility.

Then, there is godly or masterly energy. The godly
nature or faithful energy, which is in the position of the
center, does not extend itself to be overly positive or overly
negative. It just remains harmonious and centered.

I am saying, quite simply: Practicing only one of the
five virtues or overemphasizing one of them brings a negative result. When all five virtues are practiced and balanced,
the result is a neutral expression.

For example, I mentioned that the positive virtue of
Earth was faithfulness and that a negative result can be
produced when the virtue of faithfulness transforms into
stubbornness or inflexibility. If the virtue of Earth is singly
practiced, or if any one virtue is overextended, the virtue of
the person is not complete. Only when all five virtues work
together can the harmony of the complete virtue of nature
be created. When any single virtue of the five is practiced,
there must be the virtue of properness to go with it. Yet,
properness itself means nothing when it is not applied in a
circumstance with all other virtues. Expressing a single
virtue in a manner of disassociating with the other five does
not mean that a person is centered and neutral such as
priests, saints, soldiers, or spies. They are not balanced
models for everyone in the world.

If overemphasized, a single virtue brings about a
negative result. For example, too much wisdom leads a
person to have a cool mind or cool heart. Carelessness or
overdoing rites and manners make a person appear to be
superficial and hypocritical, etc. Therefore, there is the
appropriateness in wisdom, as well as with the other four
virtues. You could also say, when you act appropriately, it
appears as though you have no wisdom.

All five virtues express the one positive nature of the universe. Typically, different teachers or teachers of different cultures tend to emphasize only one virtue or another. Thus, the dramatic effect of a single spiritual emphasis is created, yet the spiritual expression is incomplete. This is why spiritual reality is a universal, moral and at the same time, integral truth. It does not support any partiality. The Integral Way is a broad education rather than the partial education of a religion.

In ancient times, to learn spiritual reality was to learn innate nature and apply that innate nature at a correct time or in the correct amount in all circumstances and situations. Therefore, to learn spiritual reality is first to learn the three origins and to return the scattered energy back to those three origins in order to nurture your life.

When good energies are gathered by a person, then the life becomes a small model of God. You do not need to be endlessly searching outwardly to find a place to "park" your life or to "perch" your mind. You are here with all three origins and the potential of a small God. Therefore, you need to respect your life, not waste or scatter it.

Secondly, when you become a student of spiritual truth, practice the five virtues from inside out in all circumstances and life conditions. Then bit by bit, you will be developing yourself and learning more about life. You can also learn the special knowledge and skills which can benefit your life and the lives of other people. By doing this, you lay down a good foundation of being achieved in the Integral Way, a whole person, a complete being.

Spiritual cultivation brings many blessings to a person's life. One of these blessings or benefits is to be able to see yourself. Thus, if you are at fault, you will know it. Seeing your own fault is a sign that your true life knowledge is growing and that spiritual light is becoming stronger inside.

I would like to give this important teaching to you one more time with slightly different words so that you can get a different handle on it.

Life is composed of three big elements. The two most influential are your physical desire and your spirit. Your mind is in between the two, being pulled back and forth.

Those of you who are serious students of internal alchemy and spiritual cultivation will benefit from hearing my personal experience about how to control the mind so that those two influential elements do not have a big battle inside of you. Here are eight verses to guide the spiritual light within you. In them I mention the spiritual light because it is usually the darkness of desire which wins the battle. It is helpful to have this light consistently available, like a torch that can light up the darkness when you need help. This spiritual light in your life is the true god, or at least a godly messenger, which you form through your learning and spiritual cultivation. Your spiritual light is always being challenged and tested by external situations of real life as well as by its own partners, which are the faculties of your body and mind. The spiritual light is the exact center of your life. Only a developed life has attained it. In general, the mind is the most developed center of life. Thus, the mind needs to find a connection to Heaven above, (which is a metaphoric way of saying that the mind needs to regulate one's spiritual life) and it also needs to find the connection to the earth below (which is a metaphoric way of saying that the mind needs to regulate one's physical life. The secret of spiritual cultivation is actually simple; do not let the light of your spiritual life be extinguished by the force of darkness within yourself or outside of yourself.

I hope that these eight verses will help you become a winner and help your spiritual light continue to grow.

1

The righteous mind in life
*   is as small as a dot.*
Evil desire is as strong
*   as a heavy load which weighs tons.*
Although the process of becoming holy
*   does not appear dependable,*
*   if that one bit of righteous mind is protected,*
*   it is enough for your celebration!*

2

The right knowledge of life
is a tiny light.
Evil desire is as dark
as the blackest night.
It is not certain that you can reach holiness.
Yet, the safety of the light of right knowledge
can bring you peace.

3

Life is made of desire and of truth.
Desire can be an endless impulse,
yet the truth is so subtle.
When there is no war between them
you have peace.
When there is war,
the defeat or sacrifice of the truth
will endanger your life.

4

If you do not damage your life,
your life does not need to depend upon Heaven for help.
Thus, you need only to recognize the right knowledge
and accordingly fulfill your life.

When a desire is suitable and possible to fulfill,
it is called natural.
When a desire is unsuitable
and reluctantly finds a substitute,
it brings self-invited trouble.

5

Desire is like fire
and blood is like water.
Human life is like wood and vegetation;
they need both water and the warmth of the sun.
Yet when either of these two become overwhelming,
they destroy the life.

6

Life is like a ship
  with a full cargo of numerous desires.
There is only one captain
  who can pilot the ship.
The world is like the vicious ocean.
Only the right commands of the captain
    will safely bring the fully loaded ship
    to reach its bright and happy destination.

7

Your body is not your enemy.
Your desire is not a traitor.
If you are a wise person,
    you reach for the counterbalance between these two.
The I Ching *teaches that*
    yin and yang cannot depart from each other.
They oppose each other.
They accomplish each other.

8

In the stage of life when you are in a body,
    there is no higher achievement that can be made
    than reaching for the counterbalance
    between yin and yang.
Because all existent life and the universe
    is under the law of polarity,
    absolute spiritual unity is the counterbalance
    you can and need to achieve.
When you achieve it,
    you are achieving the truth of universal life.

It is a valuable and truthful part of spiritual knowledge that when physical life ceases, one will become either an angel that ascends to Heaven or a ghost that descends to hell, yet more important than superficial beliefs in this knowledge is its correct application while one is still alive. Above and beyond all concepts of Heaven and hell, people need to work on their personal virtue, balanced life attitudes, uprightness, good heart and righteous mind.

If self-inspection is practiced during one's lifetime, there is little chance of losing one's good character or behavior. A person who inspects oneself and makes proper adjustments to behavior is an angel living in the world. You know what category the person who does not do this falls into. The true value of spiritual knowledge is a practical matter of the correct way of living and using your personal energy.

In literature, there are many ghost stories. In reality, living people who contain too much ghostly or negative spiritual elements can do real harm by creating problems for other people and the world. By increasing their ghostly or yin nature, they thereby damage themselves, too. Harmful things happen when they expose their ghost-like temperament or character. People who do not practice self-inspection simply do not know to work directly on eliminating their spiritual contamination, yet this can easily be learned.

My message to a spiritual student is, do not hold onto imaginary ideas about spiritual beings of different levels which have been described by religion or literature. You need to concentrate upon your own life in this world. Each person needs to work realistically on oneself, at all times and in all places, in order to think right and do right.

My teaching can be called "immortology" because we suppose that the good virtue and good character of a person is immortal. Thus, "immortology" is basically the knowledge of being an upright, healthy person. That is my subject. I treat my teaching as public education rather than a religious fantasy class. I have carried it from ancient China. My dedication and devotion is to this type of spiritual work, although some people have mixed it up with religion. Religion is valid on a certain level, but people can go higher when they choose to grow. Most people prefer fantasies to realistic spiritual discipline and cultivation. I would very much like to point out the differences between religion and spirituality here. Please do not confuse the education I offer with a religious path of psychological escape.

Each of us, at whatever age, needs to work directly on our own spiritual quality. Each moment, we need to make sure we have not been corrupted by any outside influence. Thus, there is a lot to study for your spiritual achievement.

Afterwards

The material I used in this book was taken from classes I taught after I arrived in the United States. This important class had great impact upon some students' psychology, especially those who had problems from their childhood, social conventions, or from their relationships with their parents and so forth. The transcripts of the tapes were put in a file and remained there during the years that I spent facing the needs of different students who asked many questions. Those questions attracted my immediate focus, so I worked on them with the help of newer students. All the answers to the questions have now been published as books.

Recently, I had occasion to look through the old files and saw the typed manuscripts from the class on internal alchemy. It was suggested that I consider making them into a book, too. How interesting it was that twelve years had passed since the time I taught that class. Many new things, new changes and new responsibilities required my correct response and fulfillment during those twelve years.

I believe that this book is of great value to new students as well as students who originally attended the class. Some students have drifted away from the teachings due to personal reasons or the new focus of my teaching. My definition of spiritual teaching is not the direct help that a teacher gives a student, it is guiding students to see themselves so that they know how to make a new adjustment and live better. This is not as easy to achieve as just saying something that pleases the ears or offers a psychological substitute for real growth and learning.

All leaders of spiritual or religious work know one thing: people have spiritual fantasies. Thus, they use people's fantasies to attain success in their field with business in mind. "Religious businesses" will continue to prosper until the human race comes to a new stage where people can grow and make progress themselves. When that happens, "religious businesses" and spiritual services will attain a new quality and offer a more truthful service. My work is already doing just that; it is the opposite of feeding people's spiritual fantasy because it shows them how to make realistic spiritual progress in their lives.

I have written down a simple formula which can serve as an important prescription for anyone who needs to use it. I suggest that you read the following lines over once, and maybe twice, or during situations when you most need them.

1. Respect your life source. I do not mean the subtle origin, I mean the financial source of your life, or how you earn a living. When people have no material challenges, then their emotions become luxurious. This means, when people have a good financial base, they will look for whatever luxury or pastime will serve their feelings instead of continuing to build the reality of a solid foundation for material life. Luxuries and pastimes are, for the most part, wasteful.

Respecting your life source means to respect your profession, occupation, business, skills, and whatever you can do to make a decent living. If you are good, it is your achievement. If you are not good, keep improving yourself. Do not be frustrated if you cannot achieve the level that you desire, but keep working on it.

2. Some people are supported by their families. Others join in the family business. Young people do not necessarily respect family support or the family trade, because those things differ from the fantasy that they have in their minds. They do not know that fantasy costs a lot. People who are wise enjoy the old foundation and use this foundation to develop themselves spiritually and newly in an interesting direction.

After you quietly absorb the support and the old foundation, fantasy is nothing more than pride growing in the minds of young people. They do not understand the difficulty it took to achieve a positive establishment in the world. For them, things come too easy. As the old saying goes, "Those who live with blessings never know that they are blessed, so they look for other things that can foolishly replace the real blessings." Blessings are something difficult to recognize. To be able to recognize a blessing is an achievement in itself.

When I was young, I visited many wise ones. Each of them lived a simple life, but they enjoyed their lives tremendously, much more than people who were more talented and owned a lot of things. Usually people with more possessions were not as happy as the wise ones who lived a simple life. I was impressed by their example, so I would like to try to define their achievement for you. Happiness is the reality of the size of what you require from life. If somebody has high requirements, then happiness is not easy for them to obtain. They can easily achieve other requirements, but not happiness. The way to attain happiness is first to determine the quality of happiness you are looking for, and then to determine the requirements you establish to be able to achieve the happiness. Then you adjust your requirements so that you have a realistic possibility to achieve the happiness you want.

Once I treated a retired professor who was active in the sphere of art. He told me that when he was younger, he was fascinated with women and it was not hard for him to fulfill whatever interest he had. When I treated him, he was feeling frustrated because he was no longer attractive to young women. I immediately noticed that he did not know that real happiness changes according to one's stage of life. People who are older and have more experience can use that as an asset to serve oneself and others better. They can also manage life better. Naturally they are less physical, but they need to accept this and accept themselves. In their minds, older men or women who imagine having lots of young sexual partners may have difficulty in making reality fit their fantasy. However, if they apply themselves in a direction which does not have age limitations, their achievement and happiness can still be there. The professor finally found happiness in the art business.

I do not consider myself a man of great achievement, but a man of small achievement, because I consider all the small things I feel interested in doing as my achievement. For instance, small things such as taking one hour off to walk in the forest, climb the mountain or wade in the cold stream in summertime, all bring me great joy. Surely all types of life activity are included. I consider all these small things as the real achievement of my life and my happiness.

3. A person should be satisfied with his or her spouse. When you are first married, you might have lots of feelings about your partner. Sometime later, other interests grow so strong that they might make you forget the feeling you had at first. At that time, you might become less truthful in protecting your private peace; at this stage you come closer to your feeling. This feeling is not necessarily coherent to the rational growth of your life being. It would present a challenge to your rational growth. By this I mean, please be content with the faithful partner in your family who may be the best friend you have.

4. All people have a number of friends, but your require-ments for friends may be too high, so you might think you do not have any friends. Some people think that what is called a "friend" is a person who can share your troubles and feelings, but that is different from true friendship. That is looking for sympathy from people.

I would like to give my own experience as an example. I teach students and treat patients. In the course of my work, I become acquainted with people. Acquaintances are one type of friend. Not only are the people who provide you with the help that you need your friends but to a certain extent, whoever you contact in your life activity is also a friend, because people trust you and you trust people. This can be considered a level of friendship.

The best way to enjoy friends is to let them experience their life changes, but do not change your openness or withdraw the virtue of friendliness. Most people experience changes in their close relationships. Some changes may trouble you, for example, when someone starts to oppose you, but pay attention to the ones who quietly stay at your side. Although they could not help you, they retain their faithful position. Generally, people ignore this voiceless support and only watch their troubles. However, if you only watch your troubles, you might end up considering the whole world to be dangerous and all people will become harmful if you allow them to. That perception is dangerous, because it would guide you to become cruel.

Realistically speaking, the world is so big sometimes. The waters of worldly life can be as turbulent as a violent storm on the ocean. In your life, if you are wise enough, do not create psychological loneliness and isolation for yourself, especially spiritually. You still find a peaceful harbor in your home with your spouse, your old friends, and your old trade. You may not have scintillating feelings about your wife like you do about movie stars. Your friends may not inspire great admiration and respect as do the special models of society. And your old skill or old business may not be strong enough to make you a multi-millionaire and provide all the luxuries that your emotions would like to have, but it gives you time for dreaming materially and socially and achieving spiritually.

In conclusion, you do not need to face all the difficulties in the world. Security of mind can be attained by respecting your old trade, some friends who still stay with you, and your spouse. However, you do not need to antagonize the friends or spouse who do not stay with you and the less desirable relationship if the other side is still faithful to keep you.

The above four things can be described as the old wise saying, "Ugly spouse, old trade and old friends are three treasures in your life." Learn to be wise; enjoy the real world as big as you can possess, and feel free.

I do not consider myself to be a wise man. It is your wisdom to choose to work with me faithfully. The above formula I offer to all my friends of past, present and future: whatever happens in external life and relationships, you should never withdraw your virtue within you. Although you may not accept a change or agree with what other people have created that caused the changing, all that should not be a reason to change your virtue by any immature idea or new stimulation that happens in your contacts. May the peace and sincerity of life always be with you!

About Hua-Ching Ni

Hua-Ching Ni is fully acknowledged and empowered by his own spiritual attainment rather than by external authority. He is a teacher of natural spiritual truth and a natural person. He is heir to the wisdom transmitted through an unbroken succession of numberless generations of true masters dating back to the time before written history. As a young boy, he was educated by his family in the foundation of natural spiritual truth. Later, he learned spiritual arts from various achieved teachers, some of whom have a long traditional background, and fully achieved all aspects of ancient science and metaphysics.

In addition, 38 generations of the Ni family worked as farmers, natural healers and scholars. Master Ni has continued his family tradition in America with clinics and the establishment of Yo San University of Traditional Chinese Medicine. Master Ni worked as a traditional Chinese doctor and taught spiritual learning on the side as a service to people. He taught first in Taiwan for 27 years by offering many publications in Chinese and then in the United States and other Western countries since 1976. To date, he has published about thirty books in English, made five videotapes of gentle movement and has written some natural spiritual songs sung by an American singer.

Hua-Ching Ni has lived in the mountains at different stages. When possible, he stays part-time in seclusion in the mountains and part-time in the city doing work of a different nature. He believes this is better for his nervous system than staying in only one type of environment.

The books that he has written in Chinese include two books about Chinese medicine, five books about spiritual self-cultivation and four books about the Chinese internal school of martial arts. These were published in Taiwan. He has also written two unpublished books on ancient spiritual subjects related to natural health and spiritual development.

The other unpublished books were written by brush in Chinese calligraphy during the years he attained a certain degree of achievement in his personal spiritual cultivation. He said, "Those books were written when my spiritual energy was rising to my head to answer the deep questions in my mind. In spiritual self-cultivation, only by nurturing your own internal spirit can communication exist between the internal and external gods. This can be proven by your personal spiritual stature. For example, after nurturing your internal spirit, through your thoughts you contact many subjects which you could not reach in ordinary daily life. Such spiritual inspiration comes to help when you need it. Writings done in good concentration are almost like meditation and are one fruit of your cultivation. This type of writing is how internal and external spiritual communication can be realized. For the purpose of self-instruction, writing is one important practice of the Jing Ming School or the School of Pure Light. It was beneficial to me as I grew spiritually. I began to write when I was a teenager and my spiritual self-awareness had begun to grow."

In his books published in Taiwan, Hua-Ching Ni did not give the details of his spiritual background. It was ancient spiritual custom that all writers, such as Lao Tzu and Chuang Tzu, avoided describing their personal lives. Lao Tzu and Chuang Tzu were not even their names. However, Master Ni conforms with the modern system of biographies and copyrights to meet the needs of the new society.

Hua-Ching Ni's teaching differs from what is generally called Taoism, conventional religious Taoism or the narrow concept of lineage or religious mixture of folk Taoism. His teaching is non-conventional and differs from the teaching of any other teachers. He teaches spiritual self-sufficiency rather than spiritual dependence.

Master Ni shares his own achievement as the teaching of rejuvenated original spiritual truth, which has its origins in the prehistoric stages of human life. His teaching is the Integral Way or Integral Truth. It is based on the Three Scriptures of ancient spiritual mysticism: Lao Tzu's *Tao Teh Ching, The Teachings of Chuang Tzu* and *The Book of Changes.* He has translated and elucidated these three classics into versions which carry the accuracy of the valuable ancient message. His other books are materials for different stages of learning the truth. He has also absorbed all the truthful high spiritual achievements from various schools to assist the illustration of spiritual truth with his own achieved insight on each different level of teaching.

The ancient spiritual writing contained in the Three Scriptures of ancient spiritual mysticism and all spiritual books of many schools were very difficult to understand, even for Chinese scholars. Thus, the true ancient spiritual teaching from the oriental region is not known to most scholars of later generations, the Chinese people or foreign translators. It would have become lost to the world if Hua-Ching Ni had not rewritten it and put it into simple language. He has practically revived the ancient teaching to make it useful for all people.

BOOKS IN ENGLISH BY MASTER NI

Internal Alchemy - *New Publication!*
Ancient spiritually achieved ones used alchemical terminology metaphorically for human internal energy transformation. Internal alchemy intends for an individual to transform one's emotion and lower energy to be higher energy and to find the unity of life in order to reach the divine immortality. 288 pages, Softcover, Stock No. binte, $15.95

Mysticism - *New Publication!*
For more than 8,000 years, mystical knowledge has been passed down by the sages. Master Ni introduces spiritual knowledge which does not use the senses or machines like scientific knowledge, yet both the entirety of the universe and the spirits can be known by one who attains spiritual development. 200 pages, Softcover, Stock No. BMYST, $13.95

Life and Teaching of Two Immortals, Volume 1: Kou Hong - *New Publication!*
Master Kou Hong was an achieved Master, a healer in Traditional Chinese Medicine and a specialist in the art of refining medicines who was born in 363 A.D. He laid the foundation of later cultural development in China. 176 pages, Softcover, Stock No. BLIF1, $12.95.

Ageless Counsel for Modern Life - *New Publication!*
These sixty-four writings, originally illustrative commentaries on the I Ching, are meaningful and useful spiritual guidance on various topics to enrich your life. Master Ni's delightful poetry and some teachings of esoteric Taoism can be found here as well. 256 pages, Softcover, Stock No. BAGEL, $15.95.

The Mystical Universal Mother - *New Publication!*
An understanding of both masculine and feminine energies are crucial to understanding oneself, in particular for people moving to higher spiritual evolution. Master Ni focuses upon the feminine through the examples of some ancient and modern women. 240 pages, Softcover, Stock No. BMYST, $14.95

Moonlight in the Dark Night - *New Publication!*
To attain inner clarity and freedom of the soul, you have to control your emotions. This book contains wisdom on balancing the emotions, including balancing love relationships, so that spiritual achievement becomes possible. 168 pages, Softcover, Stock No. BMOON, $12.95

Harmony - The Art of Life - *New Publication!*
Harmony occurs when two different things find the point at which they can link together. Master Ni shares valuable spiritual understanding and insight about the ability to bring harmony within one's own self, one's relationships and the world. 208 pages, Softcover, Stock No. BHARM, $14.95

Attune Your Body with Dao-In
The ancients discovered that Dao-In exercises solved problems of stagnant energy, increased their health and lengthened their years. The exercises are also used as practical

support for cultivation and higher achievements of spiritual immortality. 144 pages, Softcover with photographs, Stock No. BDAOI, $14.95 Also on VHS, Stock No. VDAOI, $59.95

The Key to Good Fortune: Refining Your Spirit
Straighten Your Way (Tai Shan Kan Yin Pien) and The Silent Way of Blessing (Yin Chia Wen) are the main guidance for a mature and healthy life. Spiritual improvement can be an integral part of how to realize a Heavenly life on earth. 144 pages, Softcover, Stock No. BKEYT, $12.95

Eternal Light
Master Ni presents the life and teachings of his father, Grandmaster Ni, Yo San, who was a spiritually achieved person, a healer and teacher, and a source of inspiration to Master Ni. Some deeper teachings and understandings on living a spiritual life and higher achievement are given. 208 pages, Softcover, Stock No. BETER, $14.95

Quest of Soul
Master Ni addresses many concepts about the soul such as saving the soul, improving the soul's quality, the free soul, what happens at death and the universal soul. He guides and inspires the reader into deeper self-knowledge and to move forward to increase personal happiness and spiritual depth. 152 pages, Softcover, Stock No. BQUES, $11.95

Nurture Your Spirits
Master Ni breaks some spiritual prohibitions and presents the spiritual truth he has studied and proven. This truth may help you develop and nurture your own spirits which are the truthful internal foundation of your life being. 176 pages, Softcover, Stock No. BNURT, $12.95

Internal Growth through Tao
Master Ni teaches the more subtle, much deeper sphere of the reality of life that is above the shallow sphere of external achievement. He also clears the confusion caused by some spiritual teachings and guides you in the direction of developing spiritually by growing internally. 208 pages, Softcover, Stock No. BINTE, $13.95

Power of Natural Healing
Master Ni discusses the natural capability of self-healing, information and practices which can assist any treatment method and presents methods of cultivation which promote a healthy life, longevity and spiritual achievement. 230 pages, Softcover, Stock No. BHEAL, $14.95

Essence of Universal Spirituality
In this volume, as an open-minded learner and achieved teacher of universal spirituality, Master Ni examines and discusses all levels and topics of religious and spiritual teaching to help you understand the ultimate truth and enjoy the achievement of all religions without becoming confused by them. 304 pages, Softcover, Stock No. BESSE, $19.95

Guide to Inner Light
Drawing inspiration from the experience of the ancient achieved ones, modern people looking for the true source and meaning of life can find great teachings to direct and benefit them.

The invaluable ancient development can teach us to reach the attainable spiritual truth and point the way to the Inner Light. 192 pages, Softcover, Stock No. BGUID, $12.95

Stepping Stones for Spiritual Success
In this volume, Master Ni has taken the best of the traditional teachings and put them into contemporary language to make them more relevant to our time, culture and lives. 160 pages, Softcover, Stock No. BSTEP, $12.95.

The Complete Works of Lao Tzu
The *Tao Teh Ching* is one of the most widely translated and cherished works of literature. Its timeless wisdom provides a bridge to the subtle spiritual truth and aids harmonious and peaceful living. Also included is the *Hua Hu Ching*, a later work of Lao Tzu which was lost to the general public for a thousand years. 212 pages, Softcover, Stock No. BCOMP, $12.95

Order *The Complete Works of Lao Tzu* and the companion *Tao Teh Ching* Cassette Tapes for only $23.00. Stock No. ABTAO.

The Book of Changes and the Unchanging Truth
The legendary classic *I Ching* is recognized as the first written book of wisdom. Leaders and sages throughout history have consulted it as a trusted advisor which reveals the appropriate action in any circumstance. Includes over 200 pages of background material on natural energy cycles, instruction and commentaries. 669 pages, Stock No. BBOOK, Hardcover, $35.00

The Story of Two Kingdoms
This volume is the metaphoric tale of the conflict between the Kingdoms of Light and Darkness. Through this unique story, Master Ni transmits esoteric teachings of Taoism which have been carefully guarded secrets for over 5,000 years. This book is for those who are serious in achieving high spiritual goals. 122 pages, Stock No. BSTOR, Hardcover, $14.50

The Way of Integral Life
This book includes practical and applicable suggestions for daily life, philosophical thought, esoteric insight and guidelines for those aspiring to serve the world. The ancient sages' achievement can assist the growth of your own wisdom and balanced, reasonable life. 320 pages, Softcover, Stock No. BWAYS, $14.00. Hardcover, Stock No. BWAYH, $20.00.

Enlightenment: Mother of Spiritual Independence
The inspiring story and teachings of Master Hui Neng, the father of Zen Buddhism and Sixth Patriarch of the Buddhist tradition, highlight this volume. Hui Neng was a person of ordinary birth, intellectually unsophisticated, who achieved himself to become a spiritual leader. 264 pages, Softcover, Stock No. BENLS, $12.50   Hardcover, Stock No. BENLH, $22.00.

Attaining Unlimited Life
Chuang Tzu was perhaps the greatest philosopher and master of Tao. He touches the organic nature of human life more deeply and directly than do other great teachers. This volume also includes questions by students and answers by Master Ni. 467 pages, Softcover, Stock No. BATTS $18.00; Hardcover, Stock No. BATTH, $25.00.

Special Discount: Order the three classics Way of Integral Life, Enlightenment: Mother of Spiritual Independence *and* Attaining Unlimited Light *in the hardbound editions, Stock No.* BHARD *for $59.95.*

The Gentle Path of Spiritual Progress
This book offers a glimpse into the dialogues between a Master and his students. In a relaxed, open manner, Master Ni, Hua-Ching explains to his students the fundamental practices that are the keys to experiencing enlightenment in everyday life. 290 pages, Softcover, Stock No. BGENT, $12.95.

Spiritual Messages from a Buffalo Rider, A Man of Tao
Our buffalo nature rides on us, whereas an achieved person rides the buffalo. Master Ni gives much helpful knowledge to those who are interested in improving their lives and deepening their cultivation so they too can develop beyond their mundane beings. 242 pages, Softcover, Stock No. BSPIR, $12.95.

8,000 Years of Wisdom, Volume I and II
This two-volume set contains a wealth of practical, down-to-earth advice given by Master Ni over a five-year period. Drawing on his training in Traditional Chinese Medicine, Herbology and Acupuncture, Master Ni gives candid answers to questions on many topics. Volume I includes dietary guidance; 236 pages; Stock No. BWIS1 Volume II includes sex and pregnancy guidance; 241 pages; Stock No. BWIS2. Softcover, each volume $12.50

Special discount: Both Books I and II of 8,000 Years of Wisdom, Stock No. BWIS3, for $22.00.

The Uncharted Voyage Toward the Subtle Light
Spiritual life in the world today has become a confusing mixture of dying traditions and radical novelties. This book provides a profound understanding and insight into the underlying heart of all paths of spiritual growth, the subtle origin and the eternal truth of one universal life. 424 pages, Softcover, Stock No. BUNCH, $14.50

The Heavenly Way
A translation of the classic Tai Shan Kan Yin Pien (Straighten Your Way) and Yin Chia Wen (The Silent Way of Blessing). The treatises in this booklet are the main guidance for a mature and healthy life. This truth can teach the perpetual Heavenly Way by which one reconnects oneself with the divine nature. 41 pages, Softcover, Stock No. BHEAV, $2.50

Special Discount: Order the Heavenly Way in a set of 10 - great for gifts or giveaways. (One shipping item). BHIV10 $17.50.

Footsteps of the Mystical Child
This book poses and answers such questions as: What is a soul? What is wisdom? What is spiritual evolution? to enable readers to open themselves to new realms of understanding and personal growth. Includes true examples about people's internal and external struggles on the path of self-development and spiritual evolution. 166 pages, Softcover, Stock No. BFOOT, $9.50

Workbook for Spiritual Development
This material summarizes thousands of years of traditional teachings and little-known practices for spiritual development. There are sections on ancient invocations, natural celibacy and postures for energy channeling. Master Ni explains basic attitudes and knowledge that supports spiritual practice. 240 pages, Softcover, Stock No. BWORK, $14.95

Poster of Master Lu
Color poster of Master Lu, Tung Ping (shown on cover of workbook), for use with the workbook or in one's shrine. 16" x 22"; Stock No. PMLTP. $10.95

Order the Workbook for Spiritual Development *and the companion Poster of Master Lu for $18.95.* Stock No. BPWOR.

The Taoist Inner View of the Universe
Master Ni has given all the opportunity to know the vast achievement of the ancient unspoiled mind and its transpiercing vision. This book offers a glimpse of the inner world and immortal realm known to achieved ones and makes it understandable for students aspiring to a more complete life. 218 pages, Softcover, Stock No. BTAOI, $14.95

Tao, the Subtle Universal Law
Most people are unaware that their thoughts and behavior evoke responses from the invisible net of universal energy. To lead a good stable life is to be aware of the universal subtle law in every moment of our lives. This book presents practical methods that have been successfully used for centuries to accomplish this. 165 pages, Softcover, Stock No. TAOS, $7.50

MATERIALS ON NATURAL HEALTH, ARTS AND SCIENCES

BOOKS

101 Vegetarian Delights - *New Publication!*
A vegetarian diet is a gentle way of life with both physical and spiritual benefits. The Oriental tradition provides helpful methods to assure that a vegetarian diet is well-balanced and nourishing. This book provides a variety of clear and precise recipes ranging from everyday nutrition to exotic and delicious feasts. 176 pages, Softcover, Stock No. B101V, $12.95

The Tao of Nutrition by Maoshing Ni, Ph.D., with Cathy McNease, B.S., M.H. - This book offers both a healing and a disease prevention system through eating habits. This volume contains 3 major sections: theories of Chinese nutrition and philosophy; descriptions of 100 common foods with energetic properties and therapeutic actions; and nutritional remedies for common ailments. 214 pages, Softcover, Stock No. BNUTR, $14.50

Chinese Vegetarian Delights by Lily Chuang
An extraordinary collection of recipes based on principles of traditional Chinese nutrition. For those who require restricted diets or who choose an optimal diet, this cookbook is a rare

treasure. Meat, sugar, diary products and fried foods are excluded. 104 pages, Softcover, Stock No. BCHIV, $7.50

Chinese Herbology Made Easy - by Maoshing Ni, Ph.D.
This text provides an overview of Oriental medical theory, in-depth descriptions of each herb category, over 300 black and white photographs, extensive tables of individual herbs for easy reference and an index of pharmaceutical and Pin-Yin names. This book gives a clear, efficient focus to Chinese herbology. 202 pages, Softcover, Stock No. BCHIH, 14.50

Crane Style Chi Gong Book - By Daoshing Ni, Ph.D.
Chi Gong is a set of meditative exercises developed thousands of years ago in China and now practiced for healing purposes. It combines breathing techniques, body movements and mental imagery to guide the smooth flow of energy throughout the body. It may be used with or without the videotape. 55 pages. Stock No. BCRAN. Spiral-bound, $10.95

VIDEO TAPES

Attune Your Body with Dao-In (VHS) - by Master Ni.
Dao-In is a series of movements traditionally used for conducting physical energy. The ancients discovered that Dao-In exercise solves problems of stagnant energy, increases health and lengthens one's years, providing support for cultivation and higher achievements of spiritual immortality. Stock No. VDAOI, VHS $59.95

T'ai Chi Ch'uan: An Appreciation (VHS) - by Master Ni.
Master Ni, Hua-Ching presents three styles of T'ai Chi handed down to him through generations of highly developed masters. "Gentle Path," "Sky Journey" and "Infinite Expansion" are presented uninterrupted in this unique videotape, set to music for observation and appreciation. Stock No. VAPPR. VHS 30 minutes $49.95

Crane Style Chi Gong (VHS) - by Dr. Daoshing Ni, Ph.D.
Chi Gong is a set of meditative exercises practiced for healing chronic diseases, strengthening the body and spiritual enlightenment. Correct and persistent practice will increase one's energy, relieve tension, improve concentration, release emotional stress and restore general well-being. 2 hours, Stock No. VCRAN. $65.95

Eight Treasures (VHS) - By Maoshing Ni, Ph.D.
These exercises help open blocks in your energy flow and strengthen your vitality. It is a complete exercise combining physical stretching, toning and energy-conducting movements coordinated with breathing. Patterned from nature, its 32 movements are an excellent foundation for T'ai Chi Ch'uan or martial arts. 1 hour, 45 minutes. Stock No. VEIGH. $49.95

T'ai Chi Ch'uan I & II (VHS) - By Maoshing Ni, Ph.D.
This exercise integrates the flow of physical movement with that of internal energy in the Taoist style of "Harmony," similar to the long form of Yang-style T'ai Chi Ch'uan. Tai Chi has been practiced for thousands of years to help both physical longevity and spiritual cultivation. 1 hour each. Each video tape $49.95. Order both for $90.00. Stock Nos: Part I, VTAI1; Part II, VTAI2; Set of two, VTAI3.

AUDIO CASSETTES

Invocations for Health, Longevity and Healing a Broken Heart - By Maoshing Ni, Ph.D.
This audio cassette guides the listener through a series of ancient invocations to channel and conduct one's own healing energy and vital force. "Thinking is louder than thunder. The mystical power which creates all miracles is your sincere practice of this principle." 30 minutes, Stock No. AINVO, $9.95

Stress Release with Chi Gong - By Maoshing Ni, Ph.D.
This audio cassette guides you through simple, ancient breathing exercises that enable you to release day-to-day stress and tension that are such a common cause of illness today. 30 minutes. Stock No. ACHIS. $9.95

Pain Management with Chi Gong - By Maoshing Ni, Ph.D.
Using easy visualization and deep-breathing techniques developed over thousands of years, this audio cassette offers methods for overcoming pain by invigorating your energy flow and unblocking obstructions that cause pain. 30 minutes, Stock No. ACHIP. $9.95

Tao Teh Ching **Cassette Tapes**
This classic work of Lao Tzu has been recorded in this two-cassette set that is a companion to the book translated by Master Ni. Professionally recorded and read by Robert Rudelson. 120 minutes. Stock No. ATAOT. $12.95

Order Master Ni's book, *The Complete Works of Lao Tzu,* and *Tao Teh Ching* Cassette Tapes for only $23.00. Stock No. ABTAO.

This list of Master Ni's books in English is ordered by date of publication for those who wish to follow the sequence of his Western teaching material in learning the Integral Truth.

1979:   *The Complete Works of Lao Tzu*
        The Taoist Inner View of the Universe
        Tao, the Subtle Universal Law
1983:   *The Book of Changes and the Unchanging Truth*
        8,000 Years of Wisdom, I
        8,000 Years of Wisdom, II
1984:   *Workbook for Spiritual Development*
1985:   *The Uncharted Voyage Toward the Subtle Light*
1986:   *Footsteps of the Mystical Child*
1987:   *The Gentle Path of Spiritual Progress*
        Spiritual Messages from a Buffalo Rider (originally
                part of *Gentle Path of Spiritual Progress*)
1989:   *The Way of Integral Life*
        Enlightenment: Mother of Spiritual Independence
        Attaining Unlimited Life
        The Story of Two Kingdoms
1990:   *Stepping Stones for Spiritual Success*
        Guide to Inner Light
        Essence of Universal Spirituality
1991:   *Internal Growth through Tao*
        Nurture Your Spirits
        Quest of Soul
        Power of Natural Healing
        *Attune Your Body with Dao-In: Taoist Exercise for a Long and
                Happy Life*
        Eternal Light
        The Key to Good Fortune: Refining Your Spirit
1992:   *Harmony: The Art of Life*
        Moonlight in the Dark Night
        Life and Teachings of Two Immortals, Volume I: Kou Hong
        The Mystical Universal Mother
        Ageless Counsel for Modern Times
        Gentle Path T'ai Chi Ch'uan
        Mysticism
        Internal Alchemy: The Natural Way to Immortality

In addition, the forthcoming books will be compiled from his lecturing and teaching service:

Golden Message: The Essence of Your Daily Life (by Daoshing and
        Maoshing Ni, based on the works of Master Ni, Hua-Ching)
Sky Journey T'ai Chi Ch'uan
Infinite Expansion T'ai Chi Ch'uan
Cosmic Tour Ba Gua Zahn
Life and Teachings of Two Immortals, Volume II: Chen Tuan
Esoteric Tao Teh Ching: Its Relevance Illuminated

How To Order

Name:

Address:

City: State: Zip:

Phone - Daytime: Evening:

(We may telephone you if we have questions about your order.)

Qty.	Stock No.	Title/Description	Price Each	Total Price

Total amount for items ordered_____

Sales tax (CA residents only, 8-1/4%)_____

Shipping Charge (see below)_____

Total Amount Enclosed_____

Visa _____ Mastercard _____ Expiration Date _____

Card number:_____

Signature:_____

Shipping: In the US, we use UPS when possible. Please give full street address or nearest crossroads. All packages are insured at no extra charge. If shipping to more than one address, use separate shipping charges. Remember: 1 - 10 copies of Heavenly Way, Tao Teh Ching audiotape set and each book and tape are single items. Posters (up to 5 per tube) are a separate item. Please allow 2 - 4 weeks for US delivery and 6 - 10 weeks for foreign surface mail.

By Mail: Complete this form with payment (US funds only, No Foreign Postal Money Orders, please) and mail to: Union of Tao and Man, 1314 Second St. #208, Santa Monica, CA 90401

Phone Orders: (310) 576-1901 - You may leave credit card orders anytime on our answering machine. Please speak clearly and remember to leave your full name and daytime phone number. We will call only if we have a question with your order, there is a delay or you specifically ask for phone confirmation.

Inquiries: If you have questions concerning your order, please refer to the date and invoice number on the top center of your invoice to help us locate your order swiftly.

Shipping Charges -
Domestic Surface: First item $3.25, each additional, add $.50.
Canada Surface: First item $3.25, each additional, add $1.00.
Canada Air: First item $4.00, each additional, add $2.00
Foreign Surface: First Item $3.50, each additional, add $2.00.
Foreign Air: First item $12.00, each additional, add $7.00.

All foreign orders: Add 5% of your book total to shipping charges to cover insurance.

To receive a catalog with full descriptions of books, videotapes and audiotapes available from the Union of Tao and Man, write us at 1314 Second Street #208, Santa Monica, CA 90401 or call 310-576-1901. Be sure to give your complete address including zip code.

Thank you for your order

Spiritual Study through the College of Tao

The College of Tao and the Union of Tao and Man were established formally in California in the 1970's. This tradition is a very old spiritual culture of mankind, holding long experience of human spiritual growth. Its central goal is to offer healthy spiritual education to all people of our society. This time-tested tradition values the spiritual development of each individual self and passes down its guidance and experience.

Master Ni carries his tradition from its country of origin to the west. He chooses to avoid making the mistake of old-style religions that have rigid establishments which resulted in fossilizing the delicacy of spiritual reality. He prefers to guide the teachings of his tradition as a school of no boundary rather than a religion with rigidity. Thus, the branches or centers of this Taoist school offer different programs of similar purpose. Each center extends its independent service, but all are unified in adopting Master Ni's work as the foundation of teaching to fulfill the mission of providing spiritual education to all people.

The centers offer their classes, teaching, guidance and practices on building the groundwork for cultivating a spiritually centered and well-balanced life. As a person obtains the correct knowledge with which to properly guide himself or herself, he or she can then become more skillful in handling the experiences of daily life. The assimilation of good guidance in one's practical life brings about different stages of spiritual development.

Any interested individual is welcome to join and learn to grow for yourself. Or you just might like to take a few classes in which you are interested. You might like to visit the center or take classes near where you live, or you may be interested in organizing a center or study group based on the model of existing centers. In that way, we all work together for the spiritual benefit of all people. We do not require any religious type of commitment.

The College of Tao also offers a Self-Study program based on Master Ni's books and videotapes. The course outline and details of how to participate are given in his book, *The Golden Message*. The Self-Study program gives people an opportunity to study the learning of Tao at their own speed, for those who wish to study on their own or are too far from a center.

The learning is life. The development is yours. The connection of study may be helpful, useful and serviceable, directly to you.

- -

Mail to: Union of Tao and Man, 1314 Second Street #208, Santa Monica, CA 90401

____ I wish to be put on the mailing list of the Union of Tao and Man to be notified of classes, educational activities and new publications.

Name:_____

Address:_____

City:_____State:_____Zip:_____

Herbs Used by Ancient Taoist Masters

The pursuit of everlasting youth or immortality throughout human history is an innate human desire. Long ago, Chinese esoteric Taoists went to the high mountains to contemplate nature, strengthen their bodies, empower their minds and develop their spirit. From their studies and cultivation, they gave China alchemy and chemistry, herbology and acupuncture, the I Ching, astrology, martial arts and T'ai Chi Ch'uan, Chi Gong and many other useful kinds of knowledge.

Most important, they handed down in secrecy methods for attaining longevity and spiritual immortality. There were different levels of approach; one was to use a collection of food herb formulas that were only available to highly achieved Taoist masters. They used these food herbs to increase energy and heighten vitality. This treasured collection of herbal formulas remained within the Ni family for centuries.

Now, through Traditions of Tao, the Ni family makes these foods available for you to use to assist the foundation of your own positive development. It is only with a strong foundation that expected results are produced from diligent cultivation.

As a further benefit, in concert with the Taoist principle of self-sufficiency, Traditions of Tao offers the food herbs along with the Union of Tao and Man's publications in a distribution opportunity for anyone serious about financial independence.

Send to: Traditions of Tao
                1314 Second Street #208
                Santa Monica, CA 90401

Please send me a Traditions of Tao brochure.

Name _____

Address_____

City_____State_____Zip_____

Phone (day)_____(night)_____

Yo San University of Traditional Chinese Medicine

"Not just a medical career, but a life-time commitment to raising one's spiritual standard."

Thank you for your support and interest in our publications and services. It is by your patronage that we continue to offer you the practical knowledge and wisdom from this venerable Taoist tradition.

Because of your sustained interest in Taoism, in January 1989 we formed Yo San University of Traditional Chinese Medicine, a non-profit educational institution under the direction of founder Master Ni, Hua-Ching. Yo San University is the continuation of 38 generations of Ni family practitioners who handed down knowledge and wisdom from father to son. Its purpose is to train and graduate practitioners of the highest caliber in Traditional Chinese Medicine, which includes acupuncture, herbology and spiritual development.

We view Traditional Chinese Medicine as the application of spiritual development. Its foundation is the spiritual capability to know life, to diagnose a person's problem and how to cure it. We teach students how to care for themselves and other, emphasizing the integration of traditional knowledge and modern science. Yo San University offers a complete Master's degree program approved by the California State Department of Education that provides an excellent education in Traditional Chinese Medicine and meets all requirements for state licensure.

We invite you to inquire into our university for a creative and rewarding career as a holistic physician. Classes are also open to persons interested only in self-enrichment. For more information, please fill out the form below and send it to:

Yo San University
of Traditional Chinese Medicine
1314 Second Street
Santa Monica, CA 90401

☐ Please send me information on the Masters degree program in Traditional Chinese Medicine.

☐ Please send me information on health workshops and seminars.

☐ Please send me information on continuing education for acupuncturists and health professionals.

Name _____

Address_____

City_____State_____Zip_____

Phone(day)_____(evening)_____

Index of Some Topics

Fifteenth Class

[date illegible]

A Simple History of Spiritual Teaching

It has always been interesting to me that the minds of human beings everywhere share a similar kind of human nature. For example, the fundamentals of human life are all similar to what happened to ancient Chinese people. All people's experience is relevant to each other. Surely, the spiritual achievement of ancient people is useful to all people. I would like to take this opportunity to give you some important historical knowledge which relates to the learning of spiritual truth.

Since you have become my friends in past or this class, what I can share with you is the fundamental spirit of universal life. I have done this by giving you a key concept in the... and... the new concept of... with universal being in each of us. The universe is our life; our life is the universal life.

The history of people is ourselves the history of spiritual reality. There are two ways to define history. One is to consider it a continuous record of social activity. The other way is to record the good and bad times of people. During the good times, there are competent leaders, and people have more awareness and can manage their businesses and lives well. This produces good results. During bad times there are busy, irresponsible leaders who create many problems and guide one group of people to suppress another group of people. This produces misfortune for everyone.

'Tao' means 'the Way.' Therefore, the Way is harmonious with history when human nature expresses normalcy, harmony and balance. This happens when people manage their own lives and the social relationship among all people meets that standard. Thus, the Way is the history of life.